Twice Around the World With Alexander

DR. R. A. TORREY AND HIS FAMILY IN ENGLAND

MR. CHARLES M. ALEXANDER

Twice Around the World
with
Alexander
PRINCE OF GOSPEL SINGERS

BY

GEORGE T. B. DAVIS

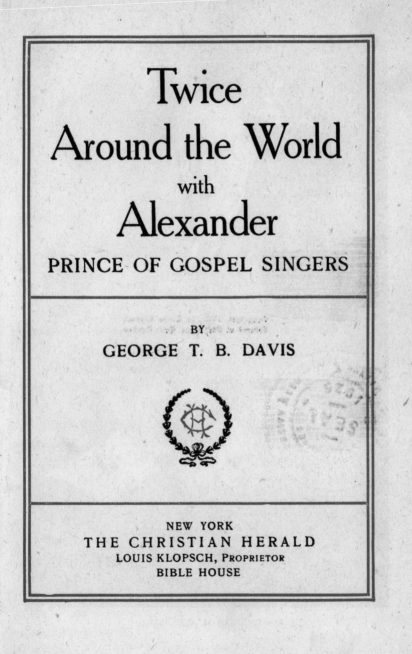

NEW YORK
THE CHRISTIAN HERALD
LOUIS KLOPSCH, Proprietor
BIBLE HOUSE

252
D

12048

FOREWORD

ONE striking feature of the German Reformation was the admission of the Congregation into a singing share of the religious service. Luther himself became a writer of hymns; and many of his gifted countrymen produced Christian lyrics to meet the popular demand. So marked was the result of this innovation that from a hostile source came the sneer "that the people were singing themselves into the Lutheran doctrine."

The following pages tell the story how thousands of men and women were drawn to the Christian life by the power of sacred song, and accepted Christ as their Saviour, Redeemer, and King. Never before in the history of revivals were there such evidences of the power of Gospel Songs to touch the heart and conquer the will in the interests of the soul's salvation.

A most fortunate selection was Dr. Reuben A. Torrey's choice of Mr. Charles M. Alexander to accompany him in his evangelistic tours. The singer proved that he was not merely a winning voice in Israel, but a master leader of congregational singing. Wherever he went he compelled everybody in the audience to sing; he led the vast throngs in Christian melody as irresistibly as he controlled the choir on the platform. An admirer spoke of him as "Alexander the Great"; and in the following pages, which tell the story of the recent missions of the two evangelists in the United States, Canada, Great Britain and Australasia, the reader will find ample warrant for that designation.

Before the occurrence of some of the wonderful song-scenes, so graphically described in "Twice Around the World," a large portion of Christian people never suspected that the Gospel could be sung just as effectively as it could be preached. To set the largest cities and the widest communities humming revival tunes and singing revival songs—to popularize well-known hymns, so that for a season they take the place of secular melodies—is indeed a notable tribute to the influence of consecrated musical genius. This is what Mr. Alexander did in many places and in many climes.

The Torrey-Alexander missions likewise proved the efficiency of personal solicitation in the work of saving souls. Armed with the song book, as well as the Bible, and using the "personal" appeal to the utmost, the evangelist in these days is indeed a triumphant conqueror of men as well as a winner of souls.

CONTENTS

CHAPTER XXVII

CHAPTER XXVIII

CHAPTER XXIX

CHAPTER XXX

ILLUSTRATIONS

ALEXANDER REVIVAL HYMNS

Twice Around the World With Alexander

I

TWICE AROUND THE WORLD

Twice around the World in quest of souls! To few evangelists has such a privilege been granted. The apostle Paul toured much of the world in his day, but it was only a fraction of our planet. Whitefield and the Wesleys, and Moody and Sankey visited America and England in their wonderful missions for the salvation of the lost; but it remained for Dr. Reuben A. Torrey and Mr. Charles M. Alexander completely to encircle the globe; and then for Mr. Alexander to make a second world tour, revisiting old scenes, leading thousands in Gospel song and preaching Christ to individuals on land and sea.

It is the aim of this book to set forth the story of these two journeys. During the first, in company with Dr. Torrey, over 100,000 people were led to make a public confession of their faith in Christ. During the second, which was undertaken primarily for Mrs. Alexander's health, many were led to the Saviour both in great gatherings, conducted by the Gospel singer, and in the more quiet method of personal dealing on the deck of a steamer, or whithersoever the evangelist and his wife went in their world tour.

SUCCESSORS OF MOODY AND SANKEY

The itinerary of the two journeys varied considerably. In the first Mr. Alexander went directly from Vancouver to Melbourne, Australia, where he met Dr. Torrey, and, with nearly fifty other evangelists, began the Simultaneous Mission, that started a great wave of revival which swept over Australia, and in which more than 20,000 publicly confessed Christ. After having toured Australia, Tasmania and New Zealand, in company with Dr. Torrey for six months, the evangelists spent several weeks in India, where hundreds of natives were converted, and where many missionaries were inspired and blessed by the Missions in Madras, Calcutta, Bombay and other places.

From India the evangelists went to Great Britain, where for three years they went up and down the land, conducting Missions in the leading cities. The largest buildings were inadequate to accommodate the crowds which flocked to hear them. They became known as "the successors of Moody and Sankey." In Liverpool, where they conducted two missions, over 12,000 converts were recorded. A great iron building holding about 12,500 people was erected for their second Mission, and on the closing night it is estimated that 15,000 people were inside, and nearly or quite 20,000 were packed outside.

THE CAMPAIGN IN ENGLAND

In Birmingham during a single month's campaign 7,700 confessed Christ; while in London, in a five months' Mission, held in Royal Albert Hall, England's finest auditorium, and in two specially erected iron buildings, about 17,000 made a public profession. In all, during the three years' work in the British Isles, about 80,000 converts were recorded, and missions were held in the following cities:

London	Liverpool	Aberdeen
Birmingham	Manchester	Dundee
Glasgow	Edinburgh	Cardiff
Belfast	Dublin	Brighton
Bolton	Sheffield	Bristol
Bradford	Plymouth	

At the beginning of the first tour Mr. Alexander left America, a comparatively unknown Gospel singer; at its conclusion he was the best known Gospel singer of the time, and the greatest choir leader since the organization of Gospel choirs. He began in Melbourne, Australia, with a choir having a membership of 1,250; while in London the membership of his choirs exceeded 4,000 with frequently 1,000 present at a single meeting. He set the whole world to singing the "Glory Song." It has appeared in print about 17,000,000 times, and has been translated into 17 languages. A London musical expert declared he had never known any other song, sacred or secular, to achieve such sudden popularity throughout England and the colonies as did the "Glory Song."

MR. ALEXANDER'S SECOND JOURNEY

On his second tour of the world Mr. Alexander, accompanied by his wife, went in the opposite direction from his first journey. Leaving London, England, he passed through the Mediterranean and the Suez Canal; touched at Ceylon; then went to Hong-Kong and Pakhoi, China, where a month was spent studying missions and assisting the missionaries, and where one of the most remarkable conversions of his entire experience occurred. After a notable Gospel meeting in a Hong-Kong theatre, the Philippine Islands were visited, and he took part in interesting Sunday services.

Mr. Alexander next spent a month in Australia, revisiting scenes of former victories and strengthening the faith of the converts. Wonderful meetings were held in Melbourne, Sydney and other places. More than 10,000 people were present at his meeting in the Exhibition Building, Melbourne, and many came forward to accept Christ. At Sydney, where the leaders thought it doubtful whether they could get the hall filled, it was quickly packed with 5,000 people; and about as many more were unable to secure admission.

Leaving Australia, Mr. and Mrs. Alexander sailed to Vancouver. They crossed America rapidly, stopping, however, to hold some interesting meetings in Chicago. Thence they went to New York and sailed for Southampton, arriving there about seven months after their departure.

WHAT WAS ACCOMPLISHED

The following is a partial table of statistics of the two journeys:

Miles traveled from begining of first journey to end of second, about...........   100,000
Countries visited in course of two journeys.   14

THE ALEXANDER CHORUS AT MELBOURNE, AUSTRALIA

Cities in which meetings were held, about. .   35
Number of people in meetings (estimated) .   6,000,000
Largest number at one meeting, about. . . .   35,000
Number of converts recorded, over. 100 000
Number of languages "Glory Song" trans-
    lated   17
Number of times "Glory Song" in print. . . 17,000,000

II

FROM FARM TO FAMOUS GOSPEL SINGER

Before giving a detailed narrative of the two world tours, let us rapidly survey the life story of this man, who has been raised up to fill a unique place in modern life and to teach myriads to "sing a new song."

His career reads like a chapter from the Acts of the Apostles. It is a romance of Faith in God. It is one of the most striking illustrations of answered prayer in this generation. "Every great event of my life has come to pass in answer to prayer," declares Mr. Alexander, and this is the keynote of his career.

It was in 1867 that Mr. Alexander was born in a log-house among the hills of Tennessee. His parents were poor, but God-fearing, with strong musical talents. But little did they dream, as their son Charles drove the cows home in the waning twilight, singing Gospel hymns as he plodded onward, that he would one day become one of the most famous Gospel singers and leaders in the world.

A RELIGIOUS HOME ATMOSPHERE

Though he was born in a humble home, yet it was delightfully situated. Many of his boyhood days were spent in adventurous ramblings through forest and glen, over hill and dale, picking berries, exploring the brooks and streams, and lying upon his back watching the fleecy clouds and dreaming of the future. The singer loves to recall the memories of those early years, and of his dearly beloved and honored parents. Speaking to me of the religious influences with which he was surrounded, he said:

"My father was an elder in the Presbyterian Church, and a leader in good works. My mother was a consecrated woman, full of deep piety, with a strong practical strain. The only papers we took were religious ones; and in the evening we would all gather round the fireside, and mother would read aloud from them. Also, on stormy and rainy days, mother would read aloud to us children. She loved most to read sermons, and Moody's sermons were our favorites. Sometimes when she had read other sermons she would say, 'Well, now, my children, these are very good, but I'll read you some more of Moody's. He goes right to our hearts, and he bases what he says on the Word of God.' I remember how we would all break down and cry together over some of his stories.

HIS MOTHER'S INFLUENCE

"Some of the most potent influences in molding my life and sweetening it were the long talks with my mother on rainy days. While the rain was beating upon the roof, and the wind was howling in the trees outside, she would tell me the stories of the chief Bible characters and point out the lessons to be derived from them. She was full of sympathy for the poor, and was easily touched by the misery of others. She was a clear-headed thinker, original and practical. The chief books in our home were religious, for my father had a penchant for purchasing portions of ministers' libraries; and my earliest reading was almost entirely of a religious character.

"My mother sang sweetly, while my father was famous

through all the region round about as a musical leader. My father purchased the first book of Modern Gospel songs that came out when Moody and Sankey were doing their great work. Then we kept getting the Gospel hymns as they were published. Almost as soon as I was able to read anything my father taught me to read music. He would take my hand in his, and we never sang a new song together without beating time with the hand. It was thus as a child that I learned to use my hands in leading Gospel singing. I well recall how on Sunday afternoons people would drive from far and near over the hills and gather on our veranda, while my father would lead them for hours in singing sacred hymns. Music thrilled me from earliest childhood."

Charles was the oldest of a family of four children—three sons and a daughter. One of his brothers is in the ministry, and the other in the service of the Government in Tennessee; while his sister is a pastor's assistant in Knoxville.

The earliest book Mr. Alexander read was the New Testament. He joined the church, and read considerable religious literature, and when in his teens was not an out-and-out Christian. Through reading an article about the late Patrick Gilmore he acquired a consuming ambition to organize great choirs of singers, and to become a proficient musical conductor. He thought that his life work would be secular, something like Gilmore's.

HEARS SANKEY SING AT KNOXVILLE

Young Alexander was sixteen years old when he first saw and heard Moody and Sankey. Long before that he had known them both by reputation, and was very anxious to see and hear them. Now at last the great opportunity had come. The meeting was at Knoxville, in the big opera-house. His heart began to thump as Sankey came on the platform and seated himself at his little organ. Up in his high position, young Alexander, with keen, watchful eyes, followed every movement of the noted singer; and when he heard him sing, "When the Mists Have Rolled Away," he felt as if he were in heaven.

The other hymns which Mr. Sankey sang on this occasion are also remembered by Mr. Alexander. Mr. Moody, that night, preached on Abraham; and as the lad looked down upon the people below him, as the speaker drew towards the close, he thought that never before had he seen so many handkerchiefs in use. The preacher had touched all hearts; and when he invited all who were willing to accept Christ to rise to their feet, there was a general movement throughout the building. It was a new sight for the young lad in the gallery; and as he went home he pondered the things he had seen and heard.

LEAVES HOME FOR COLLEGE

It is a critical period in a young man's life when he leaves home for college. In the good providence of God some words were spoken to young Alexander as he entered this new phase of his life, which were a source of strength to him throughout the coming years. He once told me this incident which I hope will help other young men as they break the ties of home to battle alone with the world:

"I well remember the day when, as a youth, I started out from my country home for the university. Good old Deacon Hudgins came along with his wagon and took me, with my belongings, twelve miles over the hills to the university town. It was a beautiful, balmy day as we drove along, each of us lost in thought. At last Deacon Hudgins gave utterance to the following words of advice: 'My boy, you are going to a place where it will be easy for you to find bad companions. You will not have the influence of your quiet, Christian home and a good mother to keep you straight. Do not disgrace the profession you have made in our country church, but be true to your church membership.' I have never forgotten those words. In my most mischievous hours, when strong temptations came to me to adopt a companion who would lead me in wrong paths, I remembered that the members of the little church would be thinking of the disgrace that I should bring upon them if I went wrong. It was a great factor in keeping me true and pure."

When asked about his first experience as a musical conductor, Mr. Alexander said: "I began my career as a conductor of singing while teaching a country school when about seventeen years of age. I developed in music rapidly, studied at a musical college for a few months, and was then appointed Director of Music in the university which I had formerly attended. It was a remarkable fact that ninety per cent. of the students there were Christians, and most of the music used in practicing and in public entertainments was religious.

"I had all grades in my classes in the college—about three hundred in all. I also organized and taught a large brass band, which was most popular among the students. The religious influence in the college was very helpful, but I did not obey the call for full surrender, though there was always a voice in my heart demanding it."

Going through the library at this University one day Mr. Alexander saw the *Autobiography of Charles G. Finney.* He took it out, read it, and it opened a new world to him. So strongly did it grip him that one reading of it was not sufficient. He read it through a second time, and then a third. Determined to know more of this wonderful man, he bought his other books so far as he could find them, and carefully read and studied them. About the same time he read the life of P. P. Bliss, the great Gospel song writer, and the author of such well known hymns as, "I am so Glad that my Father in Heaven," "Hold the Fort" and "Wonderful Words of Life." This book, written by Major Whittle, also made a lasting impression upon the mind of the young musician.

RESOLVES TO DEVOTE HIS LIFE TO SACRED SONG

It was at this time that an event occurred which changed the entire course of his life, and led him to devote his efforts entirely to sacred song. In tender tones Mr. Alexander told of this crucial experience. "While I was teaching," said he, "I had a telegram from my mother, saying that my father was not expected to live; and I hurried to my home, which was then in Atlanta, Georgia. On my journey I had time to think; and the world changed in a very few hours. Father lived for a week; and during that time my outlook upon the world was changing all the time. I was looking at things in the light of eternity. The night my father died it came to me, as never before, the worth of a human soul. He could not take any of us; he must go alone. And I pondered how essential it was before everything else to see that the soul was safe in God's keeping.

"I don't know definitely whether I was converted before that. When, following his death, I had to go across the city for an undertaker, late at night, it seemed to me as if my heart would break. I wanted to be absolutely certain that my father was in heaven, for I had not studied the Bible closely enough to know how the entrance there was gained. I knew he was an elder in a church, and all that; but as I went along the street I cried to God: 'If there is any way that thou revealest thyself to people, whether by vision, or voice, or impression, give me the certainty that my father is with thee and safe'; and I promised him that I would serve him all my life if he would but give me the assurance. As clearly as anything I ever experienced in my life, the impression came to me, 'Your father is up here with Me.' There and then I promised to serve him all my life, looking naturally up at the stars, and the load lifted from me.

"Filled as I was with thoughts of eternity, the buildings on each side of me looked like mere rubbish, though I remember that before when I went down those streets I used often to say, 'I should like to own one of those splendid blocks.' Every time I saw a man coming out of a saloon I wanted to go up to him and throw my arms about him, and tell him: 'You are going to hell, man. Why don't you accept Jesus Christ?' A great longing to save souls came to me that night, and has been with me—though I have sometimes grown cold—from that day to the present."

ATTENDS BIBLE INSTITUTE

After young Alexander had been summoned home by the death of his father, he did not immediately return to his post

THE FIRST "AT HOME" BIBLE CLASS IN IOWA

at Maryville University, but remained for some months upon the family farm, comforting his mother and making plans for the future of his brothers and sister. All thought of a secular career was now abandoned; and he was determined to devote every energy towards winning souls for Christ. He declares that those three weeks upon the farm, following his father's death, were days of heaven on earth, though they were days of loneliness. The beauty of the Scriptures was then revealed to him as never before.

Hearing of the Moody Bible Institute in Chicago, he soon gained sufficient funds to attend it for a brief period. Before going, however, he talked about the wonderful Christian training school to all his friends; and such was the enthusiasm of the young man that he did not go alone, but took eight friends with him to Chicago to attend the school. Before he left the Institute he had induced thirty-two people from the Southern States to attend it; and he has since been the means of leading scores of others to undertake its course of study.

During his first few months at the Institute it was his privilege to have, as a teacher, the beloved evangelist and Bible student, the late Major Whittle; and he declares that he will never forget the invaluable lessons learned from this prince among men. Through Major Whittle, Mr. Alexander was led to deeper consecration than he had previously known. For years he had harbored a spirit of unforgiveness towards a former friend who was hundreds of miles away; but at last, after a stirring address by Major Whittle, in which the speaker said that if the young men were not getting answers to their prayers it was because they harbored sin in their hearts, Mr. Alexander went to his room, threw himself upon his knees and cried to God for mercy. He cast out every whit of ill-feeling towards his friend, sat down and wrote him a letter, and in a few days they were reconciled.

HIS FIRST GOSPEL TOUR

After completing the course at the Moody Bible Institute, Mr. Alexander became the singing associate of Rev. Milan B. Williams, a strong evangelist. Before this he had often planned to go with various men in Christian work, and had wanted to have his own way about it. Later events proved each time that it would not have been best for him, had he been successful in his ambition. Finally one day, about the first of September, when he felt that he should be at work for his Master, he got on his knees at his bedside and stayed there until he had completely handed over his will to God. He told him that he had made a failure of securing the proper work; that he would be perfectly willing to go wherever he wanted him to go, and with whomsoever he chose. About six days afterwards, a telegram came to the Institute from Mr. Williams, and Mr. Alexander responded. He went out to be with Mr. Williams for two weeks, but remained with him for more than eight years.

In Iowa, during five years, they conducted missions in thirty-six towns and cities. In a town with a population of 6,000 they had 800 confess Christ in four weeks. In another town a tent was specially erected for their meetings, which seated 9,000 people.

III

BEGINNING A WORLD-WIDE WORK

It was in 1901 that Mr. Alexander received an invitation from Dr. Torrey, then pastor of Moody Church in Chicago, and superintendent of the Moody Bible Institute, to accompany him to Australia as his Singing Associate in a Simultaneous Mission in Melbourne. After a prayerful consideration, Mr. Alexander accepted the invitation, for it seemed to be in answer to the prayers of several of his friends. In speaking of what led up to this important event, Mr. Alexander said:

"Mr. Williams decided to take a three months' vacation and travel in the Holy Land. I felt that I must be busy in the Lord's work during his absence. Dr. Torrey, having heard that I would have some time free, asked me to accompany him to Australia. I had no desire to travel. I wanted simply to do the Lord's work. I talked with my friends and prayed about it; and a group of my especial friends who usually prayed with me about any important turn in my work told me that they had been praying for some time that God might lead me into a larger sphere, and advised me to go. Hence I concluded to go, and hurriedly arranged the details with Dr. Torrey by telephone, although over six hundred miles apart. I went South to Tennessee and bade my mother, sister and brothers good-bye, and started alone on my journey to Australia. I did not know a soul there, and it was a long, lonely trip. I went directly from Vancouver to Sydney.

A SEASON IN MELBOURNE

It was in April, 1902, that the great mission in Melbourne began, in which 7,700 'publicly confessed Christ as their Saviour, and the report of which thrilled Christendom. The Mission lasted a month. For the first two weeks the meetings were held in fifty different centers, by fifty different Missioners. During the last two weeks the meetings were concentrated in the huge Exhibition Hall, accommodating nearly 10,000 people. Night after night it was filled to over-flowing; and scenes transpired such as were never before witnessed in Australia. W. E. Geil, an American evangelist, took a prominent part in the campaign, alternating with Dr. Torrey in addressing the great multitudes.

A writer in a secular paper described as follows the spectacle of the vast throngs seeking admission to the building:

"Very remarkable was the service of the Simultaneous Mission in the Exhibition Hall on Sunday evening. Walking to it through the gardens, the illuminated palace, with its electric lights on top of the dome shimmering down over the bulge, appeared more significant than ever. And yet we have surveyed it when the Australian nation was being launched inside. No secular ceremonial, however tremendous, even the coronation of King Edward at Westminster Abbey, can seize the heart strings, like the spontaneous rush of 15,000 people drawn by the Word of God."

FAME COMES IN A NIGHT

The Australian people did not know of Mr. Alexander's ability as a choir leader, and had only expected him to sing solos at the meetings. Mr. J. J. Virgo, one of the secretaries

THE FIRST CHOIR PRACTICE IN THE CITY HALL AT MELBOURNE, AUSTRALIA

of the Mission, had been spoken of as director of the central choir. When, however, Mr. Virgo learned of Mr. Alexander's talent and training as a leader of Gospel song, he generously resigned in his favor; and the Gospel singer, who had been much discouraged on arriving in Australia, and learning the condition of affairs, was nominated by Mr. Virgo, and unanimously elected Musical Superintendent of the Simultaneous Mission. Mr. Alexander had only needed a large opportunity to reveal his real power as a leader of Gospel song. The great Exhibition Building meetings gave him his opportunity, and he became famous almost in a night. The Australian press was full of praise of the marvelous manner in which he captivated and controlled the great multitudes and brought forth such singing as had never before been heard in the city.

Mr. Alexander's revival songs swept through Australia like a whirlwind. Soon after reaching Melbourne he published a book entitled *Alexander's Revival Songs,* and in a short time almost everybody was singing them. From the very first night the 'Glory Song' ran like wildfire over the country. It was sung in shops and factories, ground out from hand-organs, whistled on the street, hummed in trains and trams, and became a universal favorite. The words and music were printed in a large number of publications, including even Melbourne *Punch.* One writer declared that the song "set Australia on fire."

Dr. W. H. Fitchett, one of the foremost religious leaders of Australia, and the author of many popular books, gave the following graphic description of one of Mr. Alexander's Song Services at an inspirational meeting in the Melbourne Town Hall, at the opening of the great Simultaneous Mission:

MR. ALEXANDER'S METHOD

"The meeting began with what can only be described as a great singing lesson, twenty-one minutes long, with Mr. Alexander as teacher, and 2,500 people of all ages as his class. Mr. Alexander is tall of stature, commanding of look; and, as he took his stand on a sort of dais, he fairly dominated the whole gathering. He is a magnetic man; and with his waving arms for batons, his expressive, radiant face, and his fine voice, he swayed organ, choir, platform and audience at his pleasure. The song in which he drilled his class was both new and beautiful. It runs:

'When all my labors and trials are o'er,
That will be glory, be glory for me.'

"The tune to which these words are set is both fine and catching. First, the massed choir sang the hymn through, while the audience listened. Then Mr. Alexander swung round, and with swaying arms drew the whole audience into melody. Presently, with a wave of his hand, he silenced the choir, and the audience alone sang the verse. Then he hushed the great mass of people on the floor, and bade the people in the galleries sing it. A thread of music, in response, ran round the three front seats of the gallery, but singing apparently grows rather faint in those altitudes.

"'Now,' said Mr. Alexander, suddenly, 'let the platform sing it alone.' Silence fell instantly on all the rest of the audience, the silence of half-amused curiosity. But the platform acquitted itself surprisingly well; some 250 manly voices poured themselves into song with quite astonishing energy; and at the close the whole audience broke into an involuntary storm of applause. Nobody had suspected the 'parsons' of such singing gifts!

"Nothing else is more striking in the great Mission now in progress than the charm and effectiveness of the singing. Mr. Alexander is, of course, a conductor of the first order; and he exercises a curious spell over an audience. He drills an audience of over a thousand people with the decision and authority of a first class drill sergeant. He scolds, rebukes, exhorts, jests with almost more than American versatility and readiness. And the amusing feature is that the great audience enjoys being scolded and drilled. And the singing, with its ease and fire and exultation and the note of triumphant faith that runs through it all, melts the audience as fire would melt wax. In the mid-day meetings the floor of the Town Hall is one mosaic of men's faces, the majority of them middle-aged, many of them old. Time and care have ploughed deep furrows on most of them. They seem at first an audience for whom music ceased to have any office. But as the singing goes on, the tired faces relax; the eyes brighten; the lips begin to move. A wave of sunshine seems to run over the human landscape before one. Music, in its truest and highest office as the servant and vehicle of religion, has fulfilled its highest function. It has set thousands of human souls vibrating in gladness. No one need doubt that the Gospel can be sung as effectively as it can be spoken. And what other creed than that of Christianity can be set to music in this fashion?"

ALL MELBOURNE SINGS THE "GLORY SONG"

One of the most striking features of the work of the evangelists in Australia was the unprecedented popularity of the "Glory Song." It may safely be said to have led hundreds into the kingdom. Many beautiful and touching incidents are recorded of its influence upon human life. At the close of the Melbourne campaign a touching incident occured which Mr. Alexander related to me as follows:

"It seemed to me that everybody in Melbourne was singing the "Glory Song." Brass bands played it, and it was sung and played in all sorts of places. The last day I was in Melbourne I had to rise very early to take a train to Warnambool at five o'clock in the morning. As I came out, the maid was scrubbing the floor of the hall outside my door, and softly crooning:

'When by his grace I shall look on his face
That will be glory for me.'

"I went down to the hotel office, took the receiver off the telephone, wishing to telephone a friend across the city, and, as I placed it to my ear, I heard the girl at the telephone exchange singing,

'Oh, that will be glory for me.

"I got on the train and started on my journey. As we passed through Terang, a man and his wife, whom I had met at the Melbourne Mission, came down to the station to meet us; and we had a few words together. The lady said, 'Mr. Alexander, I am sure you will be glad to know anything about the "Glory Song." I learned it at the Mission in Melbourne, and have been over to-day to talk to a friend on a dying bed. I was telling her about the Mission and the "Glory Song," and she asked me to sing her a verse. I sang one verse, and she said, 'Oh, that is so glorious! please sing another.' I sang another, and then sang the chorus, and while I was singing,

DR. REUBEN ARCHER TORREY

'When by His Grace I Shall Look on His Face,' she passed to see the King in his beauty.' "

THE SHOEMAKER AND THE "GLORY SONG"

It was during the mission of Dr. Torrey and Mr. Alexander in Sydney that another beautiful incident in connection with the "Glory Song" occurred. Mr. Alexander said:

"When we were conducting our campaign in the great Town Hall at Sydney, we had leaflets with the 'Glory Song' words and music printed on them, and an invitation to the meetings printed at the bottom. We distributed them by thousands, handing them to each person as he came in. We would ask them, if they already had a copy of the song in their song books to post the leaflets to friends in the country who never got new songs or put them in parcels as they sent them away. One day I had asked them to do this, and a lady, when she got home, was sending some shoes to be mended when she happened to think about her 'Glory Song,' and put the leaflet in the bundle with the shoes. The next day she went down to the shoemaker's to get them, and found the old fellow pegging away with the tears falling down his cheeks.

"She said, 'What is the matter?' He said, 'Do you remember the 'Glory Song' that you put into the bundle? Last night I got my family around the organ and we sang it. I noticed the invitation to come to the Town Hall and hear Torrey and Alexander, so I went up last night. I heard that man preach, and I gave my heart to God. I have sent my wife and children up this afternoon to the meetings, and I am just here praying that God will save them.' The next night the whole family confessed their acceptance of Christ."

IV

THE REVIVAL IN AUSTRALIA

THE news of the great work of grace in Melbourne spread throughout the commonwealth; and Dr. Torrey and Mr. Alexander had calls to conduct meetings in the chief cities of Australia, Tasmania and New Zealand. For six months they went up and down the land with ceaseless energy, conducting campaigns of a few days or a few weeks in the largest cities.

Everywhere enormous throngs gathered to hear them. No building could be found large enough to contain the multitudes that assembled, so that separate meetings had to be held for men and for women. Thousands of converts were recorded. Among the Australian cities in which they held missions were: Ballarat, Geelong, Warnambool, Maryborough, Christchurch Bendigo and Sydney. It was in Bendigo that Mr. Alexander met and led to Christ Mr. Robert Harkness, a brilliant young musical genius, who became his pianist and accompanied him in his mission work. Mr. Harkness made the decision to accept Christ as he rode along on his bicycle after a long talk with Mr. Alexander at a hotel in Bendigo.

THE EXPERIENCE OF MR. HARKNESS

He frequently tells the story of his conversion in Mission meetings:

"In June, 1902, in Australia," said he, "I accepted the Lord Jesus Christ as my personal Saviour. I had been living an easy sort of way, thinking that some day perhaps I should become a Christian, but for the time being, while I was still young, I would make myself comfortable and have a good time. I never plunged into the vicious sins that entrap many young men.

"I had a godly father on the one side, and a saintly mother on the other. We had family prayers in our home, and I had every influence for good surrounding me. I used to go to the Bible class every Sunday afternoon; and I attended church regularly for I was the organist. My mother used to plead with me about my need of a Saviour; she was very faithful and every now and then she would take me aside, and tell me as plainly as anybody could that Jesus Christ died for me, and that if I would accept him as my Saviour I could have victory over sin in my every-day life, and would have everlasting life on the promise of the sure word of God. But I went on in my easy way, music being my chief recreation and hobby.

"I never was a drinking man, and never went to a horse race in my life. I never went to a play in my life, and never saw an opera. I had every influence for good, yet in spite of all this I was missing the greatest and best thing in life.

"Dr. Torrey and Mr. Alexander came to my home town of Bendigo in June. Prior to their coming a committee of the Mission came to me, and asked if I would not help in the meetings by playing the piano a part of the time. I was not interested in evangelistic meetings; indeed, I was rather opposed to them, but the thought struck me, that perhaps my good father and mother would be pleased if I took part in these meetings, and I consented. I hadn't been in the first meeting ten minutes before I found it was going to be decidedly warm, much warmer than I had expected.

"Mr. Alexander announced Hymn No. 7, and I was soon playing a two-line hymn, with an old Southern melody. I was not deeply interested, and played it in an offhand way. In playing through the 'Glory Song,' when I came to the chorus, I closed the book; I had memorized it quickly and improvised an accompaniment to the chorus to try to displease Mr. Alexander; but, instead of displeasing him, he turned around and looked at me and said, 'Keep it up. Keep it up. That is what we want.' So I kept on. The next time we had the chorus I played a full octave accompaniment, thinking he would surely be upset, but he was not there to be upset. At the close of the meeting Dr. Torrey asked me if I was a Christian. I straightened up and said, 'No, I am here to play the piano.' Dr. Torrey left me and went away, to pray for me—I think.

"The meetings went on and every day they got warmer, and every day I got more uncomfortable. I knew there were people praying for me. I had sisters that loved the Lord Jesus Christ; and I knew that they, as well as my parents and some of my brothers, were praying that I might be led to a decision.

"The meetings closed on a Friday night, and I went to Mr. Alexander to bid him good-bye. He said, 'Don't say good-bye; come and see me to-morrow morning.' I began to make excuses, Saturday was a busy day and I would not have any time and so on. But he insisted, and I agreed to spend a few minutes with him on Saturday morning. When I went in next day he put me in the most comfortable chair in the room, in front of a nice coal fire; it was June, and winter-time in our country. He began to talk; and presently, after leading up to it he said, 'You ought to accept Jesus Christ and become an out-and-out Christian. Why don't you settle the matter right now?' I knew the Way of Life, my mother had taken care of that; I knew my Bible, but I was hardening my heart against the Lord Jesus Christ; I had made up my mind that I would not yield, and I steeled myself against all his appeals. After the few minutes had stretched into about an hour and a half a member of the committee came in and asked Mr. Alexander to go for a drive; and to my relief he agreed to go.

THE KEY TO A MUSICIAN'S HEART

"We started down the steps, and as we walked down, he put his arm over my shoulder, but said nothing. I could not understand that—why he put his arm around me. I did not want to turn and look at him, but I looked out of the corner of my eye and I saw he had his head down. All of a sudden it dawned on me that perhaps he loved me. I began to feel that this man whom I had known for only a few days really loved me. We got to the cab and I put out my hand to say good-bye when he said, 'Don't say good-bye, I want you to come to Maryborough with me. Join me at the train this afternoon.' They were going to hold a short Mission at Maryborough, sixty miles away. Without thinking I replied, 'All right, I will go!'

"He drove around the corner in the cab, and I got on my bicycle to ride home, and as I rode along I began to think over what I had done. I had never come to the point of actual belief; but that morning on the bicycle I accepted Jesus Christ as my personal Saviour. That afternoon I joined the evangelists, and we conducted missions throughout Australia and Tasmania.

"Later on we went to New Zealand, and it was there that I experienced what was, after my conversion, the greatest blessing of my life. I had been in the meetings about four months. We were in a town at the south end of New Zealand, and they had a half night of prayer; and there the question came home to me—'Are you fully surrendered to the Lord Jesus Christ?' I knew I was not, but I decided then and there that I would hand my life over to him. Then it was that I received power in my work; then it was that I received the joy that the believer can have; and then it was that I decided to go wherever the Lord would lead me; and do what he would have me do; and be what he would have me be."

Mr. Harkness has since achieved international fame as a composer of Gospel hymns as well as a pianist. He has written some of the most popular hymns used by Mr. Alexander. Among the best known are: "Is He Yours?" "No Burdens Yonder," "Oh, What a Change," "He Will Hold Me Fast," "Bearing His Cross," "The Crown of Thorns."

AN ENTHUSIASTIC RECEPTION

In response to my request for a few of the most striking incidents which occured during their journey throughout Australia, Tasmania and New Zealand, Mr. Alexander said:

"Everywhere the 'Glory Song' preceded us. Our reception by the warm-hearted people was enthusiastic in the extreme. In Ballarat Dr. Torrey denounced dancing so strongly that a storm of opposition was raised. As a result he was invited by a dancing club to visit one of their dances and see if there was anything objectionable in it. They did not think he would come, but he went, watched them for a few moments, and the dancers quickly stopped in confusion. Dr. Torrey then preached them a sermon which broke up the dance; and the club went to pieces afterwards, only one more dance being held after that night. This caused a stir on the dancing question throughout Australia.

"In connection with the Sydney campaign, two very interesting incidents stand out very clearly in my memory. One of the biggest, finest-looking Salvation Army men I ever saw was a man by the name of Miller. I always enjoyed seeing him come into our meetings. He would often speak in the open air on the outside, for the building was never large enough for the crowds. We had two brass bands—one on the inside and one on the outside—to accompany the people in singing Gospel hymns. One after another, preachers and Salvation Army men, would address the outside audience. One night this big Salvationist got up, and in his talk to the people said: 'Before I gave my heart to God I weighed ten stone; I had poor health and no peace in my soul. But since I gave my heart to God I have had peace in my heart and health in my body, and now I weigh fifteen stone (210 pounds) and every pound saved, praise the Lord!'

A MARVELOUS RESCUE

"One night while the open-air meeting was going on and the brass band was playing, people were going to the big Town Hall. A poor Finnish girl walking the street saw the people going in, and thought it was a concert hall. She went in and sat down. She could not understand much English.

We were singing, 'There's Not a Friend Like the Lowly Jesus.' When we came to the chorus she could understand the first line:

> 'Jesus knows all about our struggles';

She could not appreciate the second line:

> He will guide till the day is done';

But she understood the last words:

> 'There's not a friend like the lowly Jesus,
> No not one; no not one.'

"And it began to dawn upon her that Jesus was the Friend of sinners. Over and over again the chorus rang out: 'There's not a Friend like the Lowly Jesus,' and it sank deeply into her soul. This girl had run away from a good home in Finland, had landed in Sydney, but was unable to speak a word of English. The first day she had walked about trying to find a place, and at night she had walked up to the door of a residence and rung the bell to see if anyone could help her. It so happened that the owner of the house could speak a language she understood, and he gave her shelter and got her a position.

"But little by little, without the restraint of home life, her companions led her into sin, and this night found her one of the poor outcasts of the city. A worker happened to come to her during the service and told her the story of Jesus and His love, and how she could have him in her heart. She accepted him. I saw her that night and succeeding nights. A kind woman secured her another position; and the change that came into her face was one of the most remarkable I have ever seen. It had the sweetness and peace of heaven in it. Night by night she would go out and find other girls, who had

DR. TORREY PREACHING AT THE LAST MEETING, MELBOURNE, AUSTRALIA

been her companions in sin, and bring them to the workers, and ask them in her broken language to tell them the story of Jesus. In this way she had the joy of leading many of her former associates to Christ.

"We went to Tasmania for two campaigns—Launceston and Hobart. They call the island 'Little England.' In climate and appearance it is very much like England. Crowds taxed the largest buildings we could secure, and, as everywhere else, people were eager to hear the Gospel. I remember one night, after the after-meeting was over, Dr. Torrey called on me to sing a solo—a thing he did not usually do, for I had already sung once that evening, but the people didn't want to go home. I caught up my song-book and sang, 'Where is My Wandering Boy To-night?' A poor drunken fellow had just stepped in from the far door, 150 feet away from me. He could scarcely stand up. He had heard nothing of the sermon, but just caught the strain of

'Go for my wandering boy to-night,
    Go search for him where you will;
And bring him to me with all his blight,
    And tell him I love him still.'

"He said, 'That's for me,' and started down the aisle, and came to the front with a worker, and gave his heart to God.

THE CONVERSION OF A PUGILIST

"One night, in the same building, the champion heavy-weight pugilist of Tasmania, Jim Burke, and a member of the Tasmanian Parliament confessed Christ at the same time. In a letter to a friend some time after his conversion Mr. Burke wrote: 'I have won the biggest fight I ever had. I have in my time won many great victories, but the greatest victory I ever won was when I beat the devil.' "

The work of Dr. Torrey and Mr. Alexander in New Zealand was, if anything, more successful than the campaigns in Australia and Tasmania. Their tour throughout the country was in the nature of a triumphal progress from one city to another. The fame of their work had preceded them; and they were everywhere welcomed with open arms. Describing some of his experiences, Mr. Alexander said:

"Before leaving Melbourne, we had received a warm welcome by wire from the Mayor of Wellington, New Zealand, inviting us to hold a campaign there. We spent thirty days in New Zealand, and it constituted some of the most profitable work I think we have ever done; the power of God was with us from the first day to the last. People came from long distances to attend our meetings. They carried the fire into the country districts and into the country churches. The songs became popular immediately, and helped the revival to spread. Although we could conduct crusades in only three of the largest cities of the country, the smaller towns would telegraph ahead of us, begging us to conduct brief open-air services at the stations during the few minutes that the trains stopped. We told them that if they would secure a piano on a dray, and have it handy where we could step out from the train, we would sing a verse, and Dr. Torrey would speak a few words to them. I remember on one trip we have had seven of these meetings between cities. At one place a crowd of two thousand persons had assembled at the station. One man came a hundred miles to be present at one of those ten-minute services. We had thousands of hymn sheets ready which we would throw out broadcast over the audience. The pianist, Mr. Harkness, would be ready to jump as the train slowed up, strike the first chords, and the people would gather around the piano. Then I would mount the platform and sing a verse, and by this time Dr. Torrey would be ready, and make some telling points. It warmed one's heart to see the eagerness with which they drank in every word of song and sermon.

THE CHRISTIAN ENGINEER

"One day we noticed while traveling between Christchurch and Dunedin that we were permitted to stop longer at the stations than the schedule allowed. This surprised us at first, until one of the train men gave us the secret of it, saying that the engine driver on the train was a Christian man, and was making up time between stations in order that we might have more time to speak and sing. I wrote in one of my song books, 'To the engine driver with my love. Charles M. Alexander'; and sent it down to him. The next Sunday afternoon at the men's meeting a big grimy fellow came up and looked me full in the face—he didn't say a word, but held up his song book, open at the fly leaf. I knew who he was, and had a chance of thanking him and shaking his hand."

The report of the wonderful work of the American evangelists in the three countries of the Southern Hemisphere had spread throughout Christendom, and before their campaign was concluded they had received urgent invitations to conduct revival campaigns in England. Having, however, a desire to preach the Gospel in India, on their way, they sailed for Ceylon. The voyage was a very enjoyable one, and greatly benefited both Dr. Torrey and Mr. Alexander.

DR. TORREY AND MR. ALEXANDER REACH INDIA

On reaching India, the evangelists spent about six weeks conducting campaigns in Madura, Madras, Calcutta, Bombay and Benares. Wherever they went they were received with open arms by the missionaries and native Christians, and their crusade resulted in the conversion of hundreds of men, women and children. Especially to the missionaries their visit brought new life and new encouragement. The evangelists' faith in God, and his remarkable answers to prayers, and the reports of their wonderful revival campaigns in Australia stimulated every missionary to fresh enthusiasm in soul-winning. Mr. Alexander took with him a thousand hymn books to use in their meetings during the Indian tour; and was accompanied by his pianist, Mr. Harkness. It was inspiration to see how the natives of India caught up the melodies of the new Gospel songs. In speaking of their audiences Mr. Alexander said:

"To see the Mohammedans and the Parsees, the Hindus and the Buddhists, sitting in our meetings, each one with his red hymn book, and joining in the Gospel songs, was a beautiful sight. It was difficult to make them sing, sometimes, but it was well worth the effort. The missionaries welcomed the new songs and the inspiring accompaniments of Mr. Harkness which carried gladness into many homes and mission houses. I distributed hundreds of the song book to missionaries at out-of-the-way stations; and now the songs of praise rise from thousands of dusky-faced Christians throughout India. At one orphanage I visited they had the children lined up in rows, and gave me a surprise by having them all sing the 'Sunbeam Song.' Less than a year before these children had been rescued from starvation in a famine district.

OPENING OF THE ENGLISH CAMPAIGN

WHEN Dr. Torrey and Mr. Alexander reached England, they were practically unknown. Dr. Torrey had been there once before, twenty years previous; but he came on that occasion as an observer, and not as a teacher. It was Mr. Alexander's first visit. In a certain degree, however, they did not come as strangers, for the reports of what God had accomplished through them in Australia had filled Christian hearts with joy; and had led them to hope and pray for a similar work of grace in the British Isles.

Upon their arrival in London, a great welcome meeting was held in Exeter Hall which had been arranged by cablegram while the evangelists were still in Bombay. It was a memorable gathering. Mr. T. A. Denny presided. Among those present were Lord Kinnaird, Lord Radstock, Prebendary Webb-Peploe, Dr. J. Munro Gibson, Dr. Barnardo, Rev. S. F. Webster, Dr. Harry Guinness, Dr. A. T. Pierson, Rev. Thomas Spurgeon, Rev. F. B. Meyer, Rev. Thomas Champness, Mr. Eugene Stock, Mr. R. C. Morgan, and many other well-known religious leaders.

LORD KINNAIRD'S WELCOME

In his address of welcome Lord Kinnaird said: "We have been looking forward to your presence. We have heard what you have been doing in Australia and in other parts of the world; and we pray our Heavenly Father that, through you, there may be such an outpouring of the Holy Spirit as we have not seen for years. We will follow you with our prayers, and look forward to the hour when you will be back in London. Most heartily do we welcome you this evening."

Following the welcome meeting, the evangelists spent three weeks in Mildmay Conference Hall, North London, stirring up church members to fresh zeal in soul winning, and witnessing a large number of conversions. At the close of their work there was a prophecy of the great and glorious work which they were later to accomplish in London—they received a cordial invitation to visit Edinburgh for a four weeks' campaign. Their meetings were held in Synod Hall, which proved too small to accommodate the thousands who pressed to hear the evangelists.

This was the beginning of a revival campaign conducted by Dr. Torrey and Mr. Alexander throughout the provincial cities of England, Ireland, Scotland and Wales, which was without precedent since the great work of Moody and Sankey in 1873-'75. Wherever they went—to Glasgow, Edinburgh, Aberdeen and Dundee in Scotland; to Dublin and Belfast in Ireland; to Liverpool, Manchester and Birmingham in England— the largest halls were unable to accomodate the thousands who daily thronged to hear them.

The success of the evangelists' work was due to their faith in God, their dependence upon the Holy Spirit for results, their zeal in soul-winning, and last, but not least, to the organization of thousands of "Prayer Circles" throughout the United Kingdom to implore God for a world-wide spiritual awakening, and to pray for the work of Dr. Torrey and Mr. Alexander.

When asked to relate some narratives of striking conversions which had occured during their early work in Great Britain, Mr. Alexander kindly consented and gave me the following stories of remarkable transformations through the power of the Gospel:

TWO TRANSFORMED LIVES

"A young lady attended our meetings in St. Andrews Hall, Glasgow, who had been assisting her elder sister with her business. For years she had received nothing but her expenses for her work. She felt that she should receive more than that; and had systematically slipped a certain amount from the till each week and put it in the bank until she had stolen $650. The Spirit of God touched her one night in the meeting, and revealed her sinful heart. She accepted Christ, went home and handed her bank book to her sister, telling her that the amount in the bank had been stolen from the business, and asked her forgiveness which was immediately given. The sister, who had been cold in the Lord's service, was led to deep consecration through the act; it touched the entire community, and many others were led to Christ through this restitution.

"While we were in Belfast Dr. Harry Guinness assisted us with the overflow meetings. We had two large churches, which were packed night after night, until at last we had to take St. George's Market, which held 7,000 people. There we saw some wonderful displays of God's power. I remember one broad-faced Irishman, called 'Billy', who was very earnest in dealing with drunkards that came to the front. He had been converted in gaol one day when Sankey was singing 'Hold the Fort.' The words came across from another building to the open window of his cell, and he was led to Christ through them.

"I well recollect our last meeting in Belfast when about five hundred people came to Christ. Dr. Torrey was appealing to those to come forward who would accept Jesus Christ, and 'Billy' was down at the front dealing with some man. In the midst of the invitation he jumped up, turned to the audience and shouted, 'Why don't ye come to Jesus? Pwhat har-r-rm's he ever done ye?' Later in the meeting, when about to close, Dr. Torrey made the statement, as he addressed the new converts that never in his life had he felt so reluctant to leave a city as he had to leave Belfast. Billy jumped up again and cried, 'Nobody's a-chasin ye away!'

BELFAST'S FAREWELL

"As we took the steamer on our last day in Belfast, the street was packed solid with people right across in front of the quay. The Salvation Army Brass Band led the music; and, using a large box for a platform, I conducted the whole street full of people in singing song after song. Dr. Torrey said a few words, and then made an appeal for converts right in the street. Some laboring men coming home, all grimy from their work, with their buckets on their arms, accepted his invitation and publicly confessed Christ.

"Our choir was by the ship's side, and as we left the dock they sang, 'God Be With You Till We Meet Again,' while I directed them from the upper deck with a handkerchief. For three quarters of a mile up the docks people were strung along in great numbers, waving and singing 'Never Lose Sight of Jesus.' The people on board said they had never seen such a

A CHOIR ON WHEELS IN NEW ZEALAND

beautiful sight as those thousands of people gathered on the shore, bidding us good-bye with a Gospel song. The Captain sent a man to us, asking if he should blow the whistle. We said, 'Yes'; so while the handkerchiefs were waving and the people were singing the whistle began to blow and that was our affectionate 'good-bye' to Belfast."

At the conclusion of their work in Ireland Dr. Torrey and Mr. Alexander made a flying visit to America during July and August, 1903, where they addressed numerous conventions and religious conferences, and stirred up the people with their glorious reports of the revival campaigns in Australia and Great Britain.

CHICAGO'S WELCOME

The most notable meeting held during their stay in America was the great Welcome Meeting in the Auditorium in Chicago. The scenes enacted at that memorable meeting were impressive, and long to be remembered. Although the service was timed to commence at eight o'clock, long before that hour thousands of people stood four deep in the street, waiting for the doors to be opened. It is estimated that ten thousand people endeavored to gain admission to the huge building.

One of the leading lawyers of Chicago, Hon. Luther Laflin Mills presided; and in his address of welcome said: "Dr. Torrey has returned to us a conquering hero, home from that holiest of wars, the battle for the redemption and uplifting of men's souls. He has been recognized in every civilized land, and in China, Japan, India and Hawaii for his work and worth as the real successor of Moody, and as such we give him welcome. With him comes Charles M. Alexander, the sweet singer, whose music has set half the world to singing, and the echoes of which still linger to-day in the hearts and memories of many peoples in many lands."

In his conduct of the musical part of the program Mr. Alexander quickly captivated the great American audience as he had done similar audiences in Australia, India and the United Kingdom; and soon they were singing his revival melodies as only Americans can sing when aroused to the highest pitch of enthusiasm. The meeting was especially noticeable by reason of one woman who sat in a box that night. She was a little, sweet-faced lady who had come all the way from Tennessee, to hear her son sing before the great audience gathered in the Auditorium. It was the first time she had seen him in so large a gathering; and the tears glistened in her fond eyes as the roars of applause broke once and again over her boy's head. She was Mrs. Alexander, and her son was the sweet-voiced baritone who had girdled the globe with Gospel song.

VI

"TELL MOTHER I'LL BE THERE"

IN September, 1903, the evangelists returned to England; and began a four weeks' campaign in Liverpool, which proved to be the most successful held up to that time in Great Britain. About 5,000 converts were recorded. Such crowds flocked to the Philharmonic Hall, where the meetings were held, that towards the close of the mission it was necessary to hold double meetings each night, the first being for women, the second for men. While the first service was in progress thousands would be clamoring at the door for admittance. People would stand four deep for an hour, all along the sides of the building, in the rain, waiting for an entrance, and as they waited they sang revival hymns. Mr. Alexander told me a characteristic incident which occured one day among those waiting for admission.

"One night," said he, "after the notice was put up 'Hall Full,' great crowds still hung around the doors. Mr. Armstrong, a city missionary, went out and said to the crowd, 'The Hall is full; why don't you go home?' One lady standing near him said, 'Please, sir, we are waiting for somebody to faint,' He said, 'Surely you don't want anyone to faint, do you? 'No,' she said, 'but they do faint in there sometimes, and I am waiting until somebody does, so that I can get their seat.' Her earnestness excited his curiosity, and he inquired if she was a Christian. She replied she was not. 'Well,' said he,' I can probably get you in at the back door.' He succeeded, and she listened to the sermon. In the after-meeting he noticed that that woman was one of the first to come down to the front seats and publicly confess her acceptance of Christ.

THE SONG THAT TOUCHED ALL HEARTS

"Our last Sunday in Philharmonic Hall was one of the most memorable days that I have ever seen in our work," continued Mr. Alexander. "We were to have a women's meeting in the afternoon and a men's meeting at night. I had been praying earnestly before going to the women's meeting in the afternoon that God would lead me to the very song that would melt the hearts of the people and lead them to Christ. I was very much in doubt during the first part of the song service what song to use. At last I threw the meeting open, and asked anyone to suggest a song that had helped them. A lady immediately mentioned No. 13, 'Tell Mother I'll Be There.' Directly she announced it I felt that that was the song we needed. We began singing it; and it took a wonderful hold upon the audience. I felt that the Lord was there, and at the close of Dr. Torrey's sermon, when he gave out the invitation, two hundred and ten women came down to the front and publicly confessed Christ. I said to the women, 'I have a curiosity to know how many of you were led to Christ by the singing of "Tell Mother I'll Be There." Will those who were please rise?' And thirty-three women out of the two hundred and ten stood up.

"When it came to the men's meeting at night, we had a choir of five hundred men. I believe everyone of them was an earnest Christian. After we had sung a little I told the audience what had happened in the afternoon; and said that we ought to have three times as many men yielding themselves to God during the singing of the hymn. I then turned to the choir and said, 'Men, pray every word you sing!' They sang it together, and you felt their hearts were behind it. You could feel that the hearts of the men in the audience were melting like wax. During the song I made a call for those who would accept Christ and confess him publicly before the audience to stand up then and there. They started to stand up; we would sing another verse and they would begin to rise up again. Presently I called up a little curly-headed boy, and stood him upon the stand beside me, and he sang a verse which seemed to move the men more deeply than ever. When the song ended one hundred and sixty men had risen and publicly professed their acceptance of Christ. Spontaneously the audience arose and sang, 'Praise God From Whom All Blessings Flow.' Then Dr. Torrey preached and repeated the invitation, and four hundred and fifty men, including the hundred and sixty who had stood up before the sermon, publicly acknowledged that they had taken Jesus Christ as their Saviour, their Lord and their King. An American consul sitting on the platform near me said that he did not know God was working in that way in these days, and that it was the most wonderful sight he had ever seen."

Not only in Liverpool, but all throughout England this touching hymn was used in the conversion of many men and women.

THE STING OF MEMORY

Mr. Alexander relates an interesting incident which occurred during their campaign in Dundee. "One night, just as I was ready to retire in my hotel," he says, "a porter came up to me and said that a gentleman wanted to se me in the coffee room. I tried to make an excuse, but the porter said that the man insisted that he must see me. I went down and found a fine, big Scotch farmer sobbing like a child. I said, 'What can I do for you? Are you a Christian man?' He said, 'I wasn't a Christian man till to-night, but I am now. I listened to Dr. Torrey's sermon, and withstood that and his appeal to come to Christ; but I was standing during the singing in the after-meeting, when the choir struck up the song 'Where is My Wandering Boy To-night?' I thought of my good old father who had gone to heaven three years before, and it touched my heart. Then at the close of the verse the choir sang 'Tell Mother I'll Be There.' My dear old mother had gone to heaven a little while before, and the memory of the home life, and of their sweet Christian lives was too much for me. I gave my heart to God, and felt that I could not go home to-night until I had told you.' He said he was going back home to start family prayers and live a consecrated Christian life. Such experiences as this," said Mr. Alexander, "give one a fresh and never-tiring interest in the work of soul winning."

During the campaign in Manchester a gentleman wrote Mr. Alexander telling him how two of his songs had brought great blessing into his life. His letter ran as follows:

"I came to hear you last Monday night. I told my wife I was going, and she was praying for me all the time. When the hymn 'My Mother's Prayer' was sung it brought to my memory the time when my saintly mother passed away, and when at her bedside I knelt and promised to meet her in heaven. This hymn broke me down, but when the audience began to sing 'I Surrender All' I could not sing it. I could not surrender all, and so left the meeting; but the idea of a complete surrender still remained in my mind. I was afraid that if I surrendered all I would have to give up card playing and theatre going. I felt that I could not give up those things. On Sunday night I began to read the family Bible, and after perusing a chapter or two, I sank on my knees, and with my wife at my side, surrendered all to Jesus. Praise the Lord I can now say, 'I surrender all.' I am taking him at his word that he is able to keep me."

For a month the evangelists held a campaign in Dublin, in the Metropolitan Hall, during which about three thousand persons publicly accepted Christ. In recalling the work in this city, two touching incidents are related:

A BUSINESS MAN AND HIS MOTHER'S BIBLE

"One night, while the audience was singing 'Where is My Wandering Boy To-night,' a bright young business man from Glasgow was among the audience, and was deeply touched. Dr. Torrey's straight dealing impressed him so much that he turned to a man sitting at his side, and said, 'That man talks religion the way I sell goods. I am coming again to hear him to-morrow night.' He came again the next night with another man, and came out boldly for Christ. He wrote immediately to his old mother in Scotland, and received in reply one of the most beautiful letters I have ever seen. He had written to her to send on his Bible as he had been converted. Many times before when he would start off on a trip she had placed a small Bible in his bag, but he would hunt it out and leave it behind. The last time he had left home his mother said, 'I won't put the Bible in this time, but, if you want it, write and let me know and I will send it on.' His dear old father was filled with rejoicing at the great news they had just received. Later the young man went to Chicago to attend the Moody Bible Institute to fit himself better for Christian work.

"We have always endeavored in our meetings to get every Christian consecrated, every consecrated person a worker, and every worker trained to work anywhere and everywhere with anybody at any time or at all times. After a noon-day meeting in Dublin, a lady went to a well known restaurant to have lunch. She had her red hymn book with her, and laid it down beside her on the table. Another lady sitting close by observed the book, and entered into conversation with her. She said she was not a Christian, but would like to meet somebody who would explain to her the Way of Life. The lady lovingly and plainly explained to her the way, with the result that before she left the restaurant the anxious one had definitely accepted Christ. A day or two later the Christian lady went into the same restaurant and chanced to lay her hymn book again upon the table. A strange lady introduced herself, asking whether she was not the same woman who had led a friend of hers to Christ in the same restaurant. She said, 'You told my friend the Way of Life. Can you tell me?' Gladly she pointed the inquirer to Christ, and soon had the satisfaction and joy of knowing that she had led another soul to Jesus."

A CHRISTIAN CREW

The results of the campaigns conducted by the evangelists are felt on the high seas as well as upon the land. A member of the Torrey-Alexander party was returning from Dublin

DR. TORREY AND MR. ALEXANDER AT THE RAILWAY WORKSHOPS, CHRISTCHURCH, NEW ZEALAND

to Liverpool by the steamer "Cork." On being shown to his cabin he was met by the steward, who recognized him as one of the staff, and gave him a cordial welcome. "I am a Christian also," said the steward, "and you are now traveling on a Christian ship." The gentleman inquired what was meant, and the steward explained that he himself had been converted at one of the Torrey-Alexander meetings in Philharmonic Hall, Liverpool, the previous September. Another steward had been led to Christ during their crusade in Dublin, where one or two firemen had also found Jesus; and now so many of the crew had become Christians that the "Cork" was known among the seamen as the "Christian Ship."

At the famous seaside resort of Brighton the evangelists conducted a most successful campaign in The Dome, The Pavilion, The Corn Exchange and Hove Town Hall. Among the many beautiful incidents which occurred there, the following should be an inspiration to every Christian to improve every opportunity of winning souls to Christ:

"As I was leaving Hove Town Hall at the close of an afternoon meeting," said Mr. Alexander, "I stopped near the door, and a lady came and asked to shake hands with me. She said her mother had written to her, telling her to come to our meetings, and be sure to speak to Mr. Alexander. I was just about to say some commonplace words and bid her good-bye when the thought came to me to inquire if she was a Christian. I found she was not. I pressed upon her the claims of Christ, but she would not accept them. I was on the point of leaving when she said, turning to a girl of about sixteen years of age nearby, 'This is my daughter.' After shaking hands with her I said, 'Are you a Christian?' She replied, 'No, I am not.' I urged upon her the necessity of accepting Christ, and she yielded. All this time her mother had been standing at her side, and when the daughter yielded I turned to the mother and said, 'Surely you don't want to be out of Christ when your daughter is a Christian?' She could not stand that and she, too, came to a decision for Jesus.

A MOMENT TOO LATE

One night during the mission a solemn thing happened. A Christian man went into a restaurant for dinner, and, as the waiter served him, he experienced a strong conviction that he ought to speak to the man about his soul. He did not yield to it, however, but left the place without referring to the question of surrender to Christ. But even after he had reached the street the feeling returned with increased force; and he waited outside the restaurant for the waiter to come out. At last, the proprietor commenced to close the shop, and seeing this gentleman standing outside asked him what he was waiting for. He replied that he wanted to speak to the waiter that had served him. The answer of the proprietor came like a blow. "You will never," he said, "speak to that man again. After serving you he went upstairs and shot himself." When this incident was related in public it produced a profound impression, for it was a solemn lesson as to the danger of disobeying the promptings of the Spirit, as well as a warning to every Christian to be zealous in seeking the unsaved.

INFIDELS CONVERTED

During the month's Mission conducted by the evangelists in Bristol, four infidel members of one family flung their unbelief to the winds and came out for Christ. There were six sons and one daughter in the family, and all were infidels. The father had once been a clergyman, but had gone into infidelity, and had brought up his family to scoff at Christianity—a step which he bitterly regretted before he died.

During the Torrey-Alexander Mission an infidel lecturer from London visited this family, in order to get one of the young men to go with him to Coulston Hall to secure material for jest and sport. When he called everyone was out except the daughter. She accompanied him to the meeting. It was the first time she had ever attended a Gospel service. What she heard so deeply impressed her that she went again alone, and was converted. It was a bold step for her, but a bolder one was to follow. She returned home and told her brothers of her decision. They were indignant, but she held her ground. Finally she persuaded one of them to go with her to another service. The result was that he, too, flung his infidelity to the wind and accepted Christ; and before the Mission ended three other members of the same family came out for Christ.

Numerous were the infidels laid hold of by the power of God during the work in Great Britain and saved. At Manchester Mr. Musgrave Reed, one of the foremost infidel lecturers in the city, was converted, and has been for some time preaching the Gospel in India.

VII

PENTECOSTAL BLESSING AT BIRMINGHAM

THE revival campaign in Birmingham during January, 1904, was probably the most successful month's mission held anywhere in Great Britain. In that brief period nearly 8,000 men, women and children publicly professed to accept Christ as their Saviour, Lord and King. The meetings were held in Bingley Hall, one of the finest auditoriums in England. It seats 8,000 people, with standing room for 2,000 more; and is so perfect in its acoustic properties that Mr. Moody declared, after holding a series of meetings in it, that he wished he could carry it about with him wherever he went. From the first the meetings were wonderfully successful, the crowds coming in such throngs that it was necessary to call the mounted police in order to prevent accidents.

Although the meetings were so remarkably successful, yet they were begun under greater physical disadvantages, as regards the evangelists, than any other series of meetings in England. Mr. Alexander had hardly recovered from an illness, while Dr. Torrey was still suffering from a cold contracted several weeks before. Dr. Torrey's indisposition was so serious that it was feared that he would be unable to continue the meetings. As usual, however, the crisis was met and conquered by prayer. In answer to my inquiry, Mr. Alexander told the remarkable narrative how God heard and answered prayer for the recovery of Dr. Torrey.

AN OPEN-AIR AUDIENCE SINGING "TELL MOTHER I'LL BE THERE."

THE FAREWELL TO THE EVANGELISTS AT DUNEDIN, NEW ZEALAND

FERVENT PRAYERS ANSWERED

"I had never seen Dr. Torrey appear so physically weak as during those first days at Birmingham," declared Mr. Alexander. "His voice seemed to be getting weaker and weaker each day, and the cold which he had contracted was still hanging on. He had hoped that his Christmas vacation trip to Germany would cure him, but he had not found the relief he had expected. One Saturday afternoon as we began the meeting it seemed to me that his voice would fail entirely before he reached the end of his sermon. On leaving the hall I took a cab and went as fast as I could to the nearest telegraph office; and sent to the Moody Bible Institute in Chicago the following cablegram: 'Pray for Torrey's voice and health.' I knew that this cablegram would probably reach them before their Saturday night prayer-meeting, which still meets regularly to pray for a world-wide revival, and has done so ever since Dr. Torrey and his friends started it. The cablegram reached them long before the meeting, for Chicago time is six hours later than in London, and they spent much time in earnest prayer for the recovery of Dr. Torrey's voice and his health.

"The next morning when I came down to the early morning service with him he looked brighter, and his voice had a hearty ring in it. I asked him how he felt, and he replied, 'Last night was the first night I have been able to sleep in three weeks.' From that morning there was striking improvement both in his appearance and in the ring of his voice. He was able to preach to three large audiences nearly every day throughout the month. A great note of praise was in my heart for this answer to prayer, which was one more striking proof that God hears and answers prayer."

A FOOTBALL TEAM CONVERTED

Among the hundreds of striking incidents connected with the great awakening in Birmingham, one of the most remarkable was the conversion of an entire football team. One Thursday night thirteen members of the club attended a meeting in Bingley Hall; and three of their number stood up and publicly accepted Christ. So eager were they to win others to their new-found Saviour, that on the following Saturday, after the usual match had been played, they insisted upon the whole team's attending the evening meeting. They came directly from the field to the hall, each with his handbag, containing his football clothes; and that night several more of the club accepted Christ. The converted members then united in their efforts; and again brought the unconverted ones on Sunday night. The remainder of the unconverted club members were then saved, making in all twenty-five, thus forming a remarkable "Christian football club" of twenty-five members.

One of the most beautiful tributes to the work of the evangelists in Birmingham was from the Rev. J. H. Jowett, the successor of Dr. Dale in Carr's Lane Chapel. Writing to an English Journal regarding the movement he said:

"What has impressed me above all things has been the Missioners' quiet and immovable assurance of the fellowship of God. Their communion with the Divine has not been ostentatiously declared; it has been most powerfully assumed. Dr. Torrey and Mr. Alexander have come to their meetings with the fragrance of the Presence Chamber round about them, and, as though it were the most natural thing in the world, they have confidently assumed the companionship of the King. It may appear to be a very ordinary matter when thus recorded in cold print; but to stand in the presence of men over whose spirits there is no shadow of uncertainty, and who rejoice in the sun-clear fellowship of the Eternal, is to be confronted with an experience which subdues one in most fruitful awe. When these men speak of God's presence they speak as those who know.

"Closely allied to this, and, indeed, part and parcel of it, is their clear and calm confidence in the marvelous ministry of prayer. Mr. Alexander's estimate of prayer is that of a child; not that it lacks intelligence, but because it is so filled with sunny and unshaken trust. He speaks of the ministry of prayer as one who speaks of sunshine or of fresh air, and he exercises himself in it with the same naturalness as one who would draw up the blind to let in the light, or open the window to let in the air. The Missioners' conception of prayer is not confined to the realm of the spirit; its ministry pervades every place, and is operative everywhere. God has privileged us to commune with him in matters directly affecting the body, as well as in the higher interests of the soul. These men have a great treasure in God; it is their inheritance, and they draw upon it with unclouded assurance and serenity. Again and again I was reminded of what Tennyson once said in the presence of Mr. Gladstone; 'Praying is to me the opening of the sluice gate between me and the Infinite.' Dr. Torrey and Mr. Alexander lift that sluice gate with most contagious confidence, and the Divine power flows into their spirits like a river of water of life.

"The Mission has fertilized the Christian life of the town. Few will be the churches which are not enriched by its labors. A wave of spiritual expectancy has swept over the city. I have heard of prayer meetings in churches which were fast dying, but which have been re-created and vitalized. Ministers have once again had their eyes fixed upon their primary work. Disciples have been won to the Lord in thousands. 'It is the Lord's doing, and it is marvelous in our eyes.' "

MR. ALEXANDER'S WEDDING

It is a well-known fact that Birmingham is the home of the Cadbury family, the famous philanthropists and cocoa manufacturers. They are leaders in the religious life of Birmingham; and they naturally took a prominent part in the mission campaign at Bingley Hall. The present head of the great cocoa firm, Mr. George Cadbury, was a member of the committee which invited the evangelists to Birmingham, and entertained them in his home, while the wife and daughter of his elder brother, the late Mr. Richard Cadbury, were active workers in the meetings.

While the Mission was in progress, Mr. Alexander became acquainted with Miss Helen Cadbury, the daughter of Mr. Richard Cadbury; and, through their mutual interests in saving the lost, the acquaintance quickly ripened into love. It may be stated, however, that the event was another of those remarkable answers to prayer with which Mr. Alexander's life has been filled. Shortly after the Birmingham campaign had ended, the engagement of Mr. Alexander and Miss Cadbury was announced. Their marriage took place the following July at the Friends' meeting-house in Birmingham. The Cadburys are Quakers; and the ceremony was conducted according to the simple methods prescribed by the Friends' ordinances. Although the ceremony was so simple, the gathering was dis-

MR. AND MRS. ALEXANDER AT THE HOME OF MRS. CADBURY

tinguished, many of the religious leaders of Great Britain being present.

The city of Birmingham turned out en masse to see the wedding procession. It is said that on only two previous occasions in the city's history—one of which was the death of the bride's father—had such throngs assembled to witness any public event. The streets were so packed with eager and interested spectators that it was with difficulty that the procession moved through the surging mass.

When the Meeting House was reached, the ceremony proceeded with considerable periods of silence as is customary. As the Spirit moved them two or three persons arose and gave a brief message, or led in prayer, the bride and bridegroom making their simple declaration near the beginning of the meeting.

The day following their marriage was spent by Mr. and Mrs. Alexander at the Cadburys' country home near Birmingham, which was once the home of Jenny Lind. Two days later the bridal pair took a steamer for a six weeks' honeymoon trip to America.

Except for a week, spent at his old home in Tennessee, their stay was almost entirely devoted to addressing Christian conferences and assemblies on the great revival work which had been accomplished in England during the previous eighteen months. Two or three days were spent at Northfield, where Mr. Alexander conducted the singing with his usual enthusiasm, and made the famous auditorium erected by D. L. Moody ring with musical melody as it perhaps had never done before. It was Mr. Alexander's first visit there; and his services were so appreciated that he was urged to return the following year; and he has been going there each year since unless other engagements prevented him.

Mr. Alexander also visited Chicago, where he took part in crowded meetings in Dr. Torrey's church and in the Bible Institute. He also assisted Dr. J. Wilbur Chapman in the revival campaign he was conducting in St. Louis, in connection with the World's Fair; and visited the Winona Bible School where two thousand ministers had gathered for a ten days' conference, and which is an American "Keswick."

A TRUE HELP-MATE

Despite the fact that Mrs. Alexander had been brought up in the midst of comfort, she has always been used to mission work, and since her marriage has thrown herself most heartily into her husband's work, accompanying him on his tours, and doing active personal service in revival meetings night after night. So ardent a soul-winner is she that I have seen her keep the janitor waiting half an hour to turn out the lights after a meeting, while she pleaded with some poor lost soul to accept Christ. She believes every Christian should be a personal worker.

Mrs. Alexander's father was one of the greatest public benefactors who ever lived in Birmingham. He gave to all good causes with a lavish hand. One of his benefactions was a beautiful quadrangle of almshouses for the aged poor. Another was the founding of a Friends' Institute in the slums, as well as giving a beautiful home of his own as a Convalescent Hospital for children.

It was when she was 12 years of age that Miss Cadbury made an open confession of Christ. During a Friends'

Mission—for all the Cadburys are Friends—in that part of Birmingham where her father had built up a large mission work, she stood up with the tears rolling down her cheeks and publicly accepted Christ. Even after she had arisen, a girl friend whispered to her, 'You are a Christian already, you need not do this, and especially before these poor people.' But Miss Cadbury was not ashamed of her Lord, and, not only stood up, but went into the inquiry room where her father was working. She knelt with him in prayer, and fully surrendered her life to Christ.

While attending the High School she helped to organize a unique and interesting society among her schoolmates. It was called the "Pocket Testament League." The rules were: That every member must be a Christian and seek to win others to Christ; must be a member of a daily Bible reading society; and must always carry a Testament in her pocket. The girls had special pockets made in their dresses for carrying their Testaments; and, when any member challenged another, the one challenged had to produce her Testament in answer. The organization flourished greatly, at one time numbering sixty members. It is interesting to note here that numerous "Pocket Testament Leagues" have recently been organized in the United States, as the result of that one started years ago by Mrs. Alexander.

Mrs. Alexander is a college woman, and reads and speaks German fluently. She has visited Palestine three times—on one occasion making, in company with her parents, a long camping tour through it. It was during her second visit to the Holy Land, in 1899, that her father passed away in the city of Jerusalem. From that time until her marriage, Miss

Cadbury devoted herself more than ever to religious and philanthropic work with her mother, among the poor of Birmingham. She regularly taught a Sunday School class of 20 young women, training them to become teachers; while on Sunday evenings she conducted a Gospel service for young children at the Friends' Institute. At another Institute erected by her father, she superintended a Working Girl's Club, which had a membership of about sixty, and met weekly.

MRS. ALEXANDER AS AN AUTHOR

Recently Mrs. Alexander has achieved not a little distinction as an author. She has written a beautiful and comprehensive life of her father, entitled "Richard Cadbury of Birmingham," which has won high praise from the English press. She has also written several poems, one of which is here reproduced:

> "Dear God, who sendest us both joy and pain,
> Teach us in both to recognize thy hand;
> For over all Life's change of smiles and tears
> Hangs a thick veil of mystery; and when
> Our inner sight is blinded; and we grope
> For reasons in the twilight of our souls,
> By which to solve the puzzle Life presents
> All seems capricious. Till, at length, the sun
> Of thy great Love in rising on our hearts
> Pierces the veil, and in the chequered shade
> We slowly learn to understand thy plan
> Of intermingled grief and happiness.
> The cup of sorrow still is hard to drink
> But thou dost share it, and our trembling hearts
> Grow stronger to endure the agony.
> How gladly, if the cup be full of joy
> We take, as from a Father's loving hand,
> And find refreshment in the pure sweet draught!"

VIII

A MEMORABLE MIDNIGHT MEETING

Upon the return of Mr. and Mrs. Alexander to England, following their brief wedding trip in America, the evangelists began their third year's campaign in Bolton, where more than 3,500 confessed Christ during the month's Mission. The meetings were held in a large drill hall, accommodating about 5,000 people. The head of the committee was Col. R. H. Ainsworth, J. P., a man of wealth and influence, who was an ardent personal worker. Night after night he and his wife could be seen going about the audience, pleading with the poor working people, who attended the Mission in large numbers.

"THE MIDNIGHT SWEEP" OF THE SLUMS

One of the most memorable meetings of the Mission was a "Midnight Sweep" for drunkards and outcasts. At 10:30 one Saturday night over a thousand workers met at the Drill Hall where services were being held; and, forming into two brigades, marched through the streets of the city, singing revival melodies. As they went through the slums, one by one the workers caught hold of drunkards and outcasts, and often literally compelled them to follow the procession to the Drill Hall meeting. When the motley throng reached the hall the scene presented was pathetic in the extreme. A thousand besotted, blear-eyed, uncouth men and women sat looking wonderingly up at the evangelists and the choir.

After a brief address by Dr. Torrey, he called upon Rev. W. S. Jacoby, the assistant pastor of the Moody Church, Chicago, to talk to the poor creatures. Mr. Jacoby knew just what to say, for he had once been way down in sin himself; but since his conversion he has become one of the most consecrated men in America. Dr. Torrey had often spoken of him as "the best-loved man in Chicago." During Mr. Alexander's wedding tour he had met Mr. Jacoby in Chicago, where they had formerly been students together in the Moody Bible Institute, and took him back to England for a month. After visiting at the home of Mrs. Richard Cadbury in Birmingham, Mr. Jacoby threw himself heartily into the work at Bolton.

Hundreds were melted to tears that night as Mr. Jacoby told the throng of drunken men and women how he, too, had once been a victim of drink, but had conquered the habit through the acceptance of Christ. A part of his life-story, which he often tells with great power, is as follows:

I want to thank God to-day that I have been redeemed from a life of sin. I was born in the city of Philadelphia. I joined the navy in 1862, where I went deeply into sin. Later I became a police officer in Philadelphia. I was a very wicked man at that time. Owing to the kind of life I lived I was suspended; but I had a political friend who went to the mayor four or five times for me, and got me reinstated each time, until finally after I had been suspended again the mayor said to him, 'Look here, I wouldn't put that fellow on again if he was my own brother.' I just tell you that to give you a little idea of what I was. Now I want to tell you what God did for me, and what God can do for a man.

MR. JACOBY'S LIFE STORY

"My father was well-to-do, and started me in the teamster business down on Front street; but I drank so much whiskey that he couldn't have me in the house any more at all, and I do not blame him. He could not trust me, and had no confidence in me; I would betray him or mother or anyone else, and so I went off into the army, away out West. I had been dishonorably discharged from the navy; and I got dishonorably discharged from the army out there, and I had to beat my way home. I never had done any work; and you cannot imagine what an experience I had on that journey. I stopped in St. Louis, and I was so hungry that I asked for work; and they put me to shoveling, and wheeling a barrow along a plank.

"I made such a mess of it that the boss came up and said, 'Guess you never did that kind of work before?' Well, I had not. 'All right, I'll give you something else.' So he gave me one of those great heavy stamping things that you stamp the cobble-stones down with. That was awful; I was not used to that kind of thing, and I said, 'That's enough of that; I guess I will go on.' I did not get any money—I was only there a day or two—and on I went, beating my way home on trains. I took a coal car at Reading for Philadelphia. Oh, what a dirty looking fellow I was! One heel had gone, jumping on the car, and I was smothered in coal dust. I slipped off the car at Philadelphia, went to our house and rang the bell. Mother came down stairs, threw up both hands, and said, 'Oh!' and just fell right on my shoulder and cried. Away down as I had gone into sin my mother still loved me. They packed me upstairs in the third story; it was a large house and my brother-in-law and sister lived there.

"They kept me up there, and my father did not know I was at home. About the third day, as they were all seated at the table, at noon, my sister's little girl about three years old says: 'Grandpa, Uncle Bill's up stairs.' They all looked at one another; and father says, 'Is William up stairs? Go and tell him to come down.' So down I came. He looked at me, and he said, 'How do you do!' and I said, 'How do you do!' 'Take a seat,' and I did. They passed me a plate, and he asked for it, filled it up and I went to eating. He said, 'What are you doing now?' I said, 'nothing.' He said, 'You are getting along better than I am.' I looked at my mother, and there she sat, and there was a smile on her face for one moment, and then the next the tears were running down her cheeks; she saw us there together, but she saw the estrangement between us. He went out, and he said to my brother-in-law, 'Do all you can for him.' I tell you that to show what passed in my life.

"I heard them singing to-day, 'Tell Mother I'll Be There"; and it brought back a scene to my recollection. You know I told you that I had been out in the West among the Indians, serving in the U. S. army. I received a letter, telling me how, when that song, 'Where is My Wandering Boy To-night' came out, and it was sung in our home, mother stood at the piano, when the young man sang it, with the tears running down her face. She was thinking of her boy wandering away from home.

'I received a telegram one day saying, 'Hurry if you want to see mother before she passes away; and, as fast as I could, I hurried to Philadelphia, jumped into a carriage, went home and up stairs to the room where mother was lying, seemingly

A SECTION OF THE AUDIENCE OF 12,000 CHILDREN AT ROYAL ALBERT HALL

unconscious. I am almost tempted to believe that mother knew I was there. They said she had looked toward the door again and again when it was opened, and they knew she was looking for her boy; and when I ran into the room I couldn't see anyone else; I just threw myself upon the bed and in a few moments she had passed away.

PROCESS OF CONVERSION

"It was in a little town out West one day that I found Jesus as my Saviour. I had heard of God, and used to go to church. I remember my Sunday School days, but do you know I don't ever remember my Sunday School teachers' telling me about Jesus, though they probably did. I did not know anything about the Word of God at that time; but I tell you I had been an awfully wicked man, and the people of that town knew it. One time I had a row with several of them; and the citizens were just going to get together and outlaw me and forbid my coming into the town. But it was there that I was converted. I remember being down at the altar at the Methodist Church, and I kneeled there and some one would ask me if I didn't feel it. 'Well,' I thought, 'what have I got to feel?' I supposed there would be a kind of glorified shock coming to me pretty soon. I did not know what else to expect. I went up there for six or seven nights. I had started, and I was going to find Jesus. As I knelt there some one would whisper, 'Don't you feel any different?' 'No, I don't feel any different.' One of them said, 'Rise up and join the church on probation.' I did not know what that meant, but I said, 'I have served the devil for forty-five years, and I will serve Jesus the rest of my life, if I never have any feeling'. I thought that the 'feeling' was for the good people that had been good all their lives, and that I had been such a rascal I was not entitled to any feeling.

"I started out to serve Jesus for the rest of my life, and the people began to come to my store—(I had a little store then)— and they told me about the Bible and about the things of God, and how I would rejoice. The more they told me the hungrier I got; I would rather hear them talk about Jesus than sell four or five dollars worth of goods. Pretty soon I would go out into the school-house and testify. They wanted me to preach. I said, 'I cannot preach'; but I do remember catching a man that had a bob-sled one day, and having a prayer meeting in his sled as we went along, and leading him to the Lord Jesus Christ.

WANTED HIM FOR MAYOR

"By this time I knew I was saved, but I hadn't that joyful experience that others talked about. One day I went into a prayer-meeting. A lady said to me, 'God is not only able to save you, but he is able to fill you with joy and make you a power in his service. Don't you want that kind of experience?' 'Yes, I do.' 'Well you pray to God and ask him for the power of the Holy Ghost, and he'll give it you.' I did. I don't know that I ever went without a meal in my life before that unless I had to. But they decided to fast and pray that day. I heard the dishes rattling out in the kitchen for some of the folks' dinner, and I was going without any. That was very strange to me, but I said to the brethren after a while, as we sat there in prayer, 'I believe God is sending the unction of the Holy Ghost upon me right now; I realize the consciousness of his presence; he is giving me a blessing.

"And I fell on my knees, and all of us thanked him in

prayer. As we knelt there I was alongside a great big fat farmer. They were all round the room, praying earnestly that God might pour out his blessing upon the meeting; and all at once I thought to myself, 'Why, that old fellow, what's he shaking that way about?' Pretty soon he would shake again, and I said, 'I believe he's laughing.' The idea of laughing in a prayer-meeting. But the first thing I knew I was laughing, too. Before that meeting was over we were laughing and crying and singing. God had come down in power upon us, and then I knew what it meant to have feeling.

"About two or three years after I was converted in that town, and my testimony had gone out all around there, one of the leading bankers came to me and said, 'We want you to run for mayor of the town. If you will run for mayor we will put you on both tickets; there won't be any opposition.' That is what God can do for a man. He keeps him so that he gets the respect of all people."

When Mr. Jacoby concluded, Dr. Torrey appealed for decisions; and about one hundred and sixty of those wretched men and women went forward and publicly decided their acceptance of Christ as their Saviour.

THE STORY OF A KISS

The next evening Mr. Alexander called upon the workers to give their experiences of the previous evening. After several had spoken, the Gospel singer invited his wife to the platform; and in tender tones, which held her great audience spellbound, she told the following story:

"Last night as we sat in that awful midnight meeting my heart ached to see the people in front of me. I could not help noticing one woman in the second row. She was as drunk as could be, and looked about as disgusting a sight as was possible, with the womanliness all stamped out of her. I was praying constantly for her during the meeting. In the after-meeting it fell to my lot to deal with her. I managed to get round behind the platform and had a long talk with her, and I believe the Spirit of God pierced through the fumes of drink into her soul. She promised me that she would tidy her hair and wash her face and come again, and that she was willing in the strength of God to give up the sinful life she was living. But it may be helpful to some to know that the thing that pierced right through her muddled brain was human affection. I tried every other way I could, insisting that I loved her, and that I loved her because God loved her. At last she began to feel the effect of human affection, and—I hardly like to tell the last part in public—finally she looked up into my face and said: 'I know God loves you.' 'Yes,' I replied, 'God loves you, too.' And at length she looked into my eyes and said, 'Will you give me a kiss?'

"Well, you can imagine how I felt, I expect, if you have ever seen a poor woman like that, reeking with foul odors, and her face distorted with drink. For a moment I involuntarily shrank from it. But I looked to God and said, 'What would'st thou have me to do?' And he seemed to say, 'Do it because I love her.' And I said, 'I will give you a kiss for the sake of Jesus who loves you.'"

Steps were taken to remove the woman from her difficult surroundings and place her under the care of a Christian home. She was seen clean and tidy at subsequent meetings, and that kiss doubtless led to the redemption of a human soul.

THE GREAT MEETING IN ST. GEORGE'S MARKET, BELFAST, IRELAND

During the Bolton campaign I was greatly impressed by two bright-faced boys, only ten and twelve years of age, who were members of the choir and were ardent personal workers in spite of their youth. During the after-meetings—and away from the meetings, too— these little fellows did personal work as consistently as any worker in the Mission. Each night they could be seen going up and down, in and out, among the people, searching out some boy or girl who was not a Christian to lead that one to Christ. At the end of the month it was found that these two boys had personally led forty-three persons to the point of confessing Christ.

A MONTH IN WALES

After leaving Bolton the evangelists conducted a month's campaign in Cardiff, the metropolis of Wales, where a great iron tabernacle seating 7,000 was erected in the heart of the city for the evangelists, at a cost of $13,000. The great structure was practically filled every night, while often hundreds and thousands were unable to obtain admission. At first, the Welsh people seemed cold and unresponsive to the appeals of the evangelists; but as the month drew to a close the enthusiasm became intense and fervid. Personal work was done, not only in the great tabernacle, but on the street cars, in barbers' shops, in stores and homes and factories—everywhere. Indeed during the closing days of the Mission the air was so charged with spiritual fervor that it seemed as if we were transported back nineteen centuries and were living in the days of the early church.

The Welsh people were quck to catch up Mr. Alexander's revival melodies; and soon the streets of the city were ringing with them; and in a brief period they were known and sung throughout all South Wales. Many persons do not doubt that the revival campaign at Cardiff was largely responsible for the wonderful religious awakening which immediately after the crusade swept South Wales like a cyclone. Many of Mr. Alexander's songs became the battle hymns of the great movement. After the Welsh revival had been in progress for some time, I made a brief trip into the heart of it, and attended three meetings conducted by Evan Roberts, with whom I had a long talk. In the course of our conversation, he told me that one of Mr. Alexander's hymns, which were sung everywhere throughout Wales, was the touching hymn, "Tell Mother I'll Be There," while of course the famous "Glory Song" penetrated into almost every nook and cranny of the Principality.

One of the most interesting converts of the revival in Cardiff was Mr. F. C. N. Douglas, a member of the Cardiff Stock Exchange. He was led to accept Christ through hearing the congregation singing "Looking This Way." After his conversion he threw all his great energy into winning others to Christ. During the crusade in Liverpool, he conducted a special excursion party from Cardiff to visit the Mission. The train was called "The Welsh Glory Special," and was declared to be the finest excursion train that ever ran out of Cardiff. Mr. Douglas tells the story of his transformation as follows:

"The nickname Dr. Torrey got on 'Change' was the 'American Hustler.' I thank God he hustled me right into salvation. The night after I had surrendered all to Christ, I came again to the meeting; and Dr. Torrey, after having invited those who would accept Christ to go down to the front seats, said, 'Christians, go to work!' I thought that was for me, and if

there ever was a weak-kneed Christian I was one at that
moment. But I thank God he made me the instrument for
bringing in two souls that night. I cannot describe the delight
I felt after that; there is no comparison. You cannot compare
that sort of thing to the making of money. I spoke to three
young fishermen, and on the following night had the pleasure
of seeing them all accept Christ. I am now doing slum work
in 'Tiger Bay,' and am going on in this way as long as God
will help me. In the six weeks following the close of Dr.
Torrey and Mr. Alexander's work in Cardiff I praise God
he has used me to bring in over thirty converts into the fold."

THE REVIVAL THAT WOULD NOT STOP

Seven months after the campaign ended, I visited Cardiff,
and found Mr. Douglas conducting open-air meetings. I also
found that the revival had gone right on after the evangelists
had left, being merged into the great Welsh revival, and that
there had been two or three times as many converts since the
crusade as there were during its progress. The pastor of one
of the largest churches in the city described to me with great
joy the transformation which the revival had wrought in his
congregation. Not only had scores joined the church, but
the church life was quickened into apostolic fervor. The
people thronged the prayer-meetings; and a prominent feature
of the church work was the open-air meetings under the
management of two of the mission converts.

IX

REVIVAL HYMNS CAPTURE LIVERPOOL

LIVERPOOL had been so deeply stirred by the mission of the evangelists a year previous, that they were now invited to return and conduct a campaign for nearly three months. Great preparations were made for their visit. A colossal glass and iron Tournament Hall had just been erected in the suburbs of the city; and this the committee rented for the crusade at a cost of $15,000. The structure held 12,500 people; and was reputed to be the largest auditorium in Great Britain, except the Crystal Palace. Huge as the building was, however, it proved at times inadequate to contain the throngs which gathered to hear the evangelists; and at the closing meeting it is estimated that 35,000 people endeavored to gain admission. An old resident of Liverpool who was present at the service declared that the scene that evening surpassed anything he had witnessed during the famous Moody and Sankey campaign in Liverpool, nearly a generation before. As the result of the campaign the names of over 7,000 converts were recorded.

During the revival Liverpool was honeycombed with praying bands; personal work was done everywhere; and the streets rang with revival hymns. One evening I passed five young men linked arm-in-arm, whistling "Tell Mother I'll Be There," and a little farther on four boys were humming the "Glory Song" as they were crossing the street. Several mornings I

A GROUP OF CRICKET PLAYERS WHO WERE CONVERTED IN THE SOUTH LONDON CAMPAIGN was awakened by the milkman's whistling a popular revival air as he delivered milk to his customers. One night a band of boys sang a Christmas carol under my window and followed it with a revival hymn.

A NOVEL WEDDING FEAST

The choir in Liverpool numbered 3,658 members; and was the largest evangelistic chorus ever organized up to that time. One of the many interesting features of the crusade was a wedding feast tendered to Mr. and Mrs. Alexander by the great choir, in the form of a huge banquet to 2,100 of the poorest people of Liverpool.

It was a thrilling and memorable sight to see the entire body of the huge hall filled with white-covered tables, at which over 2,000 of the porest of the city were sitting, some of them enjoying a good meal for the first time for days or weeks. Music wasfurnished by a brass band; and the magnificent choir—about 2,500 members of which were present—sang hymn after hymn with thrilling effect under the inspiring leadership of Mr. Alexander. At the conclusion of the feast, amid much cheering, Mr. Alexander ascended the dais and expressed to the choir his heartfelt appreciation of their unique gift. He declared that if they had studied for years they could not have presented anything to his wife and himself which would have pleased the recipients so greatly.

He then said: "I believe the Lord Jesus Christ helped me to get my wife. I don't think I could have got her myself. I believe it was straight in answer to prayer. One of the first things that I saw (I'll just let you into a little secret—you must not tell it, though) in Bingley Hall, Birmingham, was that my wife (then Miss Cadbury) would go back to the end of the hall and get hold of the most forlorn looking girl or woman in the building, and stay almost till the lights were out, trying to lead her to Christ. I said, 'That's the woman for me; and I want to say to the young men, if you want to get a wife, be sure she's a soul winner. You young women, if you want to get a husband, be sure he's a soul winner consecrated to God."

Mrs. Alexander next bravely mounted the high platform, and likewise expressed her deep gratitude for the wedding present. As she had been watching the people during the evening, the scene had called her back, in thought, to the parable of the Wedding Feast related by Christ while on earth. To the poor people present she said: "What we long for above everything else is that all who come here to-night to rejoice with us should learn to know and to love the dear Saviour who fills our lives so full of joy."

Before the meetings concluded two hundred and seventeen persons professed to accept Christ as their Saviour, Lord and King. The entire occasion was so successful, and productive of such blessing to the poor people that a short time later the choir raised the money for a second feast to Liverpool's poor, which was attended by 2,300 people, and at which there were two hundred and thirty-one confessions.

A CHANGE OF SONGS

During the second crusade at Liverpool an excellent opportunity was afforded of seeing some of the fruits of the awakening of a year previous. For example, one of the Captains of the Stewards during the Tournament Hall meetings was a convert of the first revival, who had formerly been a Music Hall singer. One day he gave me the remarkable story of his conversion as follows:

"Before my conversion I was a professional singer, and was known under my professional name of Tom Johns. One evening I was singing at a concert in Liverpool, and in the middle of my comic song a note was handed to me. Without finishing my song I opened it, and learned that my mother was lying very ill, and was not expected to live through the night. I hurried away to her house. On my way I had to pass the Philharmonic Hall, where the Torrey-Alexander meetings were being held; and, as I passed, the congregation was singing, 'Tell Mother I'll Be There.' The words sank deeply into my heart, for I knew that I could not then promise to meet my mother in heaven. I could not get away from the words of that song. They rang in my ears persistently. Every time I asked myself, 'Can I tell mother I'll be there?' my conscience would answer in the negative. I realized that complete surrender to God was the only way to answer my question. Then and there I yielded my will to him, cancelled all my engagements, and my joy is now complete that I am able to sing with truth, 'Tell Mother I'll Be There.' "

The singer's conversion was the beginning of active service for his Master. Not long afterwards he was out at a Christmas party, and was invited by his friends to sing one of his old songs which had always been very popular at such gatherings. Instead of that, however, he pulled from his pocket one of Alexander's New Revival Hymn Books, and, placing it on the piano, sang "Looking This Way." So popular did the hymn prove that more were demanded, and the company continued singing revival hymns until midnight. As a result of that evening of Gospel song several of the young men of the party gave their hearts to God, and later acted as stewards at the revival meetings at Tournament Hall.

The man who was perhaps the most enthusiastic of all the personal workers during the revival in Liverpool was also a convert of the former campaign. He was a medium-sized, keen-eyed business man, with a face radiant with happiness, but with grey hair, though only forty-four years of age. His name was Edward Roberts, and the story of his transformation recalls the days of the early church. From early manhood he had been an amateur boxer and a noted referee at prize fights. One night he attended a Torrey-Alexander meeting; was soundly saved; and his life was totally changed from that hour. I want to give you a part of his story, just as he frequently tells it before his audiences where many are weeping before he concludes:

"On the 24th of September, 1902, I had promised my wife that I would take her to hear Dr. Torrey and Mr. Alexander; but there was a boxing contest on at Liverpool that night between an American and an Englishman, and it was very few of those contests that I used to miss. You would find my name in the sporting part of the papers as referee—Mr. Robert Humphreys I called myself; I suppose I was ashamed to use my own name. However, I took my wife that night to the Philharmonic Hall. When we got there, there was a crowd of people waiting outside; the meeting for women not quite over. I said to my wife, 'Do you suppose I am going to crush against this crew?' It would have been all right among the crew who were waiting to get in to see the fight. I would have crushed with the best of them; but it was to hear something that she knew might reach my heart, and I didn't want to go in. At last I got in with her, but I took little notice of what was said or done.

THE SONG CLUTCHED HIS HEART

"On the following Monday I must have given my wife a terrible shock by telling her that I thought I would go and hear Dr. Torrey. I went. I got there about a quarter to seven and had to wait over an hour; but God's Spirit was working with me so strongly that night that, if necessary, I would have waited a day and a half, not an hour and a half. Finally I got into the building and sat down. The next thing I knew of was that they got up to sing:

> " 'When I survey the wondrous cross
>   On which the Prince of Glory died,
> My richest gain I count but loss,
>   And pour contempt on all my pride.'

If I were to speak from now till to-morrow morning I could not describe the feeling that came over me as they sang that third verse:

> " 'See from his head, his hands, his feet,
>   Sorrow and love flow mingled down,
> Did e'er such love and sorrow meet,
>   Or thorns compose so rich a crown?'

"I got down and cried as I have never cried before nor since. The love of Christ did it. I stood when the invitation was given, and went to the front. A gentleman came to me and said, 'Do you know that the Lord Jesus Christ can save you?' I said, 'If he can save me he can save any man in the world'; and I felt it from the bottom of my heart. He opened his Bible and showed me text after text, and verse after verse, and in the next five minutes I saw more of the Bible than I had seen for the previous fifteen years. We got down and prayed, the tears rolling down my face, and at last the light came. I came out, and went home and told my wife the glad news. She had been praying for me at home; and not until then did I learn that, together with a group of friends, she had been praying for my conversion for six years. That nearly broke me down for a second time. Now I can scarcely realize my former life. It seems to me as if I had lived that dark life in some other world. I never knew what life was until I came to Christ."

Mr. Roberts is outdoor manager of sixty meat shops at Liverpool, and is a very busy man; but he is constantly witnessing for Christ, on the streets and at religious gatherings. He always carries his Bible in his coat pocket; and if he changes his coat he changes his Bible from one coat to the other. His face fairly glows with the joy that fills his heart. His wife says their home is now so happy that it seems like her second life on earth.

A GIRL'S PATHETIC LETTER

A beautiful feature of the work was the soul-winning enthusiasm of the boy and the girl converts. Following the Christmas intermission one of the evangelists received from an eleven-year-old girl the following pathetic letter which tells its own story:

"I have been waiting such a very long time for you to come

back so that I could send you this letter. I want to know if you will pray for my mamma, who is always getting drunk. I am eleven years old, and came to the last children's meeting, and got converted. When I got home my mamma asked me where I had been, and I said, 'To the Torrey-Alexander Mission.' She got up and hit me awful because I had been; and said that if I ever came again she would nearly kill me. So I can't come, not because of the whipping I should get, for I would not mind that, but because I should be disobeying orders. But I can do something even if I cannot come to the meeting. I can pray and sing.

"I haven't got a father; he died a week before Christmas, but mamma does not seem to mind a bit. She got drunk on the funeral day, and couldn't go to the funeral. I was singing one of your hymns on Christmas Day; mother had come home drunk, and there was nothing in the house, so I thought I could do nothing else but to pray for the Mission, and to sing to my Heavenly Father who has done such a lot for me, 'A little talk with Jesus makes it right, all right!' Will you please have sung Hymn 36, 'Over the River Faces I See.'

"Now I must close, keeping on trusting and obeying, and there is one who will help me, and only one, and that is God. God answers prayer if we have faith in him."

THE RETURN OF A WANDERER

One of the most remarkable converts of the entire Liverpool movement was a young lawyer who gave his heart to God at the very first meeting held in Tournament Hall. Mr. Alexander gave me the story of his conversion as follows:

"Over a year before we went to Liverpool, a prominent

business man of Manchester had gone to Dr. Torrey, and said to him, 'I wish you would pray for my son. He is thirty-seven years old, a wanderer on the face of the earth, traveling from country to country. I don't know where he is much of the time; but God knows, and I want you to pray for him.' Dr. Torrey promised he would do so. Months passed, and when Dr. Torrey was at Keswick the same gentleman came to him again and said: 'I have found out that my son is away over in Vancouver. Can you tell me some one to cable to? I want him put under restraint.' Dr. Torrey gave him the address of a pastor whom he knew in Vancouver; and the father at once cabled to him in order that he might look after his son. Before the cablegram had reached Vancouver, however, the young man had left the city and was again wandering in the great Northwest. Months passed on, and Dr. Torrey and I began our campaign in Liverpool. On the very first night of the crusade that same young man for whom prayer had been made months before walked into the building, listened to the service, was convicted of sin and gave his heart to God. The young man became an earnest worker, and spent several weeks with us in Liverpool, and was the means of leading many to accept Christ. For many years he had been separated from his wife, but to-day he has a happy home once more, and is serving the Lord with all his heart. The last I heard of him was that he was studying to become a minister of the Gospel."

One of the red letter days of the campaign occurred when a company of over five hundred Bolton people chartered a special train and came to Liverpool to attend the afternoon and evening services. It was probably the largest revival party that

DR. TORREY AND MR. ALEXANDER WITH A GROUP OF SOLDIER CONVERTS AT PLYMOUTH, ENGLAND

ever made a journey by rail in England. At the close of the night meeting they formed in ranks outside Tournament Hall, together with five hundred Liverpool people, and marched over a mile to a railway station, singing revival hymns. The singing was in perfect time and tune, for it was conducted by Mr. Alexander, from the top of a cab, by the waving of a white handkerchief. They thronged the station platforms, sang heartily for fifteen minutes; and, as the special train departed, all united in the chorus, "We'll Never Say Good-bye in Heaven."

A JAPANESE CONFESSES CHRIST

A Japanese gentleman of high rank and position attended the hall one Saturday night, and remained behind to see Dr. Torrey. He had gone, but Mr. Alexander talked to him and told him how to find out that the Bible is indeed God's Word. He sat up all night, reading the Gospel of John. He saw that it was the word of God; and attending the early morning meeting on the Sabbath, confessed Christ from the platform. Like so many other converts, he at once set to work to win others. Liverpool has a large Chinese population; and, though this man's prejudices were altogether unfavorable to these people, he went among them, and was the means of many conversions. In the after-meeting, on the very last night of the Mission, he was found busy among the men who remained behind. He said that six Chinese whom he had brought to the meeting, and for whom he had been praying, had just accepted Christ. He had time for only a passing word, and was off again in another instant. Later he was eagerly talking with a group of young men. He was planning to go as a missionary of the Gospel to his own people.

Near the close of the movement an honor unique in English civic life was accorded to the evangelists. The Lord Mayor of Liverpool gave a luncheon in their honor in the Town Hall, to which he invited a select company of the foremost clergy and business men of the city. About sixty were present, including Mrs. Torrey, Mrs. Alexander and Dr. John Watson, better known as "Ian MacLaren."

After the luncheon, the Lord Mayor expressed his gratitude for the visit of the evangelists, who had done so much for the political and commercial, as well as the religious, welfare of the city, by their remarkable work. A rector of Liverpool, speaking for the Church of England, then warmly commended "the successors of Moody and Sankey"; he was followed by the Rev. J. H. Atkinson, who represented the Nonconformist ministers of the city. Dr. Torrey and Mr. Alexander spoke briefly, expressing their gratitude for the signal honor, which they took not as a tribute to themselves but to their labors.

MEETINGS IN A FACTORY

One of the most notable converts of the first revival campaign of the evangelists in Liverpool was a workman in a soap factory, who had been a habitual drunkard. He had been such a slave to drink that he would spend whole nights in wild drunken carousals. A fellow workman induced him to attend a revival meeting. He went; he found Christ; his life was transformed. He and his friend bought two Alexander hymn books, and began singing praises to God, and having short prayer-meetings every day at noon in the factory. The singing drew in others until the attendance exceeded fifty

daily, and many workmen were converted. Then the convert—who was a musician, and had formerly played the violin
all night long at dances—organized a revival orchestra among
the workmen. He became its leader; and they went out and
conducted Gospel services in churches all over Liverpool,
where scores were led to Christ. The noon-day prayer meetings were continued for more than a year. Then came the
second campaign of Dr. Torrey and Mr. Alexander, when the
Christian workmen were filled with such love and zeal that
they began, and have continued, two prayer meetings daily at
the factory, one at 8 a. m. and one at noon during the lunch
hour. The last the writer heard was that their prayer meetings were still keeping up splendidly.

X

"GET RIGHT WITH GOD"

ONE striking feature of the world-wide work of Dr. Torrey and Mr. Alexander was the distribution of small white cards bearing on their face in bold red letters only four words, "Get Right With God." In Australia, Mr. Alexander began giving out these cards by tens of thousands in connection with the revival meetings; and when they reached England hundreds of thousands were distributed. In strange and unexpected ways people of all ages and classes were brought face to face with the cards and got right with God. A whole volume could be filled with beautiful and touching narratives of men, women and children who were converted through the little cards.

In speaking of the origin of the phrase and of some of the most striking transformations wrought through the sentence which has now become world famous, Mr. Alexander said:

"Some years ago Major James H. Cole was conducting a series of revival meetings at a sea-side resort. As he walked up and down the beach and saw the indifference of the throngs, he prayed earnestly that God would give him some method of rousing them to a sense of their lost condition, following which he threw himself down on the grass, and as he did so there flashed through his mind the words, 'Get Right With God.' They seemed to be a message directly from God himself, and he arranged to have this sentence printed on little white cards.

COL. H. G. B. BEAUCHAMP, C.B., OF THE BRITISH ARMY

The Major has been using them ever since with the greatest success. He declares he could fill a volume six inches thick with incidents of the people who have been converted through the message on the little cards.

THE CARD AND THE JUDGE

"When we were in Ballarat, Australia, our work seemed to need something to create greater interest and to give people something to do for the Lord. I remembered the four words that I had seen on a card in America; and I decided to use them at the next afternoon meeting. I went to the printers and had the four words, 'Get Right With God' set up in large, clear type, and printed nicely upon narrow, heavy boards. I had 14,000 of the cards on the platform at the beginning of the afternoon meeting.

"I told the people the following story to get them interested in the work which I felt sure the card would do:

"In a city in America an evangelist had distributed these cards gummed on one side. A little girl, whose father was a judge, took several home. He was an unconverted man. While he was away from the home she went into his room and pasted on the foot of his bed, 'Get Right With God.' Across the mirror she pasted the same. She put another in the bottom of the washbowl. When he came in that evening she stuck one in the top of his hat. She put another on the handle of his umbrella. When he went up to his bedroom she slipped into the dining-room and placed one on his plate. She managed to get one stuck inside his desk in his office.

"When he went to retire for the night he noticed the one at the foot of his bed. The next morning when he arose he noticed the one in the washbowl, and the one on the mirror. When he went to his breakfast there was one looking him in the face at his place at the table. When he went to get his umbrella and hat there he saw them again. When he went down to his office and rolled his desk cover back there was 'Get Right With God' looking him in the eye again. He decided to give his heart to God, and get right with him.

"I then requested the Christians in the audience to take as many as they could distribute judiciously. They were eagerly caught up and more were called for.

THE MESSAGE IN THE PAPER

"We began to hear results of the plan on every hand. I was talking to a bright young business man who had confessed Christ, and he told me how this card touched him. He looked at it, and stuck it hastily into his overcoat pocket, and forgot all about it until he had occasion to reach in his pocket for one of his business cards. He could feel this card, for it was longer than his own; and every time he touched it he was reminded of the words, 'Get Right With God,' until he was driven to give his heart to the Lord.

"From Ballarat we went on to Sydney, 1,000 miles away, to hold a campaign there. I told the Sydney workers about it, and handed a card to one of the secretaries of the campaign to show him the sort of thing it was. He said, 'I would like to take one home.' He had a paper with one of Dr. Torrey's sermons in, and slipped the card inside to take care of it. Later on he got into conversation with a man who was under conviction of sin. He wanted to point him to Christ, but did not have time to finish the conversation; so he said, 'Here, take this paper and read Dr. Torrey's sermon.' The man took it home, but did not like to have any of the family see him reading a sermon. Many people are like that; afraid of what others may think or say of them. Propriety, I believe, sends more souls to hell than anything else except neglect. So that man waited up until the rest of the family had retired, and when everyone else was in bed he opened the paper to read the sermon. As he did so the little card fell out and lay looking up at him, 'Get Right With God.' As he gazed at the card the words seemed to burn into his soul, and then and there he dropped on his knees and got right with God.

OFFICER HELD HIS CARD IN SIGHT

"In Belfast we had 150,000 printed and distributed. I explained to the workers one Sunday morning how to distribute the cards; and asked them to give one to every man and woman they met. I went out on the street to see how it was being done, and had not gone far before I met a policeman coming down the street past the crowds, holding out at full arm's length one of the little cards. Everybody he passed had wanted to give him another; and this was the only way he could keep them from approaching him. That night, while the after-meeting was in progress a gentleman came up to me and said, 'Do you see that old man on the front seat? He had been drinking this morning. His little girl brought him one of these cards, and he could not get away from it. He stuck it in his hat, and came to the meeting, and now he is saved.'

"At Edinburgh a fine-looking commercial man came to me and said, 'This card here is what brought me. I was going out of Edinburgh to do business. I bought my ticket; here it is (and he pulled it out and showed it to me), and got into the carriage. I went to pull down the curtain at the carriage window, and out rolled this card, which some one had stuck in the roll of the curtain. I had promised my old mother years ago that I would give my heart to Jesus. But I wandered farther and farther into sin until I was afraid of myself. I was getting worse. I went home, tipsy, the other night, and I never used to do that. I thought of all this as the train went on. We passed another station; and I felt I could bear it no longer—I must settle the matter now. I got out at the next station and came back again to Edinburgh.' He came to the meeting, listened to Dr. Torrey and was saved that night; and now he is working with all his heart for Christ.

TWO HUNDRED THOUSAND CARDS IN LETTER BOXES

"In our first campaign at Liverpool we distributed 200,000 of the little cards. There are many different ways of using them; and here the unique plan was followed of putting them in the letter boxes. A few days later a woman on top of a tramcar opened her bag, and in it was a little packet of 'Get Right With God' cards. 'You have been to the revival meetings, haven't you?' she was asked. 'Yes,' she replied, 'last Sunday morning my husband and I were not Christians. We found two of these cards in our letter box, and had great fun about it. After we had laughed over them we thought later on that we would go to the meeting. We both went, and both were saved that night.'

"One man in Liverpool had been going to a certain place of worship for many years. He came to the hall where our meetings were held, and stayed to the after-meeting. The minister of the church he attended said he was never more surprised in his life than when this man came forward for salvation. He asked him how it was, and the man answered, 'This card was stuck in my pew, and it has been staring at me all the time, and I must get right with God.'

"At Bristol one young man put the card into the hands of 250 cyclists. Of the hundred and sixty persons who accepted Christ that night I asked those to stand up who had been led definitely to Christ through the little 'Get Right With God' cards. Seventeen of them stood up. One fine looking old gentleman was asked where he got his card. 'Oh!' he answered, 'it was given me six miles away, and I have walked over here to the meeting.' And he walked all the way back again—twelve miles in all.

THE STORY OF A BRIDAL COUPLE

"In our second crusade in Liverpool a quarter of a million of the cards were given out on New Years Day, 1905. Scores were led to Christ through them. Two of the most interesting converts were a bride and a groom who were reached by the little cards in a most remarkable manner. A Christian worker was passing a church when he saw a bridal party come out and enter a carriage. Having several 'Get Right With God' cards in his hand, he stepped up to the carriage and handed one to each of the occupants. Being a distinguished looking man with silvery hair he was able to do this without causing the least offense. To the bride and the groom he said, 'I wish you a most happy New Year, but it cannot be the happiest possible unless you are absolutely right with God. I will deeply appreciate it if you will take these cards and put them up in prominent positions in your new home; and I would like to ask especially that you put one in your looking glass.' The worker then went on his way, having sown the seed. Six days passed. At the end of the week the same worker was delighted to see the bride and the groom to whom he had given the cards go up to the front at Tournament Hall and publicly acknowledge Christ as their Savour, Lord and King. He went forward and congratulated them heartily upon this step; and then they told him they could not get the message of the little white card out of their minds until they finally came to the hall and yielded themselves to God.

WHAT ONE POLICEMAN DID

"In Liverpool a few days later, a minister from Manchester arose at an afternoon meeting and told how a single card given out during our campaign in that city had been the means of inaugurating a great and glorious work. He said: 'A police sergeant came to one of your meetings and got hold of some of the 'Get Right With God' cards. That same night he distributed them while on duty. There was one of the men under him whom he was very anxious to see won for God, and that night he spoke to him about his soul. The man turned away from him with the remark: 'You are exceeding your duty now; that has nothing to do with a policeman's work.' The sergeant said, 'Well, my brother, will you just take this card and look at it?' The man took it out of courtesy; and, when he got home, found it still in his pocket. He read it; it got hold of him then and there, and he gave his heart to God. Since then he has been instrumental in leading a hundred men to Christ. He has a large Bible class for men.

XI

THE ROMANCE OF A TEXT

A VERITABLE Gospel romance has grown up around this Scripture text which has been the means of leading scores of people to an acceptance of Jesus Christ. It is a year text, once adopted by Mr. Alexander, which has since been adopted by tens of thousands of people in all parts of the world. In Melbourne, Birmingham, Liverpool, and, in fact, in each city that the evangelists visited, the story of the year text was told; and it never failed to arouse fresh enthusiasm for God's Word, and to lead hundreds to adopt it as their year text.

"This is how I came to adopt the use of a year text," said Mr. Alexander:

"I was spending vacation with a young man in a certain town, and we agreed to adopt II. Tim. 2: 15 as our year text—that is, a text on which to shape our lives during the whole of that year. Our bedrooms adjoined, and we were so fond of each other that we slept with the door between our rooms open; and when we went to bed in the evening, instead of calling out 'Good-night,' we used to sing out, 'Second-Timothy-two-fifteen'; and which ever of us woke first in the morning would rouse the other up with

'SECOND-TIMOTHY-TWO-FIFTEEN'

"After the week's vacation was up we had to part, he going one way and I another on the Lord's business. I went down to the depot with him, and as the train moved off he stood out on the back platform—'Second-Timothy-two-fifteen,' he said: 'Second-Timothy-two-fifteen,' I replied.

"The train drew out. 'Second-Timothy-two-fifteen' I shouted; and 'Second-Timothy-two-fifteen' came back.

"The train was getting clear of the depot. 'Second-Timothy-two-fifteen' I shouted for all I was worth; and 'Second-Timothy-two-fifteen' came back very faintly. 'Second-Timothy-two-fifteen' I let go once more; but I didn't hear any answer—only saw the white of his handkerchief fluttering in the wind; but I knew all the time that he was shouting 'Second-Timothy-two-fifteen.' Some of the people must have thought we were pretty crazy—one on the tail of a train and one on the platform, and both shouting out 'Second-Timothy-two-fifteen.' But wait till you hear the rest of my story.

"For the whole year we stuck to that text. Whenever we wrote we put it across the corner of our envelopes, and every letter I sent to any one had across it II. Tim. 2: 15, whilst a whole lot of my friends did the same with the letters they sent me.

"Twelve months later I was back in that same town, conducting some young people's meetings; and I was speaking of the great advantage of having a year text. I had been asking them to adopt the text that I had started out on when a young fellow got up and interrupted me. 'I am very glad,' he said, 'that Mr. Alexander ever took 'Second-Timothy-two-fifteen' for his year text.' 'How's that?' said I. 'Well, friends,' said he, 'twelve months ago I was down at the depot seeing some people, when I heard a fellow shouting for all he was worth 'Second-Timothy-two-fifteen' to a man on the end of the outgoing train, and the man that was going away was shouting back 'Second-Timothy-two-fifteen!' Well, I thought what is this 'Second-Timothy-two-fifteen' they are shouting about anyway? So I made a bee-line for home, and looked it up in my Bible. I wasn't a Christian then, but the first words of that text just hit me between the eyes—"Study to show thyself approved unto God." Then I went on and read the rest—"A workman that needeth not to be ashamed, rightly dividing the word of truth." I asked God to forgive me my sins, and help me to "show myself approved," and thank God he has done it!'

"That man had hardly sat down when another one got up and said, 'I have to thank God that Mr. Alexander took that text for his year text.' 'Why'? said I. 'Well,' he said, 'I never saw Mr. Alexander before to-night; but the first Sunday I spent in this town that man who has just spoken came to me and pointed me to Christ. He was saved through hearing Mr. Alexander's calling out "Second-Timothy-two-fifteen": and I was saved through his hearing it.'

A MIGHTY AUDIENCE ADOPTS THE TEXT

"Later on I went to Australia. At the very last meeting we held there, after Dr. Torrey had preached about an hour, and we had sung and sung, the people still waited. 'Why don't you go home?' I asked. They said, 'We want to sing.' We sang 'God Be With You' seven times straight through, from one end to the other. Still they did not move, and I said again, 'Why don't you go home?' 'We want to sing' came the answer, and we sang and sang until I thought they must be tired of singing. So I said, 'I want everybody to listen now while I tell you the story of a text.' And I told them this story. Then I said, 'Now everybody who will take "Second-Timothy-two-fifteen" as a year text, say it together.' You should have heard them—eight thousand there were—saying it 'Sec'-ond-Tim'-othy-two'-fif-teen.' ' It was just like big waves rolling upon the seashore. Now, if you want to see how that sounds, just try it. Say it twice, one after the other without a break, just as you would a college yell—'Sec'-ond-Tim'-othy-two'-fifteen.' Sec'-ond-Tim'-othy-two'-fif-teen'.'

"While I was telling the story that night there was a reporter in front; and he took down every word just as I had told it; and it was published in the Southern Cross. It came over to England where a London journal copied it. A good woman in England wrapped that paper up and sent it to a soldier in Calcutta, and that soldier read the story and gave his heart to God.

"You say, 'How do you know?' Because in going through Calcutta I saw him. He came up to me and said, 'Are you the one who told that story down in Melbourne?'

" 'Yes.'

" 'Well,' he said, 'that's the reason I am a Christian!'

"There it was. That story had gone seventeen thousand miles, and led a soldier to Christ.

THE TEXT HAD GONE BEFORE THEM

"After the story had been printed in that Australian paper we did not need introduction when we would go on to the next place to hold a revival campaign. Just as soon as Dr. Torrey and I got off the train, people we had never seen before, and who had never seen us, would begin to say 'Second-Timothy-two-fifteen.' We went across to Tasmania. A great crowd had assembled along the dock, and they all looked like strangers. But one great big fellow put his hand up to his mouth as the ship was running up to the dock, and shouted 'Second-Timothy-two-fifteen,' and we felt at home right away.

"When we reached England it was the same way. Thousands of letters that passed through the British post-office had II. Timothy 2: 15 written upon outside or inside or both. There was a deacon in England who told his pastor about it; and the pastor came to me when we were holding some meetings in Mildmay Conference Hall, London, and said, 'The whole church has taken Second-Timothy-two-fifteen as a year text.'

"A party of sixty Cambridge University students went to Oxford to attend a religious gathering. As the famous text was their motto, they had a cloth sign twelve feet long, printed with 'Second-Timothy-two-fifteen' in huge letters and hung it on the side of their car. It was read by thousands of people as the train rushed along with its crowd of noisy students.

THE TEXT AT THE COURT OF DENMARK

"Still later the story of the year-text was published in another London journal. The paper fell into the hands of the Master of Ceremonies at the Court of Denmark—a man of very high rank and influence. He read about the famous text, and was greatly impressed with its world-wide work. A few days later he was to act as chairman at a large and influential gathering of the leading people of Denmark. He decided to give them the story of Second-Timothy-two-fifteen.' The narrative was so popular that Second-Timothy-two-fifteen is now a familiar phrase even in far-off Denmark.

"If you are the superintendent of a Sunday School, or the teacher of a class, tell your scholars this story, and urge them to take it as a year text. It will make them better scholars, and will draw them nearer to God."

XII

THE "GLORY SONG" AROUND THE WORLD

FEW if any songs in modern times have achieved world-wide popularity so quickly as the "Glory Song." It is said to have "set Australia on fire." It seemed to captivate London in a day; and thence as from a center it swept with lightning-like rapidity throughout the British colonies and the rest of the world.

The song may now be heard in many tongues and dialects. It has been translated into at least 17 languages, including the Chinese and the language used by the Zulus in South Africa. It has appeared in print in leaflets, newspapers, magazines and books no less than 17,000,000 times. It is enjoyed by all classes and conditions from the street urchin to the nobility.

The greatest victory of the "Glory Song" was when it took the world's metropolis by storm. Within two weeks after the Mission of Dr. Torrey and Mr. Alexander began in the Royal Albert Hall the song was hummed and whistled and sung on the streets, in shops and factories, in trams and trains, on the underground railway—everywhere. Shop girls sung it on their way home from work; newsboys whistled it; policemen hummed it on their beats, and pirated editions of it were sold on all the leading thoroughfares of the city. A musical expert declared he had never known any other song, sacred or secular, to be in everybody's mouth so quickly as was the "Glory Song."

THE SONG IN DENMARK

A Danish pastor who visited the revival in England for a week, told, one day, how he had been captivated by the song; and how it was spreading throughout Denmark. "Three years ago," said the pastor, "I was sick for a fortnight, and while lying on my bed I received from London a copy of a paper in which there was a report of the Torrey-Alexander revival, and a reprint of the 'Glory Song,' words and music. In that fortnight God came into my heart in a wonderful way; and as I lay in my bed I translated the 'Glory Song' into Danish. When I was strong enough I went to revival meetings; and for four weeks we sang the 'Glory Song,' and I suppose God used it to save many people. This autumn we had four meetings, at which 2,700 people were present—more than half of them men; and we sang the 'Glory Song' evening by evening until their hearts were glowing. When I return to Denmark I am going from city to city, and town to town, conducting revival meetings, and teaching the people to sing the 'Glory Song.' "

When I asked Mr. Alexander about the authorship of the song, and how it sprang into universal favor, he said:

"The 'Glory Song,' words and music, was written in Chicago by Charles H. Gabriel, who is one of the most popular Gospel song writers in America to-day. I remember quite well the first time I saw it in looking over a new song-book. I had just glanced at it, and said to myself, 'That man has wasted a page, for I do not believe that song will be sung much.' Some months later I stepped into a large Sunday School convention, and heard an audience sing it. It took such a hold of me that I could think of nothing else for days thereafter. I got all of my friends to sing it. I dreamed about it, and woke to the rythm of it. Then I began to teach it to large audiences; and soon whole towns were ringing with the 'Glory Song.'

"I remember one little town in Kansas, called Wellington, where the university students turned out in a body, men and women, and marched through the town four abreast, singing lustily as they tramped:

Oh, that will be glory for me.'

THE MARCHERS SING THE "GLORY SONG"

"Later I was in a neighboring town conducting a mission; and the largest revival excursion I ever heard of came to visit us. They chartered a special train of fourteen large cars and two engines, and brought over eight hundred people, many of them the most prominent merchants, bankers, society ladies, people of all grades and classes. When they alighted from the train they formed in long lines four deep, and marched through the streets—eight hundred strong—each of them wearing a ribbon on which was printed with large letters, 'Glory for me.' Needless to say they set the entire town ringing with the melody.

"When I went to Australia I determined that the 'Glory Song' should be the great hymn of the Mission in Melbourne. The very first night it struck fire, and was called for a second time by the chairman of the meeting. In a few days it was in everybody's mouth, and it was being printed in secular as well as religious papers. The news of its popularity in Australia went everywhere, and thus started the song on its world-wide career.

"It is a song that takes with society people as well as musical people. The name of the song at once interests everybody. Millions of people have been reached through its publication in the daily newspapers. It was printed three times in the London Daily Mail, which has over a million circulation. I was in a great many parts of London, and asked all classes and all grades of people if they had ever heard of the 'Glory Song,' and I did not receive a single negative answer.

THE "GLORY SONG" IN GREAT BRITAIN

"A friend of mine made a bicycle tour through Western England; and he said that people were whistling or singing the melody on the streets of almost every village and city through which he passed. In the Welsh revival the 'Glory Song' was in constant use, and was one of the first songs to be used. It was called for at almost every service we held in the Royal Albert Hall, London. One afternoon I did not have it, and at the close of the meeting I had pitiful and indignant appeals for it. One clergyman said he had come 200 miles, and ought to go back that afternoon, but that he would stay until the night meeting if we woud have the 'Glory Song.' I have also found that the longer people sing it the better they like it; and the greater volume that can be secured in rendering it the better it is.

"I recently heard of a young man who, before he was converted, had bought a nine-gallon cask of beer and placed it in his cellar. After his conversion he sent for his deacon and minister. They lifted the barrel of beer up on the sink, turned on the tap, and sang the 'Glory Song' together while the beer ran away.

"One afternoon a worker came to me in the Royal Albert

LORD KINNAIRD

EX-GOV. W. J. NORTHEN, of Georgia

MR. PAUL GILBERT

SECRETARY J. J. VIRGO

Hall, London, and said that a Jew had been present at the service, and had heard the audience sing the 'Glory Song.' When they came to the words—

'When by his grace, I shall look on his face,'

the thought came to him: 'These thousands of people seem sincere; they may be right and Jesus may be the Messiah. If that is true, I shall never look on his face unless I accept him.' And that train of thought led to his taking Christ as his Saviour.

"During our campaign in Sheffield, England, I received the following letter:

"Dear Mr. Alexander: Several of my friends have told me that you would be pleased to hear this little incident of the 'Glory Song.' During the revival I posted a large bill on a board announcing the meetings; and on the top I placed a photo of Dr. Torrey and yourself, with the first verse of the 'Glory Song' printed underneath. This stood at our shop door the whole four weeks of the revival. I took it away on Monday morning; and not long afterwards a woman said to me, 'Why have you taken that board away?' I replied that the Torrey-Alexander meetings were over. She said, 'Oh, I am so sorry; that verse has made my husband quite a different man. He has been here nearly every day to read it, and when he has come home he has said, 'Well I have been to read my verse:

'When all my labors and trials are o'er,'

and tried to say it off from memory. 'Since then,' said the woman, ' he has signed the pledge and is trying to lead a better life.' 'I might add,' the writer continued, 'that he was the most unlikely person to have taken the slightest notice of the verse.' "

THE LAUNCHING OF THE DREADNAUGHT

"One striking incident heard about the song was contained in a letter I received from England. The writer said that the song was sung at the launching of the H. M. S. Dreadnaught, the largest battleship in the world, one of whose guns is said to shoot twenty-seven miles. King Edward was present at the launch, and had given orders that there be no band music, in view of the death of his father-in-law, the King of Denmark. His command was complied with, but no order had been given prohibiting singing; hence the bluejackets on the warship sang several hymns as the ship was launched, and the first number of the program was the 'Glory Song.' It was simply another proof of the world-wide popularity of the hymn."

XIII

WONDERFUL SCENES AT ROYAL ALBERT HALL

THE most notable of all the Missions of Dr. Torrey and
Alexander around the world was that held in London, the
world's metropolis. It lasted five months—from February to
June, and the expenses amounted to $85,000. The number of
professed conversions recorded reached about 17,000.

The movement was inaugurated at the invitation of the
"London Evangelistic Council," a large, unsectarian, influential
body of nearly a hundred men, at the head of which was Lord
Kinnaird, one of the foremost religious leaders of Great
Britain. The members of the committee included leading
business men of London, members of Parliament, editors,
lawyers and clergymen. The chairman of the Executive Committee was Mr. W. G. Bradshaw, deputy chairman of the London City and Midland Bank. The honorary secretary of the
great crusade was Mr. John H. Putterill, the secretary of the
London Y. M. C. A.

The Council was ably assisted during a part of the campaign by an Auxiliary Ladies' Committee, which included in
its membership a number of women belonging to the nobility.
Among the active members of the committee were Lady
Napier, Lady Agnes Anderson, Lady Trelawney, Lady Wim-
borne, the Hon. Misses Kinnaird and Mrs. C. E. Tritton.
The president of the committee was Mrs. Webb-Peploe, wife
of Prebendary Webb-Peploe of St. Paul's Cathedral, and the

vice-president was Miss Morley, the president of the Y. W. C. A. Lady Hope also worked actively in the campaign.

A CHOIR OF FOUR THOUSAND

The famous Royal Hall was engaged for the first two months; an iron and glass building seating 5,500, and costing $20,000, was erected in South London for the next two months; and another great building seating over 5,000 was erected in the Strand in the heart of London, for the last month of the campaign. In each case the choir numbered nearly 4,000 members, with about 1,000 in attendance nightly.

The first series of meetings, during February and March, was held in the Royal Albert Hall, a great circular structure erected as a memorial to Prince Albert, the royal consort of Queen Victoria. It is the finest and most famous auditorium in Great Britain. It accommodates 11,000 people, but so great were the throngs in attendance that sometimes from 5,000 to 10,000 people were unable to obtain admission. It is estimated that the attendance at the meetings was about 100,000 per week, or over 750,000 for the Royal Albert Hall campaign.

At the great welcome meeting in the Royal Albert Hall on February 4, 1905, the evangelists were greeted by one of the most remarkable audiences ever gathered in the historic building. It included leaders of all creeds in the world's metropolis; journalists and publishers famous the world over and numerous members of Parliament.

"ALEXANDER THE GREAT"

The great audience was both melted and electrified by the revival melodies as rendered under the leadership of Mr.

Alexander. Standing upon the high, red dais erected upon the platform, he captivated and dominated first his two-thousand voiced choir and then his huge audience, until he had them in the hollow of his hand, and made the vast structure resound as probably never before with thunderous paeans of revival song. The next day a writer in a London daily declared the Gospel singer was "Alexander the Great"; that he was more than a choir conductor; he was a "crowd conductor"; and that he would "make London hum, for he would make London sing."

The editor of a London daily, who had himself attended the meetings, gave his readers his own impressions of the singing. He said: "I have seen the methods and the triumphs of the most famous baton wielders of the time—Colonne, Nikisch, Mottl, Weingartner, Henry J. Wood. Never have I been so much impressed as I was by this bright-faced, athletic-framed, energetic young evangelist. As the leader of a choir he has an amazing, an almost magical, influence. It is not only over the trained choir, either, that his influence carries. He simply makes everybody sing, and sing just as he wants them to. Never has Albert Hall resounded with a greater volume— never thrilled to a more intense effort."

COL. BEAUCHAMP ENLISTS

On the night following the welcome meeting, the first evangelistic service was held in the Royal Albert Hall. Although eleven thousand people were inside the great building, yet it was estimated that ten thousand others were unable to secure admission. Dr. Torrey delivered a powerful sermon on the subject, "What it Costs not to be a Christian." At its conclusion, when he gave the invitation to all those who would accept Christ to stand up and publicly confess him, between two and three hundred persons arose in all parts of the hall.

The very first man to stand upon his feet, almost as soon as the words were out of Dr. Torrey's mouth, was a well dressed gentleman sitting upon the platform, who was later found to be a Colonel in the British Army, and a member of the nobility—Colonel Horace G. P. Beauchamp, C.B., son of Sir Thomas and Lady Beauchamp. He had been induced by friends to take an interest in the meetings; and as he listened to Dr. Torrey's convincing arguments he decided to give his heart to God and boldly confess Christ before the great multitude. From that night Col. Beauchamp's life was transformed. He went everywhere telling his friends about his conversion, and giving his testimony before large and small audiences. On one occasion he addressed a great Men's Meeting in Exeter Hall, and on another, spoke to the students at the London Polytechnic. Speaking at a convert's meeting soon after his conversion, Col. Beauchamp said: "How easy everything is now! I can't keep quiet. Every one of my friends knows it. Now my whole desire is to serve God. Thank God his Holy Spirit is working through Dr. Torrey and Mr. Alexander. It is not Dr. Torrey; it is not Mr. Alexander; it is God's Holy Spirit working in the Albert Hall. Life is so easy now. All the difficulties ahead of me have vanished; and I am able to speak of God's love and of all that he has done for me."

A SOLDIER'S STORY

One night when speaking to a group of poor men at the London Medical Mission, Col. Beauchamp told them something of his life story before his conversion, saying: "I sowed my wild oats as well as anybody. I was an awful gambler; I think gambling kept me back more than anything else from becoming a child of God. Eventually in His mercy God again spoke to me. I had got command of my regiment, and thought it was about time I gave up living for the devil and pulled myself together. So I tried in my own strength to live for God. What I did in my own strength was to live a fairly 'religious' life. I used to go to the hospital every single day. I would conduct service every Sunday. I used to go to the prayer meetings on week days; I would come up from the polo grounds and go straight into the prayer-meeting in my polo kit. From the prayer tent I would go to the mess, and forgetting all about the prayer-meeting, all about the hospital service, I would play cards up to any hour of the morning. Not only that, but I would very often ask young officers to play with me who didn't want to play, but who thought they would have to play with a senior officer. I knew that card-playing and prayer-meetings on the same night were not right, and I knew I was getting no blessings out of the prayer-meetings. Things went on in that way for a long time. Eventually I left my regiment, and sailed around the world. I was shipwrecked once; the boat ran into an iceberg, and it was generally believed that she was going down. Some one came up to me in the excitement, and said, 'Will you go into the saloon and join in prayer?' I said, 'No, I will not; I have not obeyed God in my life, and I am not going to cry to him now.' I would have given anything to cry to him, but I could not. I was ashamed. By hard work the ship was saved, but the impression of spiritual danger lasted."

HOW ASHLYN STIRRED LONDON

Perhaps the most remarkable conversion of the entire campaign was that of Quentin Ashlyn, a concert hall singer and entertainer. London was stirred by his confession of Christ.

One day, while passing on a bus the Royal Albert Hall he felt a desire to go inside and hear the evangelists. He was impressed by Dr. Torrey's sermon, but did not surrender to God. On returning home, however, he found on the mantelpiece a sermon by Dr. Torrey on "Hell." He was so stirred by its delineation of the terrible doom awaiting sinners that he there and then decided to forsake sin and accept Christ. Mr. Ashlyn then wrote at once to the manager of the concert hall where he was appearing and told him that he had been converted, and that he could not continue his work as a concert hall entertainer. The manager would not release him from his contract, but declared he must at least appear, but if he desired, he could go on to the platform of the hall and tell the story of his conversion. Accordingly when his turn came on the program Mr. Ashlyn walked out on the stage and said:

"I have come to the platform this afternoon to explain why I am unable to give the sketch included in the program. The reason is that I have been converted to God through the agency of the Torrey-Alexander Mission at the Royal Albert Hall. I feel that my life must not be spent in amusing people, but in the service of the Saviour who died for me. I feel that I cannot go on playing the fool before men and women, knowing that many of them are going to destruction." When Mr. Ashlyn had begun his speech the people began to laugh, thinking it was a new witticism, but before he concluded they were far from laughing.

The bold stand of the entertainer gave a new sensation to the great materialistic metropolis. The press contained long interviews with him, while the manager of the concert hall was so impressed that he offered his hall to Mr. Ashlyn, free of charge, for a week of revival meetings. The offer was accepted; and it was my privilege to be present at St. George's Hall on that memorable Sunday afternoon when he held his first meeting. Large crowds assembled outside the building; and when the doors were opened the hall was quickly packed. The majority of those who sought admission were not able to get inside; and a second meeting was held immediately following the first. Mr. Alexander, who had been conducting a meeting at the London Polytechnic across the street, was present and sang at the second service.

A SINGER WHO WAS TIRED OF LIFE

In a simple but deeply affecting manner Mr. Ashlyn told at the two services how his life had been transformed by his acceptance of Christ as his Saviour. He said in part:

"I was tired of getting out of bed in the morning, tired of dressing myself, tired of theatres, tired of novels, tired of going to see my friends. Two of my old concert hall friends committed suicide, and I was almost ready to follow in their steps. I used to like my profession. At one time I was rather proud of going on this platform. I liked the applause, and I liked the money more. If I could get $50 for the night I was pleased; if I could get $75 I was still more pleased; but ere long I was tired of it all. But now my life is transformed. I wish there was a window in my soul so that you could just see how full of peace I am to-day."

When Mr. Ashlyn appealed for decisions for Jesus Christ two persons stood up. In the evening he again spoke from the same platform, and the hall was once more crowded. His testimony was with power, and more than twenty-five persons confessed Christ, including an actress. Throughout the entire week Mr. Ashlyn conducted meetings, and great blessings resulted. When it became known that Mr. Ashlyn was giving up his profession he was asked what his future profession would be. He replied, "It is not in my hands; he who has saved me will lead me, and where he leads I will follow." Mr. W. T. Stead, who interviewed Mr. Ashlyn, declared that if half a dozen men, as well known in London as Quentin Ashlyn, were to experience such a revolution from boredom to joy, and from misery to peace, and were to proclaim it as earnestly, the whole city would be shaken with a new realizing sense of the miracle of the Word.

Not long after his conversion Mr. Ashlyn gave a striking comparison of his past and his present life, saying:

"Before my conversion I was the most miserable man in London. I, who amused everybody, could not amuse myself. As the years passed I seemed to get worse and worse. Nothing interested me. I had heard my mother talk about the peace and joy she experienced. I did not believe it. It seemed to me there was no such thing as happiness in the world. Now my heart's burden is gone, and I am a new man. I feel like laughing all the day. My friends are all wondering at the change in my looks. I am as if I were in a new world."

Since his conversion Mr. Ashlyn has been conducting revival meetings, throughout England and Wales; and large num-

bers have been led to Christ through hearing his story.   One
of his converts was connected with one of the best known families of the English nobility.

A notable feature of the Royal Albert Hall campaign was
the half-hour song service, led by Mr. Alexander at the conclusion of each afternoon and each evening meeting.   He
began them because the people were so eager for the Gospel
songs that they lingered after the metings were over and
seemed loth to go home.   He declared that he had never seen
anything like the enthusiasm of the Albert Hall audiences since
leaving Australia.   In these song services he frequently called
upon somebody to give a testimony; and the service usually
closed with a solo by Mr. Paul Gilbert, during which a second
invitation was given, in response to which from ten to twenty
persons often stood up to accept Christ.   One afternoon Mr.
Alexander called upon his wife to relate an incident of personal
work which had occurred in London a short time previous.
Bravely ascending the crimson-covered dais, and in a clear,
soft voice which carried to the topmost gallery, while a deep
silence fell over the vast audience with her opening words,
she said:

FLOWERS CONQUER A HEART

"I was in London a few days before the work commenced,
and went into a waiting-room, and there saw a woman sitting
at the table, with such a look of bitterness on her face that my
heart ached for her.   I spoke to her, but she shook me off as
sharply as she could.   I tried again, but she rebuffed me
again.   I prayed in my heart that God would give me some
word to say to her; she seemed to need love and friendship so

much. Still she would not hear me, and the tears filled my eyes as I turned away, her words cut me so.

"I went out into the street and looked about for a flower-shop. I could not find one, but presently a young girl came along selling flowers, and I bought a bunch of lilies of the valley. The woman did not look very pleased when I entered the waiting-room again. But I went up to her and said, 'Would you mind accepting a few flowers from me?' You should have seen the change that came into her face on the instant. The look of bitterness fled. Then I found the way was open, and that I could speak to her. It seemed that some professing Christians had made her turn away from the Saviour by some act of injustice they had done to her. She was judging the Lord by those who were not following him.

"I mention this that we may all ask God to make us real Christians, so that when we go among other people they may know just what we are and no longer say of us that we are merely professing Christians."

THE DARKY "NINETY AND NINE"

On another occasion Mr. Alexander called upon his wife to recite the beautiful darky version of "The Ninety and Nine." She again mounted the dais and recited it as follows:

> "Po' lil' brack sheep dat strayed away,
>   Done los' in de win' an' de rain—
> An' de Shepherd he say, 'O, hirelin',
>   Go fin' my sheep again.'
> An' de hirelin' say, 'O, Shepherd,
>   Dat sheep am brack and bad.'
> But de Shepherd he smile, like dat lil' brack sheep
>   Wus de onliest lamb he had.

"An' he say, 'O, hirelin', hasten,
  For de win' an' de rain am col',
An' dat lil' brack sheep am lonesome
  Out dere, so far f'um de fol'.'
But de hirelin' frown, 'O, Shepherd,
  Dat sheep am ol' an' grey.'
But de Shepherd he smile, like dat lil' brack sheep
  Wus fair as de break ob day.

"An' he say, 'O, hirelin,' hasten,
  Lo! here is de ninety an' nine,
But dere way off f'm de sheepfol'
  Is dat lil' brack sheep ob mine'.
An' de hirelin frown, 'O, Shepherd,
  De rest of de sheep am here!'
But de Shepherd he smile, like dat lil' brack sheep
  He hol' it de mostes' dear.

"An' de Shepherd go out in de darkness
  Where de night was col' an' bleak,
An' dat lil' brack sheep, he fin it,
  And lay it agains' his cheek
An' de hirelin' frown, 'O, Shepherd,
  Don' bring dat sheep to me!'
But de Shepherd he smile, like dat lil' brack sheep
  An'—dat lil' brack sheep—wus—me."

As Mrs. Alexander concluded, tears were seen in many eyes, and when the invitation was given a number of veterans of the Crimean War arose to confess their acceptance of Christ.

"TELL MOTHER I'LL BE THERE"

Throughout the Royal Albert Hall campaign the song next in popularity to the "Glory Song" was the touching melody, "Tell Mother I'll Be There," the chorus of which runs as follows:

"Tell mother I'll be there, in answer to her prayer;
  This message, blessed Saviour to her bear;
Tell mother I'll be there, heaven's joys with her to share;
  Yes, tell my darling mother I'll be there."

This song was used not only as a congregational piece by the great audience, but its popularity was partly due to its beautiful rendering as a solo by Mr. Paul J. Gilbert. Mr. Gilbert possesses a high, clear, tenor voice; and, as he sang the hymn touchingly and prayerfully at scores of meetings, it is safe to say that literally hundreds of people were led to give their hearts to God. Mr. Alexander also used the song occasionally as a solo. After one such occasion he received the following letter from a young man who had been in the audience the previous night. He wrote:

"Dear Mr. Alexander: I feel that I cannot let this day pass without in some measure thanking you for the rendering of that beautiful solo, 'Tell Mother I'll Be There.' I listened with great interest to Dr. Torrey's sermon, 'What shall it profit a Man?' and in some degree was convinced that I was not going straight; but when you sang the hymn I was struck at once, and immediately you had finished I went to my apartments. I could not sleep at all, but just as the dawn was breaking I returned to the Good Shepherd's Fold. I have been away from home some time now, and had determined to go home to-morrow (Saturday) and see my mother, and tell her the good news. I received the enclosed this morning, and My heart is almost breaking—for I am too late. It reads:

"Dear John: Mother died this morning at eight o'clock."

Undoubtedly the prayers of that mother were heard and answered before she passed into the presence of the King.

A WORKINGMAN'S STORY

Another revival song which led to numerous conversions was the one entitled, "In the Good Old Fashioned Way." In one of the meetings, when testimonies were being given by the converts, a workingman arose and said: "I am an uneducated section hand, but I'm not ashamed of it. I worked on the Union Pacific Railroad in 1878. I wasn't converted then, but since I was converted at the Royal Albert Hall, instead of swearing while I work I have been singing 'The Good Old Fashioned Way.' My mates used to call me 'Blackguard Stan'; now they call me 'Converted Stan.' One of them said to me the other day, 'What is this? You used to curse and swear; now you are singing all the day. You are happy and comfortable. One time you used to come to me on a Monday morning to borrow, you now have change in your pocket at the end of the week. What is it you have got? I want a bit of that.' I said, 'What I have got is good for you, and you can have it the same way as I got it?' As the section-hand finished his narrative he said: "I am always singing the 'Good Old Fashioned Way.' I'll sing it for you now if you like." Mr. Alexander, smiling radiantly at the man, urged him to do so by all means. In his rough, untrained voice, the man sang lustily:

> "I am going home to glory,
>   In the good old-fashioned way."

The happy face of the man, and his words which came from a heart overflowing with joy, touched many in the audience, and were as good as a sermon. There were many working-men in the audience, and they were greatly impressed. Several were moved to accept Christ.

THE DEDICATION OF A PIANO

Another interesting convert was a church organist. One afternoon after a meeting had ended, and Mr. Harkness, the pianist was locking up the piano, a gentleman stepped up to him and in the course of conversation confessed that he was leading an immoral life, although he was an organist in a London church, and the teacher of a Sunday School class. Mr. Harkness talked earnestly with him, declaring that he could get victory only by a whole-hearted surrender to Christ. The man would not yield at the time, however, but arranged to return and talk it over with Mr. Harkness. Two days later the latter received a letter from the organist, in which he said: "Glory to God! I found peace this morning at three o'clock, after spending half the night in prayer. There was a tremendous battle, but God had the victory. Praise His Name forever. It has been a grand day for me to-day. I have this day surrendered all to Jesus and asked the Lord to

" 'Take my hands, and let them move
At the impulse of thy love.'

No more concerts or dance meetings. I have dedicated my piano to the praise of Jesus. My heart is full of singing."

The audiences in the Royal Albert Hall were composed, not only of people from every section of London from Whitechapel to Mayfair, but included people from almost every great nation on earth. One night while singing, "Blest Be the Tie that Binds," the question was asked how many different nationalities were represented in the audience; and it was learned that men and women were present from the following countries: America, Switzerland, France, Germany, Russia, Japan, Sweden, Norway, Denmark, Scotland, Ireland, Wales,

Holland, Australia—fifteen nationalities in all including England.

During the two months' campaign at the Royal Albert Hall, which constituted the first stage of the five months' crusade, the names of 6,500 converts were registered. Lord Kinnaird, the president of the London Evangelistic Council, in speaking of the first phase of the movement, said: "It has exceeded our most sanguine expectation. There never has been a continuous series of meetings with so large an attendance. The meetings of Moody and Sankey did not attract larger numbers, and in no instance did these missioners stay so long in one place. I think, too, that the results, so far as we can judge them yet, are most satisfactory. These have proved our contention that the people only want the Gospel preached to them by level-headed men and they will respond. We have reached the people we intend to reach, and to a most astonishing extent. I know this to be a fact for the reason that I have seen present many of those whom I have personally invited."

The hearts of all the leaders of the movement were overflowing in praise to God for the glorious victory. Dr. Torrey declared the meetings had been " a success beyond our utmost anticipations." Mr. Alexander, when asked for his opinion, said: "The Mission has been far beyond the expectations of any of us, and we have the greatest cause for thankfulness to God." The Secretary of the movement, Mr. John H. Putterill, declared that they were "the most extraordinary series of meetings ever held in this great metropolis."

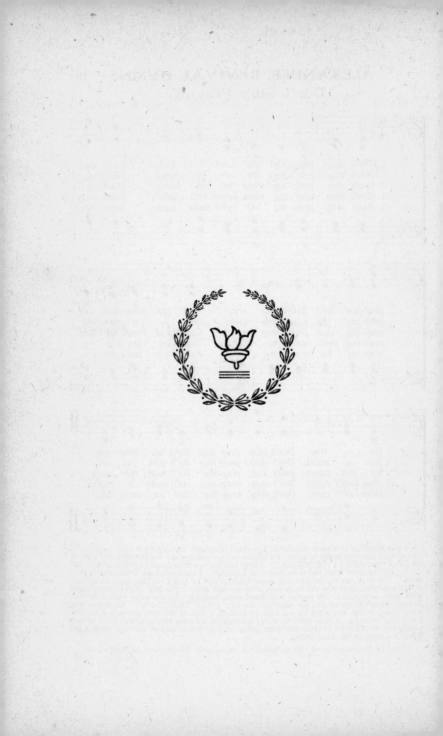

Don't Stop Praying.

E. R. W.   EDNA R. WORRELL.

1. Don't stop pray-ing! the Lord is nigh; Don't stop pray-ing! He'll hear your cry; God has prom-ised, and He is true; Don't stop pray-ing! He'll an-swer you.

2. Don't stop pray-ing for ev-'ry need, Don't stop pray-ing! the Lord will heed; No pe-ti-tion to Him is small; Don't stop pray-ing! He'll give you all.

3. Don't stop pray-ing when led to sin; Don't stop pray-ing that good may win; Christ was tempt-ed and un-der-stands; Don't stop pray-ing! He'll hold your hands.

4. Don't stop pray-ing when bowed with grief; Don't stop pray-ing! you'll get re-lief; Troub-les nev-er es-cape God's sight; Don't stop pray-ing! He'll make it right.

5. Don't stop pray-ing but have more trust; Don't stop pray-ing! for pray we must; Faith will ban-ish a mount of care; Don't stop pray-ing! God an-swers pray'r.

I was standing at a bank-counter in Liverpool, England, waiting for a clerk to come. I picked up a pen and began to print on a blotter in large letters, two words, which had gripped me like a vice: "PRAY THROUGH." I kept talking to a friend and printing until I had the big blotter filled from top to bottom with a column. I transacted my business and went away. The next day my friend came to see me, and said he had a striking story to tell me. A business man came into the bank soon after we had gone. He had grown discouraged with business troubles. He started to transact some business with the same clerk over that blotter, when his eye caught the long column of "PRAY THROUGH." He asked who wrote those words, and when he was told, exclaimed, "That is the very message I needed. I will pray through. I have tried to worry through in my own strength, and have merely mentioned my troubles to God, now I am going to pray the situation through until I get light."—CHARLES M. ALEXANDER.

Tell Mother I'll be There.

C. M. F.

CHARLES M. FILLMORE.

1. When I was but a lit-tle child, how well I rec-ol-lect How
2. Though I was oft-en wayward, she was al-ways kind and good, So
3. When I be-came a prod-i-gal, and left the old roof-tree, She
4. One day a mes-sage came to me, it bade me quick-ly come If

I would grieve my moth-er with my fol-ly and neg-lect; And
pa-tient, gen-tle, lov-ing, when I act-ed rough and rude; My
al-most broke her lov-ing heart in mourning aft-er me, And
I would see my moth-er ere the Sav-iour took her home; I

now that she has gone to heav'n, I miss her ten-der care,
child-hood griefs and tri-als she would glad-ly with me share;
day and night she prayed to God to keep me in His care;
prom-ised her, be-fore she died, for heav-en to pre-pare;

O Sav - iour, tell my moth - er I'll be there!

CHORUS.

Tell moth-er I'll be there, in an-swer to her pray'r, This

message, blessed Saviour, to her bear! Tell mother I'll be there, heav'n's

joys with her to share, Yes, tell my dar-ling moth-er I'll be there.

Is He Yours?

ADA R. HABERSHON.

ROBERT HARKNESS.

Solo, or unison.

1. A Sav-iour who died our sal - va - tion to win, A Sav-iour who
2. A Shep-herd who giv - eth His life for the sheep, A Shepherd both
3. A Pi - lot who knoweth the dan-gers at hand, A Pi - lot who
4. A Shel-ter from tem-pest, from wind and from storm, A Shel-ter from

knows how to save us from sin,— Yes, He is the Sav-iour, the
might - y to save and to keep,— Yes, this is the Shepherd, the
bring - eth all ves - sels to land,— Yes, this is the Pi - lot, the
judg - ment, a Shel - ter from harm,— Yes, this is the Shel - ter, the

rall. *a tempo.*

Sav - iour we need, And He is a Sav - iour in - deed!...
Shep - herd we need, And He is a Shep-herd in - deed!...
Pi - lot we need, And He is a Pi - lot in - deed!...
Shel - ter we need, And He is a Shel - ter in - deed!...

Is He Yours?

CHORUS.

Is He yours?.. Is He yours?.. Is this Saviour, who loves you, yours?
Is He yours?   Is He yours?

He Will Hold Me Fast.

"Thy right hand shall hold me."—Psalm cxxxix, 10.

ADA R. HABERSHON.   ROBERT HARKNESS.

1. When I fear my faith will fail, Christ will hold me fast;
2. I could nev - er keep my hold, He must hold me fast;
3. I am pre - cious in His sight, He will hold me fast;
4. He'll not let my soul be lost, Christ will hold me fast;

rall.

When the tempt-er would pre - vail, He can hold me fast. . . .
For my love is oft - en cold, He must hold me fast. . . .
Those He saves are His de - light, He will hold me fast. . . .
Bought by Him at such a cost, He will hold me fast. . . .

He Will Hold Me Fast.

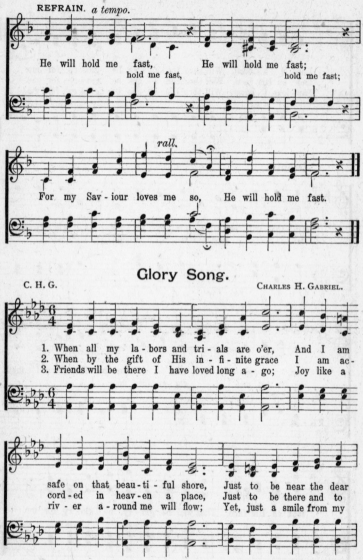

REFRAIN. *a tempo.*

He will hold me fast, He will hold me fast;
hold me fast, hold me fast;

rall.

For my Sav-iour loves me so, He will hold me fast.

Glory Song.

C. H. G.   CHARLES H. GABRIEL.

1. When all my la-bors and tri-als are o'er, And I am
2. When by the gift of His in-fi-nite grace I am ac-
3. Friends will be there I have loved long a-go; Joy like a

safe on that beau-ti-ful shore, Just to be near the dear
cord-ed in heav-en a place, Just to be there and to
riv-er a-round me will flow; Yet, just a smile from my

Lord I a - dore, Will thro' the a - ges be glo - ry for me...
look on His face, Will thro' the a - ges be glo - ry for me...
Sav - iour, I know, Will thro' the a - ges be glo - ry for me...

CHORUS.

Oh, that will be glo - ry for me, glo - ry for
Oh, ... that will be glo - ry for me,

me, glo - ry for me, When by His grace I shall
glo - ry for me, glo - ry for me, ...

look on His face, That will be glo - ry, be glo - ry for me.

No Burdens Yonder.

"And God shall wipe away all tears from their eyes; and there shall be no more death, neither sorrow, nor crying, neither shall there be any more pain; for the former things are passed away."—Rev. xxi, 4.

ADA R. HABERSHON.   ROBERT HARKNESS.

Quietly.

1. No bur - dens yon - der, not a sin - gle care, ..
2. No tri - als yon - der, all the testing done, ..
3. No toil - ing yon - der, and no wea - ri - ness, ..
4. No part - ings yon - der, and no sad good - byes, ..

When home is reached, noth - ing there to bear, ..
The school-days o - ver, and the priz - es won, ..
No dis - ap - point - ments, and no more dis - tress, ..
No pain, no sick - ness, and no weep-ing eyes, ..

No bur - dens yon - der, all will be laid down, .. Be -
No much-tried faith like gold in fur - nace heat, .. The
The fu - ture bright, the past all un - der - stood, .. We'll
But best of all my Sav - iour I shall see, ... No

fore we share His glo - ry   and   His   throne...
pu - ri - fy - ing will all   be   com - plete....
see that all the way He   led   was   good....
cloud will come be - tween my   Lord   and   me. .....

rall.

CHORUS. *a tempo.*

No   bur - dens yon - der,   All   sor - row past, ..

a tempo.

ad lib.

No   bur - dens yon - der,   Home   at   last. ....

Oh, What a Change!

ADA R. HABERSHON.

ROBERT HARKNESS.

1. Soon will our Sav - iour from heav-en ap - pear,
2. Lone - li - ness changed to re - u - nion com - plete,
3. Sun - rise will chase all the dark-ness a - way,
4. Weak-ness will change to mag - ni - fi - cent strength,

Sweet is the hope and its pow - er to cheer;
Ab - sence ex - changed for a place at His feet,
Night will be changed to the bright-ness of day,
Fail - ure will change to per - fec - tion at length,

All will be changed by a glimpse of His face—
Sleep-ing ones raised in a mo - ment of time,
Tem - pests will change to in - ef - fa - ble calm,
Sor - row will change to un - end - ing de - light,

This is the goal at the end of our race!
Liv - ing ones changed to His im - age sub - lime!
Weep-ing will change to a ju - bi - lant psalm!
Walk-ing by faith change to walk - ing by sight!

CHORUS.

Oh, what a change, ... Oh, what a change, ... When I shall see . . . His won-der-ful face! .. Oh, what a change, ... Oh, what a change, ... When I shall see His face!

Oh, what a change, (×4)

Shadows.

Words and Music by ROBERT HARKNESS.

SOLO and CHORUS.

1. When we cross the val - ley there need be no shad - ows,
2. When our loved ones leave us there need be no shad - ows
3. When He comes to meet us there need be no shad - ows,

When life's day is end - ed and its sor - rows o'er;
If their faith is fixed in Je - sus as their Lord;
When He comes in all His glo - ri - ous ar - ray;

When the sum - mons comes to meet the bless - ed Sav - iour,
For they go to be with Him who died to save them,
When the trump of God shall sound and loved ones wak - en,

Shadows.

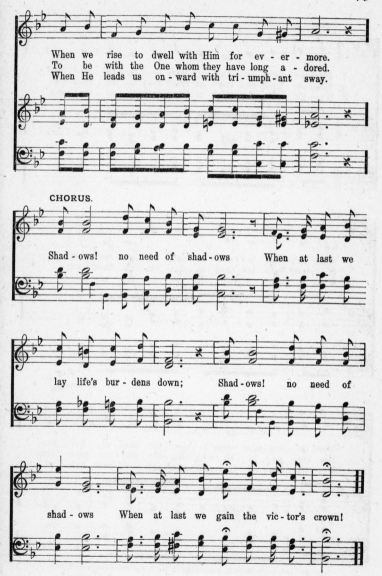

When we rise to dwell with Him for ev - er - more.
To be with the One whom they have long a - dored.
When He leads us on - ward with tri - umph - ant sway.

CHORUS.

Shad - ows! no need of shad - ows When at last we

lay life's bur - dens down; Shad - ows! no need of

shad - ows When at last we gain the vic - tor's crown!

V

OPENING OF THE ENGLISH CAMPAIGN

WHEN Dr. Torrey and Mr. Alexander reached England, they were practically unknown. Dr. Torrey had been there once before, twenty years previous; but he came on that occasion as an observer, and not as a teacher. It was Mr. Alexander's first visit. In a certain degree, however, they did not come as strangers, for the reports of what God had accomplished through them in Australia had filled Christian hearts with joy; and had led them to hope and pray for a similar work of grace in the British Isles.

Upon their arrival in London, a great welcome meeting was held in Exeter Hall which had been arranged by cablegram while the evangelists were still in Bombay. It was a memorable gathering. Mr. T. A. Denny presided. Among those present were Lord Kinnaird, Lord Radstock, Prebendary Webb-Peploe, Dr. J. Munro Gibson, Dr. Barnardo, Rev. S. F. Webster, Dr. Harry Guinness, Dr. A. T. Pierson, Rev. Thomas Spurgeon, Rev. F. B. Meyer, Rev. Thomas Champness, Mr. Eugene Stock, Mr. R. C. Morgan, and many other well-known religious leaders.

LORD KINNAIRD'S WELCOME

In his address of welcome Lord Kinnaird said: "We have been looking forward to your presence. We have heard what you have been doing in Australia and in other parts of the world; and we pray our Heavenly Father that, through you, there may be such an outpouring of the Holy Spirit as we have not seen for years. We will follow you with our prayers, and look forward to the hour when you will be back in London. Most heartily do we welcome you this evening."

Following the welcome meeting, the evangelists spent three weeks in Mildmay Conference Hall, North London, stirring up church members to fresh zeal in soul winning, and witnessing a large number of conversions. At the close of their work there was a prophecy of the great and glorious work which they were later to accomplish in London—they received a cordial invitation to visit Edinburgh for a four weeks' campaign. Their meetings were held in Synod Hall, which proved too small to accommodate the thousands who pressed to hear the evangelists.

This was the beginning of a revival campaign conducted by Dr. Torrey and Mr. Alexander throughout the provincial cities of England, Ireland, Scotland and Wales, which was without precedent since the great work of Moody and Sankey in 1873-'75. Wherever they went—to Glasgow, Edinburgh, Aberdeen and Dundee in Scotland; to Dublin and Belfast in Ireland; to Liverpool, Manchester and Birmingham in England— the largest halls were unable to accomodate the thousands who daily thronged to hear them.

The success of the evangelists' work was due to their faith in God, their dependence upon the Holy Spirit for results, their zeal in soul-winning, and last, but not least, to the organization of thousands of "Prayer Circles" throughout the United Kingdom to implore God for a world-wide spiritual awakening, and to pray for the work of Dr. Torrey and Mr. Alexander.

When asked to relate some narratives of striking conversions which had occured during their early work in Great Britain, Mr. Alexander kindly consented and gave me the following stories of remarkable transformations through the power of the Gospel:

TWO TRANSFORMED LIVES

"A young lady attended our meetings in St. Andrews Hall, Glasgow, who had been assisting her elder sister with her business. For years she had received nothing but her expenses for her work. She felt that she should receive more than that; and had systematically slipped a certain amount from the till each week and put it in the bank until she had stolen $650. The Spirit of God touched her one night in the meeting, and revealed her sinful heart. She accepted Christ, went home and handed her bank book to her sister, telling her that the amount in the bank had been stolen from the business, and asked her forgiveness which was immediately given. The sister, who had been cold in the Lord's service, was led to deep consecration through the act; it touched the entire community, and many others were led to Christ through this restitution.

"While we were in Belfast Dr. Harry Guinness assisted us with the overflow meetings. We had two large churches, which were packed night after night, until at last we had to take St. George's Market, which held 7,000 people. There we saw some wonderful displays of God's power. I remember one broad-faced Irishman, called 'Billy', who was very earnest in dealing with drunkards that came to the front. He had been converted in gaol one day when Sankey was singing 'Hold the Fort.' The words came across from another building to the open window of his cell, and he was led to Christ through them.

"I well recollect our last meeting in Belfast when about five hundred people came to Christ. Dr. Torrey was appealing to those to come forward who would accept Jesus Christ, and 'Billy' was down at the front dealing with some man. In the midst of the invitation he jumped up, turned to the audience and shouted, 'Why don't ye come to Jesus? Pwhat har-r-rm's he ever done ye?' Later in the meeting, when about to close, Dr. Torrey made the statement, as he addressed the new converts that never in his life had he felt so reluctant to leave a city as he had to leave Belfast. Billy jumped up again and cried, 'Nobody's a-chasin ye away!'

BELFAST'S FAREWELL

"As we took the steamer on our last day in Belfast, the street was packed solid with people right across in front of the quay. The Salvation Army Brass Band led the music; and, using a large box for a platform, I conducted the whole street full of people in singing song after song. Dr. Torrey said a few words, and then made an appeal for converts right in the street. Some laboring men coming home, all grimy from their work, with their buckets on their arms, accepted his invitation and publicly confessed Christ.

"Our choir was by the ship's side, and as we left the dock they sang, 'God Be With You Till We Meet Again,' while I directed them from the upper deck with a handkerchief. For three quarters of a mile up the docks people were strung along in great numbers, waving and singing 'Never Lose Sight of Jesus.' The people on board said they had never seen such a beautiful sight as those thousands of people gathered on the shore, bidding us good-bye with a Gospel song. The Captain sent a man to us, asking if he should blow the whistle. We said, 'Yes'; so while the handkerchiefs were waving and the people were singing the whistle began to blow and that was our affectionate 'good-bye' to Belfast."

At the conclusion of their work in Ireland Dr. Torrey and Mr. Alexander made a flying visit to America during July and August, 1903, where they addressed numerous conventions and religious conferences, and stirred up the people with their glorious reports of the revival campaigns in Australia and Great Britain.

CHICAGO'S WELCOME

The most notable meeting held during their stay in America was the great Welcome Meeting in the Auditorium in Chicago. The scenes enacted at that memorable meeting were impressive, and long to be remembered. Although the service was timed to commence at eight o'clock, long before that hour thousands of people stood four deep in the street, waiting for the doors to be opened. It is estimated that ten thousand people endeavored to gain admission to the huge building.

One of the leading lawyers of Chicago, Hon. Luther Laflin Mills presided; and in his address of welcome said: "Dr. Torrey has returned to us a conquering hero, home from that holiest of wars, the battle for the redemption and uplifting of men's souls. He has been recognized in every civilized land, and in China, Japan, India and Hawaii for his work and worth as the real successor of Moody, and as such we give him welcome. With him comes Charles M. Alexander, the sweet singer, whose music has set half the world to singing, and the echoes of which still linger to-day in the hearts and memories of many peoples in many lands."

In his conduct of the musical part of the program Mr. Alexander quickly captivated the great American audience as he had done similar audiences in Australia, India and the United Kingdom; and soon they were singing his revival melodies as only Americans can sing when aroused to the highest pitch of enthusiasm. The meeting was especially noticeable by reason of one woman who sat in a box that night. She was a little, sweet-faced lady who had come all the way from Tennessee, to hear her son sing before the great audience gathered in the Auditorium. It was the first time she had seen him in so large a gathering; and the tears glistened in her fond eyes as the roars of applause broke once and again over her boy's head. She was Mrs. Alexander, and her son was the sweet-voiced baritone who had girdled the globe with Gospel song.

VI

"TELL MOTHER I'LL BE THERE"

In September, 1903, the evangelists returned to England; and began a four weeks' campaign in Liverpool, which proved to be the most successful held up to that time in Great Britain. About 5,000 converts were recorded. Such crowds flocked to the Philharmonic Hall, where the meetings were held, that towards the close of the mission it was necessary to hold double meetings each night, the first being for women, the second for men. While the first service was in progress thousands would be clamoring at the door for admittance. People would stand four deep for an hour, all along the sides of the building, in the rain, waiting for an entrance, and as they waited they sang revival hymns. Mr. Alexander told me a characteristic incident which occured one day among those waiting for admission.

"One night," said he, "after the notice was put up 'Hall Full,' great crowds still hung around the doors. Mr. Armstrong, a city missionary, went out and said to the crowd, 'The Hall is full; why don't you go home?' One lady standing near him said, 'Please, sir, we are waiting for somebody to faint.' He said, 'Surely you don't want anyone to faint, do you? 'No,' she said, 'but they do faint in there sometimes, and I am waiting until somebody does, so that I can get their seat.' Her earnestness excited his curiosity, and he inquired if she was a Christian. She replied she was not. 'Well,' said he,' I can probably get you in at the back door.' He succeeded, and she listened to the sermon. In the after-meeting he noticed that that woman was one of the first to come down to the front seats and publicly confess her acceptance of Christ.

THE SONG THAT TOUCHED ALL HEARTS

"Our last Sunday in Philharmonic Hall was one of the most memorable days that I have ever seen in our work," continued Mr. Alexander. "We were to have a women's meeting in the afternoon and a men's meeting at night. I had been praying earnestly before going to the women's meeting in the afternoon that God would lead me to the very song that would melt the hearts of the people and lead them to Christ. I was very much in doubt during the first part of the song service what song to use. At last I threw the meeting open, and asked anyone to suggest a song that had helped them. A lady immediately mentioned No. 13, 'Tell Mother I'll Be There.' Directly she announced it I felt that that was the song we needed. We began singing it; and it took a wonderful hold upon the audience. I felt that the Lord was there, and at the close of Dr. Torrey's sermon, when he gave out the invitation, two hundred and ten women came down to the front and publicly confessed Christ. I said to the women, 'I have a curiosity to know how many of you were led to Christ by the singing of "Tell Mother I'll Be There." Will those who were please rise?" And thirty-three women out of the two hundred and ten stood up.

"When it came to the men's meeting at night, we had a choir of five hundred men. I believe everyone of them was an earnest Christian. After we had sung a little I told the audience what had happened in the afternoon; and said that we ought to have three times as many men yielding themselves to God during the singing of the hymn. I then turned to the choir and said, 'Men, pray every word you sing!' They sang it together, and you felt their hearts were behind it. You could feel that the hearts of the men in the audience were melting like wax. During the song I made a call for those who would accept Christ and confess him publicly before the audience to stand up then and there. They started to stand up; we would sing another verse and they would begin to rise up again. Presently I called up a little curly-headed boy, and stood him upon the stand beside me, and he sang a verse which seemed to move the men more deeply than ever. When the song ended one hundred and sixty men had risen and publicly professed their acceptance of Christ. Spontaneously the audience arose and sang, 'Praise God From Whom All Blessings Flow.' Then Dr. Torrey preached and repeated the invitation, and four hundred and fifty men, including the hundred and sixty who had stood up before the sermon, publicly acknowledged that they had taken Jesus Christ as their Saviour, their Lord and their King. An American consul sitting on the platform near me said that he did not know God was working in that way in these days, and that it was the most wonderful sight he had ever seen."

Not only in Liverpool, but all throughout England this touching hymn was used in the conversion of many men and women.

THE STING OF MEMORY

Mr. Alexander relates an interesting incident which occurred during their campaign in Dundee. "One night, just as I was ready to retire in my hotel," he says, "a porter came up to me and said that a gentleman wanted to se me in the coffee room. I tried to make an excuse, but the porter said that the man insisted that he must see me. I went down and found a fine, big Scotch farmer sobbing like a child. I said, 'What can I do for you? Are you a Christian man?' He said, 'I wasn't a Christian man till to-night, but I am now. I listened to Dr. Torrey's sermon, and withstood that and his appeal to come to Christ; but I was standing during the singing in the after-meeting, when the choir struck up the song 'Where is My Wandering Boy To-night?' I thought of my good old father who had gone to heaven three years before, and it touched my heart. Then at the close of the verse the choir sang 'Tell Mother I'll Be There.' My dear old mother had gone to heaven a little while before, and the memory of the home life, and of their sweet Christian lives was too much for me. I gave my heart to God, and felt that I could not go home to-night until I had told you.' He said he was going back home to start family prayers and live a consecrated Christian life. Such experiences as this," said Mr. Alexander, "give one a fresh and never-tiring interest in the work of soul winning."

During the campaign in Manchester a gentleman wrote Mr. Alexander telling him how two of his songs had brought great blessing into his life. His letter ran as follows:

"I came to hear you last Monday night. I told my wife I was going, and she was praying for me all the time. When the hymn 'My Mother's Prayer' was sung it brought to my memory the time when my saintly mother passed away, and when at her bedside I knelt and promised to meet her in heaven. This hymn broke me down, but when the audience began to sing 'I Surrender All' I could not sing it. I could not surrender all, and so left the meeting; but the idea of a complete surrender still remained in my mind. I was afraid that if I surrendered all I would have to give up card playing and theatre going. I felt that I could not give up those things. On Sunday night I began to read the family Bible, and after perusing a chapter or two, I sank on my knees, and with my wife at my side, surrendered all to Jesus. Praise the Lord I can now say, 'I surrender all.' I am taking him at his word that he is able to keep me."

For a month the evangelists held a campaign in Dublin, in the Metropolitan Hall, during which about three thousand persons publicly accepted Christ. In recalling the work in this city, two touching incidents are related:

A BUSINESS MAN AND HIS MOTHER'S BIBLE

"One night, while the audience was singing 'Where is My Wandering Boy To-night,' a bright young business man from Glasgow was among the audience, and was deeply touched. Dr. Torrey's straight dealing impressed him so much that he turned to a man sitting at his side, and said, 'That man talks religion the way I sell goods. I am coming again to hear him to-morrow night.' He came again the next night with another man, and came out boldly for Christ. He wrote immediately to his old mother in Scotland, and received in reply one of the most beautiful letters I have ever seen. He had written to her to send on his Bible as he had been converted. Many times before when he would start off on a trip she had placed a small Bible in his bag, but he would hunt it out and leave it behind. The last time he had left home his mother said, 'I won't put the Bible in this time, but, if you want it, write and let me know and I will send it on.' His dear old father was filled with rejoicing at the great news they had just received. Later the young man went to Chicago to attend the Moody Bible Institute to fit himself better for Christian work.

"We have always endeavored in our meetings to get every Christian consecrated, every consecrated person a worker, and every worker trained to work anywhere and everywhere with anybody at any time or at all times. After a noon-day meeting in Dublin, a lady went to a well known restaurant to have lunch. She had her red hymn book with her, and laid it down beside her on the table. Another lady sitting close by observed the book, and entered into conversation with her. She said she was not a Christian, but would like to meet somebody who would explain to her the Way of Life. The lady lovingly and plainly explained to her the way, with the result that before she left the restaurant the anxious one had definitely accepted Christ. A day or two later the Christian lady went into the same restaurant and chanced to lay her hymn book again upon the table. A strange lady introduced herself, asking whether she was not the same woman who had led a friend of hers to Christ in the same restaurant. She said, 'You told my friend the Way of Life. Can you tell me?' Gladly she pointed the inquirer to Christ, and soon had the satisfaction and joy of knowing that she had led another soul to Jesus."

A CHRISTIAN CREW

The results of the campaigns conducted by the evangelists are felt on the high seas as well as upon the land. A member of the Torrey-Alexander party was returning from Dublin to Liverpool by the steamer "Cork." On being shown to his cabin he was met by the steward, who recognized him as one of the staff, and gave him a cordial welcome. "I am a Christian also," said the steward, "and you are now traveling on a Christian ship." The gentleman inquired what was meant, and the steward explained that he himself had been converted at one of the Torrey-Alexander meetings in Philharmonic Hall, Liverpool, the previous September. Another steward had been led to Christ during their crusade in Dublin, where one or two firemen had also found Jesus; and now so many of the crew had become Christians that the "Cork" was known among the seamen as the "Christian Ship."

At the famous seaside resort of Brighton the evangelists conducted a most successful campaign in The Dome, The Pavilion, The Corn Exchange and Hove Town Hall. Among the many beautiful incidents which occurred there, the following should be an inspiration to every Christian to improve every opportunity of winning souls to Christ:

"As I was leaving Hove Town Hall at the close of an afternoon meeting," said Mr. Alexander, "I stopped near the door, and a lady came and asked to shake hands with me. She said her mother had written to her, telling her to come to our meetings, and be sure to speak to Mr. Alexander. I was just about to say some commonplace words and bid her good-bye when the thought came to me to inquire if she was a Christian. I found she was not. I pressed upon her the claims of Christ, but she would not accept them. I was on the point of leaving when she said, turning to a girl of about sixteen years of age nearby, 'This is my daughter.' After shaking hands with her I said, 'Are you a Christian?' She replied, 'No, I am not.' I urged upon her the necessity of accepting Christ, and she yielded. All this time her mother had been standing at her side, and when the daughter yielded I turned to the mother and said, 'Surely you don't want to be out of Christ when your daughter is a Christian?' She could not stand that and she, too, came to a decision for Jesus.

A MOMENT TOO LATE

One night during the mission a solemn thing happened. A Christian man went into a restaurant for dinner, and, as the waiter served him, he experienced a strong conviction that he ought to speak to the man about his soul. He did not yield to it, however, but left the place without referring to the question of surrender to Christ. But even after he had reached the street the feeling returned with increased force; and he waited outside the restaurant for the waiter to come out. At last, the proprietor commenced to close the shop, and seeing this gentleman standing outside asked him what he was waiting for. He replied that he wanted to speak to the waiter that had served him. The answer of the proprietor came like a blow. "You will never," he said, "speak to that man again. After serving you he went upstairs and shot himself." When this incident was related in public it produced a profound impression, for it was a solemn lesson as to the danger of disobeying the promptings of the Spirit, as well as a warning to every Christian to be zealous in seeking the unsaved.

INFIDELS CONVERTED

During the month's Mission conducted by the evangelists in Bristol, four infidel members of one family flung their unbelief to the winds and came out for Christ. There were six sons and one daughter in the family, and all were infidels. The father had once been a clergyman, but had gone into infidelity, and had brought up his family to scoff at Christianity—a step which he bitterly regretted before he died.

During the Torrey-Alexander Mission an infidel lecturer from London visited this family, in order to get one of the young men to go with him to Coulston Hall to secure material for jest and sport. When he called everyone was out except the daughter. She accompanied him to the meeting. It was the first time she had ever attended a Gospel service. What she heard so deeply impressed her that she went again alone, and was converted. It was a bold step for her, but a bolder one was to follow. She returned home and told her brothers of her decision. They were indignant, but she held her ground. Finally she persuaded one of them to go with her to another service. The result was that he, too, flung his infidelity to the wind and accepted Christ; and before the Mission ended three other members of the same family came out for Christ.

Numerous were the infidels laid hold of by the power of God during the work in Great Britain and saved. At Manchester Mr. Musgrave Reed, one of the foremost infidel lecturers in the city, was converted, and has been for some time preaching the Gospel in India.

VII

PENTECOSTAL BLESSING AT BIRMINGHAM

THE revival campaign in Birmingham during January, 1904, was probably the most successful month's mission held anywhere in Great Britain. In that brief period nearly 8,000 men, women and children publicly professed to accept Christ as their Saviour, Lord and King. The meetings were held in Bingley Hall, one of the finest auditoriums in England. It seats 8,000 people, with standing room for 2,000 more; and is so perfect in its acoustic properties that Mr. Moody declared, after holding a series of meetings in it, that he wished he could carry it about with him wherever he went. From the first the meetings were wonderfully successful, the crowds coming in such throngs that it was necessary to call the mounted police in order to prevent accidents.

Although the meetings were so remarkably successful, yet they were begun under greater physical disadvantages, as regards the evangelists, than any other series of meetings in England. Mr. Alexander had hardly recovered from an illness, while Dr. Torrey was still suffering from a cold contracted several weeks before. Dr. Torrey's indisposition was so serious that it was feared that he would be unable to continue the meetings. As usual, however, the crisis was met and conquered by prayer. In answer to my inquiry, Mr. Alexander told the remarkable narrative how God heard and answered prayer for the recovery of Dr. Torrey.

THE EVANGELISTS AND A PARTY OF FORTY CAMBRIDGE UNIVERSITY STUDENTS

the revival meetings, a group of Christians from a suburb of London went back to their homes, fired with a desire to do something in their own village. Although they could not preach they decided on singing on the village green. God so blessed them that in ten days there were sixty conversions; and the whole church was filled with the glory of Christ.

During the South London campaign the names of about 5,000 converts were recorded. At the closing meeting Lord Kinnaird thanked the great choir most heartily for the splendid service throughout the crusade; and made the significant statement that even yet people did not fully realize the power there is in sacred song. He said: "I believe that of all modern discoveries, the power of sacred song, and the power of a choir to help forward revival work is only just being found out by the Christian Church at large. We hope you will all go back to your churches and missions and schools, more on fire than you have ever been before, and take the inspiration to your homes and districts, so that you may have during 1905 a greater number of converts in London than London has ever seen. Why should we be behind Wales? If Wales has a hundred thousand converts, why should not London? We thank God, however, that this is only the beginning."

THE NOVEL LOST ITS ATTRACTION

The meetings in the Great Hall, Strand, located in the very heart of London, during the last month of the campaign, were services of power and victory. Over 2,500 converts were recorded, the great majority being adults. After the first week, when it rained nearly all the time, the tabernacle, seating between 5,000 and 6,000, was practically filled each night.

The audiences were composed of a larger proportion of the unsaved than were those in either the Royal Albert Hall or in South London. Scores of unemployed men, with which London teemed at this time, drifted into the meetings, unsaved, and went out rejoicing in Christ as their Redeemer.

An infidel girl went into a meeting in the Strand Hall, determining to show her defiance by reading a novel during the service. Her attention was caught by Mr. Alexander's stopping the singing of the song, "His Grace is Sufficient for Me," to ask a party of blind people if God's grace was sufficient for them in their affliction. The happy "yes" from the sightless people profoundly impressed her; and she followed Dr. Torrey's sermon closely, was deeply convicted of sin and accepted Christ.

Three milkmen accepted Christ one night when the invitation was given at the Strand Hall. Their employer's custom had been to give each man ten quarts of milk, with instructions to make twelve quarts of it by giving their customers short measure. After accepting Christ, they went the next morning to their employer, told him that they were Christians, and that they could not consent to give short measure any more. Without a word each man was given the full twelve quarts, and continued to receive them from that day.

How deeply thousands of young men in London were affected by the movement was shown by the fact that they were not afraid to show their colors in public. A young lady who went to business every day by train declared she saw numbers of young men each morning reading their Bibles in the train on their way to work, and often being laughed at for doing it. She said it had all come about since the revival.

THE BIRTH OF A HYMN

A few days before the movement in the Strand ended, a new Gospel song was added to Mr. Alexander's collection of revival hymns, which achieved instant popularity. It was entitled, "Oh, What a Change"! The words were written by a lady already widely known for her sacred verse, Miss Ada R. Habershon. She was a worker in the campaign, and heard Dr. Torrey speak one afternoon upon the second coming of Christ. She was much impressed by the Doctor's words; and on returning home wrote the beautiful lines of the hymn, the first verse and chorus of which are as follows:

"Soon will our Saviour from heaven appear,
   Sweet is the hope and its power to cheer;
All will be changed by a glimpse of his face—
   This is the goal at the end of our race.

CHORUS

Oh, what a change! Oh, what a change!
When I shall see his wonderful face!
Oh, what a change! Oh, what a change!
When I shall see his face."

Soon afterwards Miss Habershon handed the lines to Mr. Harkness with the request that he set them to music. During Dr. Torrey's sermon one night, as the pianist scanned the lines, he had an inspiration; and pulling from his pocket a piece of paper jotted down the melody. The hymn was quickly printed, as originally written, without any alteration whatever, and delighted every one who was privileged to hear it. During the last days of the campaign on the Strand it was sung on an average of at least once in each meeting.

A GRAND FAREWELL

The great five months' crusade came to an end with a historic meeting for praise and thanksgiving held in the Royal Albert Hall. Ten thousand people gathered in the great structure, where so many victories for Christ had been won, to give God the glory for the wonderful success of the entire movement. The memorable gathering lasted nearly four hours. It was presided over by Lord Kinnaird; and the great audience included members of the nobility, members of Parliament, leading bankers, professional men, prominent English clergymen, editors, and men of affairs. It was announced during the evening that 202 meetings had been held in the course of the campaign, attended by 1,114,650 persons, giving an average attendance at each service of about 5,500. Best of all, however, was the fact that the number of converts recorded since the beginning of the movement exceeded 17,000.

During the evening brief addresses were delivered by Lord Kinnaird, Mr. W. G. Bradshaw, Rev. F. S. Webster, Pastor Thomas Surgeon, and by Dr. Torrey and Mr. Alexander.

Lord Kinnaird gave utterance to the joy which filled the hearts of the committee at the successful conclusion of the great crusade. He declared that one of the best features of the work, next to the great number of converts, was the fact that so many had been inspired to do personal work. In speaking of one person whom God had blessed in this form of work, he said: "A lady set herself to work, at the beginning of the campaign, on one family, and the result is that the father and mother and three children, all of ripe years, have been brought to a knowledge of Jesus Christ so far as we can know. How happy she must be this evening!"

SHEAVES GATHERED IN LONDON

One of the most interesting addresses of the evening was that of Mr. W. G. Bradshaw, the second in command of the great London City & Midland Bank, who, as Chairman of the Executive Committee, gave a glowing summary of the great movement. He said in part:

"We have reached to-night the last meeting of what has been, I suppose, the greatest revival campaign held in London since the days of Mr. Moody; and we are gathered here with very mingled feelings. On the one hand, we are sad that the happy service of the last five months has come to an end. On the other hand, our hearts are full of praise and thanksgiving to God for the great blessings he has sent us. 'The Lord hath done great things for us, whereof we are glad.' The campaign has been, through the mercy of God, a wonderful success. Overflowing congregations have gathered day by day to listen to the simple Gospel preached in the plainest terms, until they have aggregated over a million souls. More than fourteen thousand men and women (seventeen thousand, including the children,) drawn from all classes of society, have accepted the Lord Jesus Christ as their Saviour, their Lord and their King. For five months, more than ten thousand Christian workers have stood shoulder to shoulder in the cause of the Gospel with unbroken harmony and brotherly love. The old truths—the Divinity of Jesus Christ, the inspiration of the Scriptures, the power of the Lord to save and to keep any one who will put his trust in him—have been pealed forth with no uncertain sound, and it has been demonstrated that they still retain their hold upon the masses of the population. Thousands have had their faith strengthened, their hopes revived, their zeal rekindled. The responsibility upon every Christian of taking part in the great work of winning souls to our Lord Jesus Christ has been emphasised and brought home in a way which I think has never been equalled before."

Rev. F. S. Webster, in speaking of Mr. Alexander and the revival melodies, said: "You have taught us the 'Glory Song,' and London streets and alleys and mews and the riverside— all are echoing with inspiring strains. The women of our mothers' meeting were singing it this afternoon on the river at Hampton Court; and the children at their treat Thursday were shouting it on the railway train, and on the sea at Clacton. And last Tuesday I sang it with a great company round the open grave of one of our chief workers, whose husband was a worker in the after-meetings in this hall. And the 'Glory Song' seemed to be equally in place, both at the school treat and the funeral."

Perhaps the most striking part of the entire meeting, however, was the music. Mr. Alexander led the choir and audience with such enthusiasm and buoyant energy that one of the speakers declared he looked more as if he were beginning a five months' campaign rather than ending one. The new revival hymn, "Oh, What a Change!" was sung with thrilling power and effect by the vast assembly. As the ten thousand people reached the high note at the end of the chorus, the great multitude was electified. At the conclusion of the set program the people seemed loth to leave; and for nearly an huor thereafter Mr. Alexander led them in Gospel song.

The meeting finally concluded with the great audience's uniting in singing "Praise God From Whom All Blessings Flow"; and thus the wonderful campaign came to end.

GRAMOPHONE ENLISTED

The revival hymns of Mr. Alexander had so captivated London during the five months' crusade that the manager of a big Gramophone Company sent repeated requests to him to sing his songs into the gramophone, and so send the hymns all over the British Empire. Finally the manager became so urgent that he came to the Gospel singer's room one morning and pleaded his cause with all his might. He declared that untold good could be accomplished through making the gramophones sing the Gospel message day and night, everywhere, to all classes of people. He declared he had requests for the records from India, Australia, and all other parts of the British Empire.

Mr. Alexander finally agreed to make some records, provided the manager did not pay him a penny and would publicly announce that such was the case, in order that people could not say he was doing it for money.

Shortly afterwards Mr. Alexander went to the offices of the Gramophone Company (known as the Victor Talking Machine Company in America,) and after earnest prayer made a number of records including "The Glory Song"; "Tell Mother I'll Be There"; "The Old Time Religion"; "The Ninety and Nine"—embracing the "Darky Version" recited by Mrs. Alexander; and "The Sunbeam Song"—with the story of Fanny Shmolefsky.

As the manager of the company predicted, the records have since been used to accomplish a vast amount of good all over the world. Over two years after the records were made, when I asked Mr. Alexander what he had heard of the influence of the songs through this medium, he said:

"They have been much used in England by the Colporters on their Gospel wagons, as they go through the country. 'Tell Mother I'll Be there' has been especially helpful in reaching crowds of men that would gather at such places.

HEARD IN LONELY AFRICA

"A friend of mine in London, a short time ago, told me of a missionary who was in a lonely part of Africa in a boat with some natives going up the river in the twilight in the lonely hill country, where he was sure no white man lived, to visit the grave of his wife, whom he had buried there long ago. Suddenly there on the hillside he heard familiar strains coming out clearly and distinctly. He thought he knew what they were. As he came closer he found it was a gramophone ringing out the 'Glory Song.' The gramophone had been purchased by some natives from white traders.

"On the ocean between Australia and America a Methodist preacher told me of an old man who attended one of his country congregations, who heard that I had sung these songs in the gramophone. He immediately purchased one of the machines and all the records I had made. The old man was not a good talker, but loved to reach people and bring them to Christ in whatever way he could. He would take his gramophone on his back; and he and his wife would trudge many miles across the country, visiting the lonely school-houses and churches, where he would give people these songs and stories. He said he had often seen the tears running down his cheeks while listening to the darky version of the 'Ninety and Nine' recited by my wife, or to the story of what 'Tell Mother I'll Be There' had done in reaching a wayward boy."

XVI

CLOSING MISSIONS IN ENGLAND

At the conclusion of the London Mission, Mr. Alexander went to America to take part in a Christian Workers' Conference at Northfield, Mass., while Dr. Torrey spent the summer in Germany. In September, 1905, they returned to England; and began the three closing missions at Sheffield, Plymouth and Oxford, prior to going to America at the end of the year.

These closing missions were particularly interesting, because of the special classes reached at each place. At Sheffield the work was largely among the thousands of employes of the great cutlery factories famous the world over; at Plymouth they were in the midst of thousands of soldiers and sailors, in the forts and on the warships in the harbor; while at Oxford splendid work was done among the students in the great University.

ZEAL AMONG TOILERS

The Sheffield meetings were held in Albert Hall in the afternoon, and in the big Drill Hall seating about 5,000 at night. Over 3,500 confessed Christ during the four months' crusade. The most striking feature of the work was the zeal for soul winning that came upon some of the converts from the factories. One man working in a big warehouse was converted and filled with such holy fervor that he led about 25 others to Christ in the establishment before the meetings closed.   Following their conversion, a number of young men were so enthusiastic to win others for Christ that 14 of them formed a Gospel Band, and hired a hall in which to carry on their work of soul saving.

One afternoon a special train brought to Sheffield 300 Liverpool people who were chiefly members of the Torrey-Alexander choir during the evangelistic campaign in that city. The people marched to the Drill Hall, singing revival melodies. At the conclusion of the evening service, they formed in a body and marched from the Drill Hall to Victoria Station, making the night air resonant with the Gospel message in song as they marched.   All along the route people came to their doors and leaned out of upper story windows to witness the unusual sight and hear the hymns.   Many hearts were touched; and it may be that some soul was born again, as the result of the enthusiasm of the visiting choir.

STREET MEETING FOR WORKINGMEN

Three of the most interesting visitors to the Sheffield Mission were Mr. Alexander's mother, sister and brother, whom he had invited to England for a month's sojourn.   On two occasions during the mission Mr. Alexander conducted immense open-air meetings at the noon hour for workmen in the foundries and factories.   At one of these meetings, held just outside of the armor-plate works of Vickers Sons and Maxim, his mother was present.   The Gospel singer stood with thirty or forty members of his choir on two lorries placed end to end; and within a few moments a large crowd of about 2,000 persons had gathered.   As the men streamed out of the gates of the big ironworks they quickly collected around the lorries; and in a short time the street was a solid mass of people listening reverently and intently to the Gospel message spoken and sung by Mr. Alexander. The singing evangelist opened the meeting with a solo, "Tell Mother I'll Be There"; and then took the famous hymn as a text for a straight ten-minute talk to the men, in which he pleaded with them to give their hearts at once to Jesus Christ. His appeal went straight to the tenderest place in their hearts—the memories of their mothers. In the course of his talk he said: "People say to me, 'Why do you have so many mother songs?' Because everybody has a mother; and a good little mother who used to get the Bible down and read and pray with you is a fine thing to have in your memory. I have brought my little mother here; she had never seen one of our open-air meetings, though way down among the hills of Tennessee she had been reading about them; and I want to say to you men that one of the greatest joys of my life is to get down on my knees beside my mother and pray with her.

PRAYED WITH MOTHER

"The other night before we started out for the meeting, we got down on our knees and had a word of prayer that God would bless the people and bring many a mother's boy to Christ. When we arose, mother looked up into my face and said, 'Oh, Charlie that was good.' I tell you it meant more than anything else I could have done for her. And if we get some letters started away from some of you to-night saying, 'Mother, I accepted the Lord Jesus Christ as my Saviour at an open-air meeting to-day; I went down there to have a good time, and I did have a good time, for I left the devil and came to Christ,' how good it will be! There is no reason why we should not. Hasn't the old master given you a bad time? I never knew anybody in the churches yet that he did not. Will you not change masters to-day and come over on to our Master's side?" At the conclusion of his talk, Mr. Alexander gave an invitation to accept Christ then and there, and four or five hands were uplifted in response. The evangelist then closed the meeting, but they were so interested that they were loth to leave, and one man called out, "We do not mind losing another 'quarter' to have some more."

During their stay at Sheffield one of the daily papers gave a graphic word picture of the manner in which Mr. Alexander gets hold of a crowd and makes them sing: "That vast platform choir he holds in the hollow of his hand. They respond to his slightest gesture like magic; they watch and know every change of his mobile countenance, even when he smiles, they, too, smile a collective smile. This is leadership. Energy seems to flow out from his very finger tips. He is like a creature, to quote a phrase of Augustine Birrell's, that emits sparks and electric shocks at every moment. Whether the music was that of the familiar 'Glory Song,' or whether it was the glorious strains of 'When I Survey the Wondrous Cross,' the infinite variety of tone and manner which marked the singing had its origin in his dominating figure."

SOLDIERS AND SAILORS REACHED

The mission at Plymouth resulted in about 3,700 public confessions, and made its influence felt throughout the entire world. In the immediate vicinity of Plymouth there are numerous barracks and fortifications; and in the harbor there are usually a number of warships, in which about 25,000 soldiers and sailors are commonly stationed. The meetings were held in the same drill hall in which Mr. Moody had held a mission nearly thirty years before. For the Torrey-Alexander Mission, however, it was made nearly one-half larger. It held about 6,000 persons, but was none too large. Frequently hundreds were turned away after the hall was filled.

Night after night the meetings were attended by large numbers of soldiers and sailors, and many of them found Christ. The red coats of the soldiers and the blue jackets of the sailors made splashes of color throughout the audience, which lent a gay appearance to the throng; while at the front, right against the platform, Mr. Alexander had a splendid Soldiers' and Sailors' Choir. Their favorite song throughout the mission was "Lean on His Arms"; and it was worth going a long distance to hear them sing it. At a word from the singing evangelist, the Army and Navy Choir would stand up and sing the verses lustily, while the big audience joined in on the chorus.

Almost every night several of the red coats or blue jackets would go forward to confess Christ. At the Royal Marine Barracks, where 1,200 men were stationed, there were found only ten real Christians when the meetings began; while a short time after the meetings closed there was a band of seventy Christians, and they held an enthusiastic meeting with the Commandant in the chair.

MARINERS TURN PLEADERS

Throughout the mission none others were more enthusiastic in the personal work than the soldiers and the sailors. It was a beautiful sight to see a big stalwart marine going about the audience, Bible in hand, pleading with his comrades to accept Christ. A midshipman on a battleship confessed Christ, and worked earnestly for his comrades. On another warship about a dozen converts formed a Christian Endeavor Society; and one of them wrote back from a foreign port, telling of the splendid meetings they were having on shipboard.

A corporal, who after having been converted early in the meetings was transferred to another post, wrote back telling of the change that had come into his life:

"I do miss the Mission. I have told many about the glorious evenings we used to spend at the Mission. When I find anything a bit trying coming across my path, I think of that little chorus, 'A Little Talk With Jesus Makes It Right,' and I can safely say, with my little experience on the Lord's side, that he does make it right, when I go to the Lord in prayer; and I often burst right out with, 'Praise the Lord for I feel so happy.' I often wonder how I could have been so blinded to go and serve the devil as long as I did; but, praise God, my eyes are open now, and I am going to try my best to make up for my bad time with the devil, by trying to get others from his terrible grasp. I remember the Mission in prayer when I pray, for I believe in prayer and plenty of it."

AMONG DOCK-YARD PEOPLE

Excellent work was also done among the thousands of employes of the Royal Navy Dock Yards, at Devonport and Stone House. On two occasions the evangelists went out to address the men at the noon hour, and at one meeting thirty confessed Christ. On still another occasion, Mr. Alexander conducted an open-air meeting just outside the gates of the dock yards, at which nearly 2,500 were present. God's Spirit was there in power; and nearly a score raised their hands in declaration of their acceptance of Christ.

As a result of the Mission, one seventeen-year-old lad was so fired with zeal that, although he worked in the dock yard about ten hours a day, he was accustomed to spend one hour and a half daily reading his Bible. In a letter written a short time after the Mission had closed, he told how the work of grace was still going forward:

"The 'fire' is still ablaze. In all the little villages and towns the sheafs are being gathered in. At the prayer and testimony meetings held in connection with the Mission, large numbers have taken Christ. On H. M. S. Hibernia, the ship on which I am at present working, quite a revival has sprung up among the workmen, several finding Jesus in the gloomy depths of a modern battleship. The 'Glory Song' is heard everywhere. The songs of the theatre are superseded by the favorites of the Alexander Hymn Book. Over a score of boys, whom I regard as friends, have taken Jesus as their Saviour during the Mission. I read the Bible about an hour and a half a day; and every word I read from it, and every text I learn, makes me a happier boy; while a word spoken for the Master fills my heart with joy."

Rarely, if ever, have I seen greater enthusiasm in soul winning than was displayed by the soldiers and the sailors during the closing days of the Mission. Here is the way in which some marines spent a Saturday afternoon and night. Twenty-six marines started out about two o'clock, walked several miles to a neighboring village, and spent the afternoon parading the streets and holding brief open-air meetings at street corners. Then they had tea, and walked back to the Drill Hall, singing revival hymns as they marched. In the meetings they did active personal work as usual, and when it was over went on to a Soldiers' Home, where they attended two prayer-meetings. The second meeting teminated just before twelve o'clock; and they reached the barracks gates just before they closed at midnight.

WORST CHARACTERS RECLAIMED

In addition to those connected with the Army and the Navy, some of the worst characters in Plymouth were transformed. When Mr. Alexander called for testimonies one day a man arose and said: "I have been the biggest drunkard that 'the Three Towns' can show. I have not entered a chapel for thirty years. I have lost my wife and children. I lost a situation at $20 a week. I lost all my friends. I almost lost my sight—through sin, but I thank God that he brought me here on Thursday night. I met a man who said, 'Where are you going?' I said, 'I am going to hear Torrey and Alexander.' He said, 'Don't go there, they are humbugs, they only want your money.' I said, 'I have got none for them; it is all gone in drink.' And God looked on me, a vile, unworthy sinner, and accepted me. I hope that one and all of you will take warning by me."

At another meeting, a man who was perhaps the most notorious character in the city, arose and said in response to Mr. Alexander's request for testimony:

"I thank God to-night that I am here and able to confess to my fellow tradesmen; that, although I have been one of the

THE EFFICIENT HOSPITAL CORPS AT BOLTON, ENGLAND

most notoriously evil men in 'the Three Towns,' a marine led me to Christ last Thursday evening in the gallery of this hall. I have been one of the worst men that ever stood in two shoes—a curse to my wife and family. I have brought my little son 14 years of age with me to-night, to teach him a lesson which I hope will last him to the day of his death. I was brought up by good, respectable parents. I have a Bible here to-night given to me on my tenth birthday in Greenock, Scotland. I am very glad to think that it is doing me good. I am proud to say that I am no more, 'T.W.' the notorious, but I am 'T.W.' a child of God, since last Thursday." There was much rejoicing, when, during the after-meeting, his fourteen-year-old son was among the number who accepted Christ

MISSIONS IN UNIVERSITY TOWNS

At Oxford, the Mission lasted only a fortnight, but during that time eight hundred people professed to accept Christ; and no one can estimate the ultimate results of the movement. A number of students in the University came out clearly for Christ, while Dr. Torrey and Mr. Alexander did much personal work with the students in their rooms.

It was Mr. Alexander's privilege to do a notable work among the students at Cambridge as well as at Oxford University. A few months previous he had gone to Cambridge to hold services in public and in the rooms of the students during Saturday and the Lord's day; and there occurred one of the most memorable scenes in the religious history of the University.

Mr. Alexander's visit was arranged for by the Cambridge Inter-Collegiate Christian Union. He was entertained at

Trinity College; and spoke at five conferences and meetings during his brief stay. On Saturday evening he addressed a select body of students, on "Personal Work in Soul Winning." He did not preach at the men, but talked to them of their duty in this matter, plainly and directly.

Mr. Alexander urged the men to surrender themselves absolutely to God, and to begin personal work at once. Then he threw the meeting open; and asked those who had not been doing personal work as they should have done in the past, but would engage heartily in it in the future, to stand up, and publicly declare their purpose before the others. There was a pause. Mr. Alexander's words had gone home in an extraordinary manner; and the spiritual atmosphere of the room was intense. God's Spirit was working in power. After a moment, a young undergraduate arose; and in a voice choked with emotion declared that he had not done soul winning because of sin, but that hereafter, with God's help, he was going to engage in it at any cost. A moment later another arose, confessed in like manner; and in tense tones declared his new determination. Then, for twenty minutes, men stood up in all parts of the room, confessing their past failure and publicly declaring that they would become active soul winners in the future. It was a deeply affecting scene; and no one can estimate its influence on the religious life of the University.

A NOTABLE SERVICE

It had been arranged for a well known speaker to students, Major Liebenrood, to address the students in Victoria Assembly Rooms on Sunday evening; but it was planned to put the after-meeting into Mr. Alexander's hands immediately following the address. The hall was filled with a magnificent body of about 500 students—men who in coming years would be the leaders of England.

In taking charge of the meeting, Mr. Alexander talked briefly to the men and then sang, "Would You Believe?" Following this he asked Mr. Paul Gilbert to sing "Tell Mother I'll Be There."

Then he called for decisions—not half hearted ones, but full surrender to Christ. A moment elapsed and no one arose. Then the power of God was felt; and in quick succession twenty men stood up. Still Mr. Alexander pleaded, while Mr. Gilbert sang the refrain again and again. Gradually another and yet another arose, until the number reached thirty-five. But even the public confession in arising did not entirely satisfy Mr. Alexander. He broke through precedent at staid Cambridge, by asking the men to come boldly up to the front and publicly declare their faith. Every man responded— indeed one more than had previously arisen; and it was a thrilling sight to behold thirty-six men march up to the front, turn around and face their fellow students, and in ringing tones declare their allegiance to Jesus Christ as Saviour, Lord and King.

At the conclusion of the general meeting Mr. Alexander and Major Liebenrood went to the room of a post-graduate, where about thirty students gathered, and for an hour Mr. Alexander led the men in a wonderfully inspiring service.

LIVERPOOL'S GOOD-BYE

As Dr. Torrey and Mr. Alexander were about to leave Great Britain for America, a great farewell meeting was arranged in Liverpool. It was held in the big Tournament Hall, where many victories of the Cross had been achieved through the agency of the evangelists. Fully ten thousand people were present; and speeches were delivered by Christian leaders from a number of cities in which missions had been held. They declared with one voice that untold good had come to their cities through the work of grace conducted by the evangelists.

Mr. Ernest Matthews, of Manchester, affirmed that the Mission in that city had exceeded their expectation. "I remember the first Sunday night, when great St. James Hall was empty at 5 o'clock, and we wondered what the first meeting was to be like. And when the long queues of people stood outside and tore their coats off in trying to get in until the place was crammed, I sat and said, 'Glory to God,' 'Glory to God.' The Missioners' work at Manchester was among the working classes; 'the common people heard them gladly, the common people loved them and love them still, and in the humble homes of the working class districts of Manchester Mr. Alexander's hymns are sung week day and Sunday without any distinction. Their memories are loved, but what is more the Lord they preach is loved as well. The Mission has made the work of God easier for all who believe in the old Gospel and love to preach it. I never knew the working classes so open and responsive to Gospel effort as they have been since that Mission two years ago, and I join in praise to God, in thankfulness to our brethren, and in prayer that greater things may come."

Near the close of the exercises, a memorable scene occurred when each evangelist was presented with a handsome

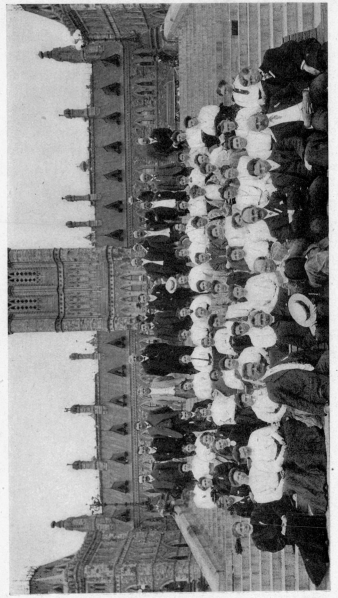

TORONTO CHOIR ON THE STEPS OF THE PARLIAMENT BUILDINGS, OTTAWA, CANADA

illuminated address, stating in glowing language the glorious results of the Missions in each city they had visited. The address bore the signature of members of the committee from every city in the British Isles where they had conducted the campaign. Of Mr. Alexander and his work, the address said: "We thank God for your magnetic and inspiring leadership in song, for all those who under profound impression have 'stood all amazed at the love Jesus offers them.' You have taught us songs that will never die, and you have made the singing of the great congregation seem at times to be the prelude of the 'Glory Song,' which shall be sung by the 'great multitude which no man can number.' "

This farewell meeting lasting four hours, full of spiritual fervor, white hot with enthusiasm for soul winning, with a number who accepted Christ even though it was not a regular revival meeting—was a fitting climax to a three years' crusade in which 80,000 people had publicly confessed Christ as their personal Saviour.

XVII

BEGINNING THE AMERICAN CAMPAIGN

THE opening of the American work of the evangelists was watched with keen interest. There were many who doubted whether their Missions would be crowned with the same success in America as in Great Britain. But Dr. Torrey and Mr. Alexander depended not on themselves, nor upon human methods, but upon the living God. And the same prayer-hearing and prayer-answering God who gave victory in Great Britain poured out Pentecostal blessings in America.

It was in direct answer to prayer that the evangelists' first American Mission at Toronto, Canada, proved to be one of the greatest revivals in their entire tour of the world. Not only in Toronto but in all the surrounding district there was a great burden of prayer on the hearts of thousands for weeks before the arrival of the evangelists. In a town 100 miles away 100 people prayed constantly for the Mission. In another town a man agonized in prayer to God for three days and three nights without taking a morsel of food or a drink of water. Toronto itself was honey-combed with prayer-meetings. It is little wonder that in answer to prayer a wave of revival swept over Toronto which thrilled the city and led 4,500 persons to confess Christ.

WORKERS FROM ABROAD

The meetings were held in Massey Hall a beautiful auditorium, located in the heart of the business district and seating 4,000 people. Every night the big building was packed to the doors, with hundreds turned away. The choir had a membership of about 2,000; there were nearly 1,000 personal workers and 300 ushers. They were like a well organized and well drilled army of Christian workers.

The influence of the meetings of the evangelists in Great Britain was strongly felt in Toronto. One of the leaders of the movement pointed to a man in the meeting one night, and said: "That man over there was converted in the Torrey-Alexander meetings in Belfast; he is one of our best workers." In speaking of those he met from Great Britain Mr. Alexander said:

"At the close of Sunday's meeting a bright young lady, Bible in hand, came up to me and said, 'Do you remember me, Mr. Alexander? I was converted at South London, and have since come over here with my family. Last night I was baptized, and I am now a member of the church here in Toronto"; and her face looked like a sunbeam. A young man came up and shook my hand and said: 'I was with you all through the Bristol Mission.' Another man said that he had worked with us in the Brighton meetings, and was ready to work again here. A young lady in our choir was in the Bradford choir, and another young man, whose face was all aglow with the love of God, told me that he had been converted in the Dumbarton meetings."

At the beginning of the movement in Toronto the people, though praying earnestly, were slow to go out and deal personally with the unsaved. One afternoon Mr. Alexander gave them a stirring talk on going out and speaking to the lost at any cost. He said:

POWER OF PERSONAL WORK

"I have seen people who have prayed for years for their loved ones, but would never go and speak to them about their soul. I know a man in this city who is afraid to speak to his grandson, though he has been praying for him. If you cannot get them yourself, send some one else, even if you have to get the whole town after them.

"Let me tell you there is something wrong in your life if you cannot do personal work. It may be pride. Do not get away from yourselves in searching for the cause. Personal work is the quickest way for you to get to God. You will never know how far you are from God till you try to lead some sinner to him. A great many will not try because it hurts.

"The last thing the devil will let you do is personal work. I have seen people who could pray and do everything else but this, even on Mission fields. What if you dropped dead in your seats? What kind of a record would you have to show to God? You say you are not naturally gifted for personal work? Then get supernaturally gifted. How many will try? Do not get up unless you mean it." In response to his appeal over half the audience rose to their feet.

The "Glory Song" proved to be the favorite hymn of the revival in Toronto as it was elsewhere. A daily paper issued it one afternoon as a free supplement in sheet music style. One afternoon as Mr. Alexander opened the meeting, he said:

THE "GLORY SONG" IN INDIAN

"Just as I came in the door I was handed the 'Glory Song' in three of the Indian languages. There was a gentleman in the Bible Institute in Glasgow, Scotland, when we held our meetings there, who afterwards went out as a missionary to China. He wrote me a letter saying that as soon as he got to his Mission station what was his surprise to hear the native Christians start up the 'Glory Song.' So he translated it into Chinese and sent it to me. 'Of course they sang it backwards,' he added with a smile; 'I'd like to hear how it sounds that way.'"

Mr. Alexander then asked the audience to tell where they had heard the "Glory Song." A man rose and said, "I heard it in Florida, and was delighted with it." "I heard it in New York," said another. Others rapidly arose saying that they had heard it in Glasgow, Scotland; Belfast, Ireland; Newfoundland, Maidstone, England; Melbourne, Australia; Bristol, England; Edinburgh, Scotland. "Keep on, we will belt the globe first thing we know," urged Mr. Alexander. Instantly a young man was on his feet saying he had heard it in Johannesburg, South Africa. "Albert Hall, London," came from another, while others heard it in the Bible Institute, Chicago; Brighton, England; Bangor, North Wales; Newcastle, England; Bingley Hall, Birmingham, England, and Cardiff, Wales.

CAME TO BORROW FIRE

The reports of the revival in Toronto led people to go long distances to catch the fire and carry it back to their own homes and communities. One man went all the way from South Dakota; another from Minnesota, and others from various parts of Canada.

One afternoon, during the praise service, Mr. Alexander singled out one of the previous night's converts who was sitting in a front seat, and said, "Brother, how does it feel to be a Christian a whole day? Stand up and tell them." The man arose, and turning towards the audience, said, "The best day I have ever enjoyed in my life." And he looked it.

"Anybody else?"

"The best day I have ever spent in my life," testified another.

"Have any of you come from a distance?" Mr. Alexander asked. A lady rose in the centre of the ground floor. "I came from Rochester to attend these meetings. Already three people have been saved through personal work."

"Where are you big-voiced men?" demanded Mr. Alexander during a lull in the speaking. Have you nothing to say?"

"Well, I thank God for a heart full of love to him," said a full-bearded man. "I came from Peterboro to learn from the evangelists, and I pray that I may take back to the good people of Peterboro something of the glorious news."

A lady missionary from Jamaica stood up and said: "I thank the Lord to-day because I came all the way from Jamaica, and I expect to be able to take some of the glory back with me. I have been sending copies of the newspaper containing the 'Glory Song' to the different missionaries throughout that island. I expect to return there in a few weeks; and I pray that I may go filled with the power of the Holy Spirit."

A striking feature of the work was that it reached all classes from the rich to the poor, from the upright business man to the criminal.

A CRIMINAL'S TESTIMONY

"I came into your men's meeting on Sunday night; and, through the singing of 'Tell Mother I'll Be There,' I was led to

Christ. I was the cause of breaking our poor mother's heart through sin. I was brought up in a Christian home, but fell through drink and drifted into crime. I have just been released from Kingston Penitentiary, where I have spent the last ten years for safe blowing. I thank God for bringing you to Toronto, and that I have been saved through your agency. God helping me, I am going to be from this time on an honest, sober, upright, law-abiding citizen. Pray for me."

Perhaps the best feature of the Toronto awakening was the manner in which it aroused and moved the business men of the city. One day Mr. Alexander was the speaker at a luncheon tendered him by the Canadian Club, one of the foremost business men's leagues of the Dominion. Mr. Alexander was accompanied to the luncheon by Charles Butler, a new soloist, Robert Harkness, and Melvin E. Trotter, of Grand Rapids, Michigan. Following the luncheon, Vice President Turnbull introduced the guest of the day as follows:

"During the past four years, throughout the English speaking world, our guest, Mr. Alexander, has been demonstrating to a critical public the power and influence of song on vast audiences. His leadership of the song service in connection with the Torrey-Alexander Mission in Massey Hall during this month can be described only as magnificent. He is an expert on the subject in which he is going to address us; and I have therefore much pleasure in introducing Mr. Alexander, who will speak to us on 'The Place and Power of Music.'"

'JUST TRY ME ON LEATHER'

Mr. Alexander, in rising to speak, was loudly applauded. He said: "I have asked your chairman to allow me to stand on a chair, for I want to see all. I heard of a man who got on one of those old-fashioned stage coaches one day, and he had but one solitary occupant for a companion. It was a cold, drizzly day on the outside, and he started in to talk to this old man for company, but all he could get out of him was 'Yes' and 'No.' He tried every subject that he knew anything about with the same result; and finally he sank back exhausted in the corner of the coach. Then the old man, his companion said, 'Suppose you try me on leather'; and the old man started in, and the traveler said he never heard a man talk on leather the way that man did. I am right in the kind of work I love; and you have asked me about the kind of work that I know best. I had my subject chosen before I knew what the title was going to be, but, as Artemus Ward said about the subject of one of his lectures, 'The most remarkable thing about the subject is that it has nothing to do with the lecture.'

"Away down in the hills of Tennessee, I was born in a log house; and one of the first things I remember was hearing the old Gospel songs sung without any instrument, and I am glad of that recollection. They sent me to school with Webster's blue-backed spelling book and a little New Testament. After I got away from that school and heard that other boys in the towns were taught from handsome books, with pictures, I felt I had been badly used. I thought my education had been neglected because I had to use the New Testament for reader, but later I found out I was mistaken; for somehow the truths of that little Testament got into me, got hold of me, and I now have no cause to regret it.

"My father used to teach me to sing Sankey's hymns, without any instrument, for we could not afford one, and later I

THE CHILDREN'S "SUNBEAM CHOIR" IN OTTAWA, CANADA

went to country singing schools and learned to sing there without any instrument, too. I have always been glad of that, because it does not matter how Harkness plays, I can always keep on singing.

WANTED—SERMONS ON WHEELS

"When I saw the worth of a human soul, and wanted to get men started in the direction that I thought was right, I began to look around to see how I could help the most men in the strongest way. I wanted something to start men's hearts going; and I found out that when you get a sermon set to music it was like a sermon on wheels. It was like going down hill. I have very little voice for singing, but there is this about it, they can always hear me no matter how big the building is. I thought I have got to do something to reach the people, and I turned about and taught them to sing.

"The Albert Hall Mission in London set going one of the greatest things in the way of music that I have ever heard of. When you get London started and its people singing and talking, you have something accomplished. There was the 'Glory Song.' I believe there is scarcely anybody in London that has not heard it. One night some men were looking up men for a free breakfast, searching for them in the park, on the benches, under arches, where ever they could be found, to take them down to a free breakfast. It was two or three o'clock in the morning; and when these workers had a crowd of men around them one said, 'Jim, let's have an open-air meeting right here.' He said, 'What can we do,' 'Start the Glory Song,' said the other, and they did, and every one of those tramps sang it. This was how they knew it. It was printed three times in the Daily Mail with the words and music, and every one had a Daily Mail, however they got it. I don't suppose they were ever in a Mission, and they would not go to Albert Hall. On the other hand, to see how the titled people would listen to the music was wonderful to me.

"I find people like music if it has point, if it is going somewhere; and when men who are not Christians come to our meetings I find that the stronger a song is the more it will be called for. That 'Pilot Song' has been called for more than any other by men who were not Christians. There is a way to get hold of men, and it is through the power of music. It was a great discovery for me when I found out that busy men like you, who do not sing, who do not take time to sing, though you ought to, when you get together you are just like a crowd of boys and like to sing just as well. I used to wonder at this; but I do not now, because down in every man's heart there is a love of song, and even the men who have been against us like these Gospel Songs. I could tell you wonderful stories how one of these simple songs, with a hook in it, will follow a man day and night and get hold of him, so that he cannot get away from it. The night before last I heard a crowd of young fellows going home, singing the 'Pilot Song.'

SONGS WITH HOOKS IN THEM

" 'The power of song'! Why, I can go to a crowded meeting, and put in ten or eleven hours and feel fresh. The music is different from what it used to be, because it has point to it. I feel when I sing that it is going to get hold of some men and change their homes. That is what you want to see done. I know of homes right here in this town that have been changed. Some of you say that you don't believe in these methods, but there's a fact that you cannot get away from, and in a little while I will ask Mr. Trotter to illustrate it. I have seen people come to Albert Hall at two o'clock and stay till six o'clock. Dr. Torrey would take up three quarters of an hour; but all the rest of the time men and women in the galleries and boxes and on the floor of the hall would be calling for some simple Gospel songs; and then we would go back after supper and sing them until nearly eleven o'clock. I have never seen any other kind of music that would get hold of people like this. Men just as smart looking as you are would stay there and ask for these songs. I have a stack of letters that high (indicating it with his hands) from all classes of people, telling that these songs just suited their case.

"One time in Chicago I was teaching a choir of little girls to sing, little street girls, whose clothes were scarcely good enough for them to come to church; and we had them away up in the back of the gallery of Mr. Moody's Church. It was a time of great financial disaster in Chicago; and a business man who had lost all his money was walking along the street, wondering what would become of him, when he heard the singing from the church, 'God Will Take Care Of You.' Nothing else had touched him like those little voices. He came into the church, and heard them sing it again. He had not thought of that, but he said to himself: 'Of course God will take care of me,' and went away happy. I like to use material like that. Long ago I found out when I got people worked up by a concert or something of that kind it stopped there. I would be all exhausted and to no purpose. I would ask myself, 'Where did I take those people, where did I land them anyway? There must be something more in this world than this?' Now yesterday I was at work from 10 o'clock in the morning until nearly midnight, and when I got home I was satisfied that I had been doing the best work in the world.

THE "TELL MOTHER" SONG

"Musicians come to me, and ask me why I don't use the other kinds of music. If oratorio would have the same effects in the hearts of men like you, I would have oratorios every time I got a chance. But you fellows know if you try a thing and it doesn't do the business you quit it, don't you? I get the songs that do the business; and, if I find one that won't, I drop it. There is a song, 'Tell Mother I'll Be There,' which I hesitated a long time before using. I have been criticised all over the world for using it, but you would not criticise me if you knew what it has done and what testimonies and letters about it I have received. A friend cut it out of a scrap book, and sent it to me, and I carried it a year before I used it. One night there was a crowd of railway men, and I said to myself, 'I wonder what would reach those men?' I used it, and when it was over a burly engineer came up to me and said, 'Mr. Alexander, I promised my mother on her death bed that I would become a Christian; but, instead of that, I have been going to the devil faster than ever. Preaching never touched me, but that little song did; and if you will sing it to-morrow night I will bring the boys.' He did bring them for many nights; and he used to say, 'Don't forget to sing "Tell Mother"' I used that song every time, and I have used it many times since. Newspapers have taken columns to say what doggerel it is; but at the end they had to admit the effect it had on those men. Argue against everything but a fact!

"There's Harkness, a Bendigo boy, still under the British flag, though a long way from home. He wrote some of those songs; for instance 'Pilot Song,' and I would rather have written that song than anything else I know of. It is like a snow ball, it keeps on growing as it rolls along. I am going to give you each a copy as you go out. If you don't want it yourself, put it in a letter and send it to your aunt or your sweetheart or somebody. You have all heard of the man who said, 'Let me make the songs of a nation and I care not who makes its laws.' And the point I make to-day is the power of good Gospel music over every other kind of music in making over families. It has a power that no other music has. I have a warm place in my heart for every man in this room. Don't forget us. We love you more than ever. We are going to pray for you. Good-bye."

Not only in Toronto, but throughout the province of Ontario, the results of the Mission were felt. Numerous local revivals sprang up in smaller cities as the outcome of the work of grace in Toronto. One minister who went 300 miles to "catch the fire" arose in a meeting in Massey Hall, and said: "Three hundred and thirty miles from here my people held a prayer-meeting last week to pray for the success of the work here. It started a revival. Four people were converted, and two were led to confess Christ, who had never confessed him before. The whole church was awakened, and they have sent me here as the result. Several other ministers came from long distances and brought prominent members and officers of their churches.

CHILDREN'S PRAYER CICRCLE

The work among the boys and girls of the city was deep and lasting. Even the children were fired with a remarkable passion to win their playmates and companions to Christ. Three girls—two 11 and one 10 years of age—banded together and formed a prayer-circle to hold weekly meetings at one anothers' houses. Inside of ten days they had won seven other girls, one of whom subsequently led her uncle and aunt to Christ. A letter from one of the three original members of the circle contained the following:

"Our meeting was a great help. I don't thing there was a girl went away unsaved. There were fourteen present. I notice a big change in the girls at school. Two little girls I have been praying for have joined the church. I am trying to tell other girls of Jesus, not because I want to be praised, but because I want to do it for Jesus' sake."

Another girl convert of about twelve years of age wrote:

"I am glad I took Jesus when I did, so that I can lead some of my playmates to him. I am going to see how many I can win for Jesus. I wrote to my brother George in Chicago, and told him I was saved. I am going to keep reading my Bible. I am going to make a prayer-list in the back of my Testament; and, if that will not hold them all, I will get something else."

The children were filled with missionary zeal as well. A 12-year-old boy, a convert of the revival, and a member of another prayer-circle wrote: "We are thinking about supporting a missionary (native). I am sure we will be successful, as the Lord has answered our prayers, and will answer them again. Be sure and pray for our meetings, that the Lord may fill us with his Holy Spirit, that many hearts may be touched and led to publicly confess Christ."

Among the young people as well as the children, the revival produced large results. A unique organization called the Pocket Testament League was organized in the High School after the young ladies had heard of the one started by Mrs. Alexander in an English High School many years previous. A member of the league told of its purpose as follows:

"Some of the girls decided to form a Pocket Testament League in the High School. We have nine members in our League now, and have appointed a President and a Secretary. We thought well to make out some rules, and have those who joined agree to keep these rules, so we made out three—

1. We are to carry our Testaments wherever we go.

2. We are each to make a prayer list.

3. We are to read as much as we can in the Bible every day.

"Our object is to get to know the Bible better, and to bring other girls to Christ."

It was in Toronto that the Mission staff was enlarged by the addition of a soloist engaged by Mr. Alexander, named Charles Butler. He is a Southerner from Macon, Georgia. He won favor from the start; and especially did great good among the men by his beautiful rendering of Mr. Harkness's hymn entitled, "Is He Yours?" which there came to be known as the "Pilot Song."

XVIII

THE GREAT WORK IN PHILADELPHIA

THE three months' campaign in Philadelphia, which directly followed that in Toronto, was the chief religious event of the day. It aroused the country from coast to coast, led to scores of local revivals, and stimulated evangelistic work all over the land.

The movement was a union effort in which practically all the evangelical churches co-operated. The two foremost men in the management of the Mission were Dr. Floyd H. Tompkins, the famous rector of Holy Trinity Church, and Mr. John E. Converse, President of the Baldwin Locomotive Works. In addition, however, scores of other well known ministers and business and professional men gave time and money to help forward the movement, including John Wanamaker, Dr. Russell H. Conwell, Dr. J. R. Miller, Dr. John A. Cass, Dr. Patterson, Dr. Charles R. Watson, Herbert Caskey, H. C. Lincoln, Dr. C. A. R. Janvier and Mr. Allen Sutherland.

The meetings were held in two remodeled military armories, located on the north and south sides of the city. They were fiitted with galleries and seats to accommodate between 5,000 and 6,000 persons. During the first month the meetings were held in the Northern Armory; during the second in the Southern, and the final series in the Northern one. On the opening day nearly 12,000 people crowded into the big structure, during the afternoon and evening meetings. Night after night thereafter the big building was filled to overflowing, while frequently thousands were turned away. Sometimes, after the hall was filled, there would be one or more open-air meetings in front of the building in addition to a large over-flow meeting at a nearby church.

A detail of thirty policemen was usually present to prevent accidents, as the crowds waiting in the street rushed into the building, which would often be completely filled in a few minutes.

REMARKABLE FIGURES

It is estimated that in the 62 working days of the campaign 375,000 persons were brought under the sound of the Gospel, giving an average daily attendance of over 6,000 people. The sermons preached by Dr. Torrey numbered 156; while the talks by Mr. Alexander, of which there were sometimes half a dozen in the course of a single meeting, amounted to about 500. The number who publicly confessed Christ during the Mission exceeded 7,000.

From the beginning to the end of the movement, the Phila-delphia newspapers gave large space to the meetings and to the messages of the revivalists. So expectant were the people over the beginning of the work, that one daily compared the advent of the evangelists with that of Whitefield in the eighteenth century. It was ascertained that several revivals in Pennsylvania towns were started through reading the reports in the Philadelphia press.

Mr. Alexander's Revival Hymns quickly captivated Phila-delphia; and were heard, not only in the churches and in the homes, but on the streets of the city at all hours of the day and evening. Almost every night, after the armory meeting was over, groups of choir members would board street cars and turn them into Gospel cars by making them echo for miles with revival hymns. One man arose at a testimony meeting, and told of his experience in one of these cars:

"I was delighted when I left here the other night to get into a street car with some of the choir. They had the spirit of song in their hearts; and they could not keep quiet. And as the old car rolled down Fifteenth Street, all the way along the street people stopped to see what was going on. It was simply the Spirit of God going down Fifteenth Street in the hearts of those choir people; and their lips were giving utterance to the fulness that was in their hearts. I hope you will all take up that spirit of song and go through the street, singing with the Spirit of God in your hearts."

The meetings had not long been in progress before scores were being converted in the Philadelphia churches, in addition to the hundreds at the Armory meetings.

One afternoon, before Dr. Torrey preached, Mr. Alexander said: "If any one knows where revival fires have spread in your church, in your family, anywhere, tell us." One by one in quick succession some fifty men and women arose and told of conversions.

"We go out after blacksmiths and laborers," declared a man, in workingman's garb, in the rear of the house. "We have led several to Christ, and induced many to come to the meetings."

A colored man arose in the middle of the audience, and said that in his church there were more than 100 conversions recently. "I've come from the coal regions to get some fire," said the man. "I shall take it back, too."

Several ministers reported conversions in their churches. A man arose in the front row, and said they were having hundreds of conversions in Northeast Kensington.

PEOPLE HOME HEARD SERVICES

By a unique contrivance the messages of the evangelists in sermon and song were delivered, not only to the great throngs which gathered night after night at the great armories, but to the people of Philadelphia as they sat in their homes in every part of the city. A Telephone Company installed a megaphone above the speaker's stand, so that the words of Dr. Torrey and the words of Mr. Alexander and the songs of the choir and the audience were carried over the wires into the homes of the people. As one sat in one's home, the entire proceedings at the armory could be heard by simply taking down the receiver and asking Central to connect one with the revival meetings. Thousands who could not attend the central meetings were reached in this manner.

One day Mr. Alexander received a touching letter, telling how one woman was converted through the use of this invention. The writer said: "One Sunday in February our maid was alone in the house, and, as she had been told by us of the possibility of hearing your meeting by 'phone, she took up the receiver for the first time and listened to the afternoon service. The meeting, as she heard it, so affected her that she resolved to go herself the following Thursday. She did this; and was so touched and convinced that, instead of going to a dance party that same evening, she called for her sister and went to the evening meeting. When the call was given to go forward she was one of the first. She was very happy in telling her mistress, the first thing next morning; and has since been the happiest girl you ever saw. She has no need now for the dance party nor for the theatre of which she is very fond, and is glad that she went to the armory that evening instead of to the dance party."

Later in the campaign still another invention called the "multiphone" was used to spread the Gospel message. By means of this, the entire revival service was reproduced nightly at Bethany Presbyterian Church, about a mile and a half away. One evening nearly 400 people listened there with great interest to the service at the armory.

Throughout the Philadelphia Mission the singing of Mr. Charles Butler was greatly appreciated at the revival meetings at the armory and at special services. One afternoon when he had sung "When the Comforter Came," Mr. Alexander asked him to tell how he was converted, and he said:

"I went to a Georgia city to work, and I went to the devil at the same time. It was not necessary to tell you all the sins I engaged in then. I had the habit of profanity so that I swore unconsciously. I couldn't quit it, although I always resolved to do so on the first of every January. One day I went to a revival meeting conducted by Evangelist Robert Miller, and heard him tell of a three-fold salvation—that Christ crucified saved from the penalty of sin, Christ risen from the power of sin, while Christ coming again will save from the presence of sin. I told the preacher afterwards that I wanted that sort of salvation. He showed me I. Corinthians 10: 13— "There hath no temptation taken you but such as is common to man: but God is faithful, who will not suffer you to be tempted above that ye are able." From that time on, 'the fire that he kindled consumed my sin' " said the soloist, quoting a verse of the hymn he had just sung.

AT PRINCETON UNIVERSITY

During a rest week between the meetings in the North and the South Armory, Mr. Alexander paid a brief visit to Princeton University, where a revival flame was kindled in the hearts of many of the students. He was accompanied by his pianist, Mr. Robert Harkness, the soloist, Mr. Charles Butler; and Mr. Melvin E. Trotter. On Saturday evening he conducted a meeting for undergraduates, similar to one he had held at Cambridge University. It was a time of heart-searching and confession, such as two juniors declared they had never before witnessed in the institution. On Sunday Mr. Alexander and his party were busy from morning until night, conducting meetings and talking with students in their rooms about their soul salvation, and about the necessity of winning others to Christ. The Gospel singer took part in seven meetings during the day. The largest was in the afternoon at Alexander Hall, when President Woodrow Wilson was present and concluded the meeting with the benediction. Of all the meetings conducted among the students, perhaps that on Sunday evening for those in the theological department left the deepest impression. Two theologues, on returning to their rooms, burst into tears and falling upon their knees prayed for forgiveness and for the baptism of the Holy Ghost, in order that they might go out and win souls as never before. At the present time of writing, over a year later, I learn that the effect of Mr. Alexander's visit was felt throughout the entire year in the theological seminary.

As in Toronto, one of the most far-reaching features of the movement was the manner in which it gripped the business men of the city. Hundreds of business men received a passion for soul-winning that they had never known before, and at the present time—over a year after the Mission—many of them are still filled with holy zeal for seeking and saving the lost. One night Mr. Alexander noticed sitting upon the platform a well dressed man with his top hat and gloves beside him. During the after-meeting, he told him to go down into the audience and do personal work. The man obeyed, and that night had the joy of leading a man and his wife to Christ. This filled him with such enthusiasm that he became one of the most active workers in the movement. He was Mr. H. Wellington Wood, manager of the Philadelphia branch of the famous Heinz Pickle Company. Before the Mission concluded, he led nearly two scores of persons to Christ by personal work; and in less than eighteen months afterward he had the inexpressible joy of having pointed two hundred and sixty persons to a knowledge of Christ wherever he went throughout the country—in hotels, in street cars, on railways, in homes and churches. He has their names and addresses written in red ink in a little vest pocketbook, which he always carries with him. The list includes a millionaire, a prominent physician, business men, criminals and numerous railway and street car employes. One day Mr. Wood called fifteen of his traveling salesmen into his office, and had a straight talk with them about Jesus Christ. He found that eight were already Christians, but seven were not. Before the talk concluded, however, all seven stood up and accepted Christ, and soon after joined various churches. One had been an infidel for years.

RELIGION AND BUSINESS

In speaking of his soul-winning work, Mr. Wood said to me: "Men do not get away from me in business, and I am determined that they shall not get away from me in coming out for God. I am determined to use every bit of diplomacy I possess to win souls for Christ. I have a peace now that I never knew before. I have surrendered myself entirely to him. I once attended theatres; I have now no desire for them. I used to bowl three and four nights a week; I have now resigned every bowling club I belonged to, and never bowl now unless it is for exercise. Every night I have something better on hand, something to do for God. Then my family relations are happier than ever before. We thought we had a happy home before, but now I love my family more and seem to see them in a different light. This work of soul-winning has brought me 'the old time religion which makes me love everybody.'"

Asked whether this personal work had interfered with his business, Mr. Wood said: "No, it increases it. We had $5,000 increase last week above any previous week. Not only that, but my relation to my men is more happy. I watch their spiritual life and their home life; and I have a different interest in them altogether."

As Mr. Alexander's choir numbered 3,000 it was impossible for all the members to occupy the 600 or 700 choir seats on the platform at the armory meetings. The members were assigned to attend the meetings on certain nights. But on two evenings full rehearsals of the great chorus were held under Mr. Alexander's direction in the famous Baptist Temple, of which Dr. Russell H. Conwell is pastor. On one of these occasions, following the thrilling choir practice when the big building vibrated as perhaps never before with a mighty volume of song from nearly 3,000 trained voices, Mr. Alexander introduced to the choir Mr. Melvin E. Trotter, who had been assisting the evangelists in the armory meetings for several days. Mr. Trotter was once a drunkard, but was saved in the Pacific Garden Mission in Chicago, nine years ago, when on the point of committing suicide. To-day he has the largest Rescue Mission in the world at Grand Rapids, Michigan.

Mr. Alexander said he wanted Mr. Trotter to tell the choir the story of "Old Man Wiseman." He said he had heard it over and over, but it always did him good. Before Mr. Trotter concluded the touching narrative tears were flowing down many cheeks in the audience. Mr. Trotter said:

OLD MAN WISEMAN

"There was an old fellow who hung around our Mission called 'Wiseman.' This old fellow would come in, and he was a splendid old fellow to cry—oh, how he could cry! He could cry to order at a moment's notice. He would come in and try to tell me how sorry he was about it, and he'd say, 'Oh, Brother Trotter, I want you to pray for me.' And then he'd say, 'I'll never touch it again, Brother Trotter—never as long as I live—and I'm going to love Jesus, and, oh, how I love you! Give me a quarter.' And he would get his quarter, and out he'd go; and I would say to myself, 'Well, I'll believe that as long as there's life there's hope.' In about three days in he would come again with the same cry, and the same dirt— only a little more of it—and he would tell me the same old story. I would say, 'What do you want, Wiseman?' And he would say 'I want you to pray for me, Brother Trotter. I want to be right with God.' And I'd pray for him the best I knew how, and point him to Jesus, and he would tell me how much he loved me, and 'Now gi' me a quarter, Brother Trotter, and I'll be all right.' He would be prayed with, and every time I would say to him, 'You have got to get away from this thing—quit sin right here.' And he would get right up from his knees and say, 'Oh, Brother Trotter, I'm all right now, and, oh, it is so glorious.' And he would weep and weep— and oh, what a weeper he was! He just had tears to burn.

"I was writing my annual report of the year's work one morning, and was getting along nicely with it. But I'm not much of an artist with the pen, and I wanted to be quiet and not be interrupted with people coming into my office all day, so I said to my assistant, 'Mr. Bush, don't open that front door. I want to be left alone; I don't want anybody bother- ing me while I am at work on this report.' He went across to the Eagle Hotel to get a pitcher of lemonade; and while he was away there came a rap at my office door. I didn't pay any attention to it. I thought to myself, 'Wonder who that can be who wants to interrupt me now?' But when a second rap came I got up and opened the door sharply, and—there was my friend Wiseman quite drunk. I said, 'What do you want?' 'Oh, Brother Tr——' 'Don't "brother" me now! What do you want?' And he started to cry. I said, 'Now, you get out o' here sharp!'

A MOST HASTY EXIT

"My room is just a hundred feet long. I got hold of him by the coat collar and started him on a run for the door, and the farther we went the faster we got—I tell you we traveled—and when we got to the door, instead of opening it, I just gave him a shove and helped him along a little in the good old-fashioned way, and he went all in a heap in the street. And I said 'There! serves you right.' I said to myself, 'I've been fooled long enough; that fellow's been hanging round this Mission till he's disgraced it, and the quicker we get rid of him the better.' I was all out of breath; you know I'm pretty fat to run a dash.

"I went back to the office to get my breath, and to pray. I went to get down on one knee. You know that one-knee praying don't get very far—you only get half a blessing on one knee—guess you've tried it some of you. I said, 'I'll just have a little word of prayer, and ask the Lord to help me finish up that writing, because it's late, and I've been wasting time.' I got down on one knee and said, 'Now, Lord, help me to finish this writing, because I've been interrupted by that old fellow, but I'm glad I did the right thing to him, Lord. I did just the right thing. And I want you to help me. And I did just the right thing to that old Wiseman.'

"I got back to my desk, and I said, 'Now where did I leave off? That don't sound very good; did I ever write that?' And I took my morning's work and crumpled it all up, and said 'Everything's all out of shape. I guess I'll do it to-morrow morning.' I repeated again, 'Father, I did just right by that old fellow.' And I kept telling God how right I had done by kicking old Wiseman out into the street.

"I went to the telephone and rang up my wife. 'Any mail come in?' She said, 'Where are you?' 'That isn't what I asked you; is there any mail in?' I didn't wait for any answer. I swung up the receiver and said, 'Everybody's acting like a fool; I don't know what's the matter with them.' Then I said, 'Lord, I did just right with that old fellow—just the thing I ought to have done weeks ago.'

"A little later Mrs. Trotter rang up. She said, 'Is there anything gone wrong?' I said, 'Nothing with me, but what's the matter with you? You're the wrong one; it isn't me!' And I swung the receiver up again. I said, 'Wonder whatever has got into her. We have been married nearly fifteen years, and she never acted like this before. I don't like it a bit.'

EVERYTHING WENT WRONG

"I went across to the Eagle Hotel and ordered my dinner. I didn't want to go home and see my wife at all; things weren't going good enough. Things went all wrong at the hotel. I ordered something I didn't get, and I got something I didn't order. The soup was salt, and the dinner was cold. I said, 'The cook's crazy'; swallowed something, and went back to the office.

"My assistant was there—he wasn't due for two hours yet. I looked at him, and he looked at me. I said, 'Where have you been?' 'Why,' he said 'I am two hours early.' I said, 'You are two hours late, do you hear me?' He looked at my eye and went out; he said to the other fellows, 'I guess the old man's in the air.' He was right; the old man was 'in the air.'

"I said to my assistant, I want you to take the meeting to-night.' He said, 'Why, this is your night.' I said, 'Am I working for you, or are you working for me? You do as I tell you!' He took the meeting that night, and I sat down through the song-service. The piano was flat, and all out of tune, and everything was in a minor key.

"After the meeting was over I went home. We went to have our little prayer before retiring, and I took up the Bible, but could not find anything I wanted to read, so threw the Bible into the lap of a little girl who has lived with us for several years, and I said, 'You read.' I said to my wife, 'You pray; I don't feel like it.' I got on one knee again, and the family worship went through. I had the strangest kind of feeling that when my wife prayed she was looking at me out of one eye, and I was just watching for her to do it, and I would have called her down for it if she had, too.

"About two o'clock in the morning I got up and went to my old large rocking chair—I have put my head into that old chair and met my Lord there more times I think than anywhere else in the world—and I said, 'Lord, I want to know what is the matter. I love old Wiseman, but it was the only way to bring him round.' And the Lord brought it home to me, 'Didn't I die for him? Is that the way I used you? When you were down in sin, a mighty sight worse than old Wiseman, I took you to myself.' I said, 'Oh, God, forgive men, and help me to find old Wiseman.' Next morning I began hunting for old man Wiseman. I said to the boys, 'Now you go down into such and such a saloon, and you go over to So-and-So's barrel-house, and you go somewhere else, but find old man Wiseman.' They couldn't find him. And it was nearly a week before I set eyes on him again.

"We were on the Gospel wagon one Sunday afternoon, and I was singing away on the front of it, when I spotted my old man coming round the corner. I never in all my life saw a

THE TEMPORARY TABERNACLE ON THE STRAND, LONDON

JEWISH CHILDREN WHO ATTENDED THE CHILDREN'S MEETINGS

man that looked quite so good to me as he did. There he was—dirt, moustache, and all,—but he looked just sweet to me. Instead of waiting to go down the back steps to get at him I jumped off the front and started for him. I had on a new suit of clothes, but I got hold of old Wiseman, took him in my arms, and just pulled that dirty old head over on my shoulder. I said, 'Old man, I want you to forgive me; I love you, old fellow.' He looked at me, and held me away for a moment, and he said, 'Brother Trotter, you do love me, don't you?'

'Yes, Wiseman, I do!'

'Yes, Brother Trotter, I know you do!'

'And Wiseman, I want to do anything I can for you.'

'He says, "Gi'me a quarter!"'

"I gave the old man a quarter all right, and gave him half a dollar, too. I said, 'I want you to come and see me. Come down early to-night; there'll be a big crowd, and you'd better come early: come at 7 o'clock.' At seven o'clock he was at the Mission, and he came forward that night, and gave his heart to Jesus. Oh, friends it is love that conquers!"

PREACHED THROUGH THE PRESS

During the last month of the revival Mr. Alexander was dining one day with the editor of a leading daily paper when he was asked if he would not like to have two columns in the newspaper each day in which to speak to the people of Philadelphia. He gratefully accepted the offer, and became an editor for two weeks. Each day he inserted the words and music of a Revival Hymn; and gave a number of touching incidents regarding their influence during his world-wide revival tour.

A day or two after writing the preceding pages of this chapter I received a letter from a former Philadelphia newspaper man, telling of the effect of personal work in his life. It is one of the strongest statements I have seen how soul-winning will completely change a man's life, making it far richer, happier and more useful to the world. At my request Mr. E. E. Marriott, of the New York Mail and Express, sent me the statement which follows:

"It was the whole-souled, earnest talk of Charles M. Alexander in the great meetings of the Torrey-Alexander Mission in Philadelphia, 1906, that converted me to personal work.

"Under the new conviction as to Christian duty, then forced upon my mind and heart, I was impelled to give up an important newspaper editorial position because it required me to do secular work on Sundays.

"When this new impulse to personal work came to me, I had been a Christian for more than five years, and was an active member of Bethany Persbyterian Church, of the Young Men's Christian Association, and of the Brotherhood of Andrew and Philip. I was, and had been for years, News Editor on the staff of a large leading newspaper; and my position required me to be at work at the office on Sunday nights and five other nights in the week. On my one free evening each week and every noon and afternoon I attended the Mission meeting; but came to the conclusion that I must have my Sundays for the Lord's work. My wife was one of the most effective personal workers in all the meetings, and she and I prayed that I might find the right way.

"Finding that I could not get any relief from Sunday work

in the Philadelphia newspaper field, I resolved to give up my position. My wife and I agreed on this. We broke up our comfortable home on Bainbridge Street, Philadelphia, sold most of our furniture; and I gave my employers two weeks' notice. Some of my friends shook their heads, and said they thought I was acting rashly in giving up so good a position; but I knew in whom I believed, and was persuaded that 'all things work together for good to them that love him.'

"We moved to New York, and the first newspaper to which I applied gave me an editorial position which I still hold, and which allows me to have my evenings and Sundays free. It cost me about $500 in expenses and loss of income in the few weeks necessary to make the change, but how great has been the reward!

"In the twelve months that have passed since I took this step, I have been greatly blessed in doing personal work. My wife and I have given our Sundays and evenings as volunteers at evangelistic meetings in tents, Mission halls and in open-air services; and we have had the inexpressible joy of leading more than 120 individuals to accept Jesus as their Saviour, and to connect themselves with the visible Church of Christ! Wasn't it worth while?"

XIX

A NEW DEPARTURE—"REVIVAL LUNCHEONS"

SOME of the most far-reaching results of the great work of grace in Philadelphia occurred through a visit paid by Mr. Alexander to a small church in West Philadelphia, called the Oak Park Church. That night a revival flame was kindled which thrilled the community, and led scores into the Kingdom. The spark of revival was ignited in a most unusual manner. The meeting was held in the basement of a new building, and only about two hundred people were present. Mr. Alexander did not sing for the people at all, but talked to them about Christ's power to save.

They were cold and unresponsive as he spoke. But he was determined not to let the meeting end without some personal work. As soon as the service concluded, he walked down into the audience and began speaking to a large, fine looking man, asking him if he was saved. A dozen men soon gathered around him, and in a few moments they were on their knees in prayer. As the little group prayed the fire fell from heaven, and a work began, the ultimate result of which only eternity will reveal. Over one hundred persons confessed Christ in less than three weeks as a direct outcome of that meeting. The church was transformed, and men were enlisted for Christ who became among the most enthusiastic supporters of the revival.

One of the little group who knelt in prayer that night was Mr. John H. McBride, a prominent real estate dealer of Philadelphia. He declared that he had been a church member for twenty-five years, but not until that night had he really accepted Christ as his personal Saviour. In speaking to me later of that memorable scene he said: "The tender way in which Mr. Alexander placed his hand on my shoulder simply won me, and when he asked me if I was a Christian I became instantly convinced that my sins were not forgiven, for I realized that my life had been no different from that of other men of the world. I could not resist when he said immediately after that, 'Let us pray.' On my knees I asked God to forgive my sin and take away my pride, for that was one reason why I had not fully surrendered. From that moment my life was entirely changed; and I determined to for ever do personal work and witness for my Saviour. During these resolves I could hear the cries of other men who had evidently been living the life I lived, and were now sobbing tears of repentance; and in a few moments our little church was turned into a place of wonderful joy because of the realization of sins forgiven."

In speaking of the results which immediately followed, Mr. McBride said: "The locality was transformed as the result of that one meeting. The whole community seemed to be aflame with the Spirit of God. We began a prayer circle each Saturday night with our pastor, Rev. G. E. Raitt, as leader. Already our prayers have been answered in a wonderful manner. At our first circle meeting three were saved, and one of the three led three others to Christ. Last Saturday night seventeen men and five women were present, and some of them remained two hours and a half." Over a year later I visited the Oak Park Presbyterian Church, and found the Prayer

Circle was still continued and the leaders were still on fire with a passion for souls.

A NOVELTY IN THE WORK

Mr. McBride was so grateful to Mr. Alexander for starting a revival flame in his church that he arranged a unique business men's luncheon at a downtown hotel, in honor of the singing evangelist. Forty-three young business and professional men were present. The luncheon began with the singing of a song; and before it had proceeded very far the revival spirit burst forth, and the power of God fell upon the men just as they were eating. One after another arose from their seats at the table, and with tremulous voices confessed that they had not been leading right lives, while five men stood up, and then and there publicly accepted Christ.

Tears ran down the cheeks of those strong young business men at this manifestation of God's power; and the luncheon closed with the singing of two revival hymns. Mr. McBride declared that as a result of the gathering fifty persons were led to accept Christ as their Saviour within a few days. The gathering was termed a "Revival Luncheon." It was the first ever held in Philadelphia; and it created wide-spread interest as the press of the city described the gathering. Mr. Alexander declared that it was one of the most remarkable scenes that he had witnessed in his entire tour of the world.

"Revival Luncheons" now became one of the most interesting features of the revival. They were held every few days at some down-town hotel or restaurant or in a business building, and were presided over by Mr. Alexander. At five of the luncheons eighteen persons declared they would accept

Christ, while scores publicly stated that they would engage in soul-winning as never before. The luncheons uniformly began with a revival hymn, and ended with a prayer. Scarcely would the first course be concluded before Mr. Alexander would call upon some business man to tell the story of his conversion; and then one rousing testimony would follow another for nearly or quite two hours.

A FISHING EXCURSION

At one of these luncheons at the Y. M. C. A. Building, there was present Mr. G. W. Cole, of the staff of the "Christian Endeavor World." He was deeply impressed with the scenes witnessed, and wrote a graphic description of the event for his paper, entitled "A-fishing with Alexander." He said:

"I witnessed in Philadelphia the other day the greatest man-fishing scene that it was ever my good fortune to behold. It was not one of those places where there is a great sea of faces, and, when the net is cast and hauled, a multitude of sinners are gathered in. It was a deep, quiet pool, with rod and reel; and a past-master in the art of fishing for men was there, casting the bait and angling for the souls of men.

"They called it in Philadelphia an 'Alexander Revival Luncheon.' I had never heard of such a thing until I got the invitation to attend. It was in the banquet hall of the Young Men's Christian Association on Chestnut Street. There were seventy-five to a hundred men there, mostly business and professional men, just two or three Reverends. Alexander, the man whose singing and leading in revival songs have made him famous around the world, was there, but he didn't sing; no, not a note.

"We had hardly begun to eat when swish went the line, and the fishing began in dead earnest.Never before was I in any kind of religious meeting where formality and conventionality got such a cold shoulder. I told them afterwards that it was the biggest spiritual ice-breaker I had ever seen, and I wished they could let us have it in Boston for a while. Man after man was on his feet, a lawyer, a salesman, a newspaper man, a read estate dealer, and what not, testifying to what the grace of God had recently been doing to transform his life and turn him into a fisher of men. A confirmed drinking man was next on his feet, and then a backslider, a man who said he got religion in his youth, but now he had found Christ. And so it went.

"With such a liberal scattering of fresh bait, the fish began to rise one after the other, for it had been arranged that every Christian man invited to the luncheon should bring as his guest an unconverted friend. At first Alexander stood on the bank. He landed one noble fellow who sat in the chair right next to him. But pretty soon he waded right in. Opening my eyes, after a period of silent, united prayer, I saw him right across the table from me, in the middle of the room, with his arm over the shoulder of a fine young fellow. He couldn't get him, so he turned to his companion. Such a frank, plain, direct, honest appeal. He didn't make it easy, but he did make it attractive. In a minute, while the rest of us continued in prayer, these two young men were on their feet, confessing to their fellows their decision to cast in their lot with Christ.

"And so it continued. The luncheon lasted perhaps two hours. The men who were there will remember it as long as they live."

GET TO WORK AT ONCE

One of the speakers at this luncheon was Dr. Charles R. Watson, head of the Personal Workers of the Mission. He told how his ideas of personal work had recently undergone a complete transformation:

"Before Mr. Alexander came here I believed in personal work; believed in it mightily, theoretically, and practiced it some. But at that time I always had an idea that you had to know a man about ten years before you could be polite enough to talk to him about his soul's salvation. I never thought one could just hitch up to a street car and stay out in the cold with a conductor and talk to him about his soul. I used to think you ought to approach it gradually—a sort of 'inclined plane' process, and have the inclined plane about a mile long, and by the time you had gotten to the top the fellow had gone by and the opportunity, too. I think the greatest thing this Mission has taught us is that even on a train, on a street car, or wherever you may happen to be, you can open the conversation with a stranger and go right on to his heart; not ask him whether he is a church member; not try to get him to be good merely; but to just ask him the straight blunt question whether he is saved. I must confess I have gotten a tremendous lot out of the Mission in learning that lesson that one could do personal work suddenly, and that by following the Providence of God he will show us where to do it."

Another speaker was an insurance manager, who was converted in the meetings, Mr. M. B. Lockyer. He told of an interesting "Committee of Seven," which had recently been organized in his church:

"We have a man in Germantown who hadn't been inside a

church for twenty-five years. We have a committee of seven in connection with our Young People's Society there which meets on Saturday night for the definite purpose of praying for the success of our Sunday night meeting. We started to pray for this particular man; and entered into a covenant with ourselves to pray regularly for him three times a day as long as it might be necessary to bring him over. It was necessary to pray three times a day for five weeks; and our prayers were answered two weeks ago last Sunday night. He came to church that night; and he was so uneasy all the time. He said to me, 'Lockyer, I've got to do something; I don't know what it is; there is something at work with me.' He didn't know that he was working against the prayers of seven people and those of his wife. Our pastor put the invitation so lovingly that he couldn't resist it. He went up and took Jesus, and to-day he is feeling better than in all his life."

MINISTER CHANGES HIS METHOD

At another "Revival Luncheon" at a downtown restaurant, at which four men made the great decision, the pastor of a large church testified that the idea of personal soul-winning had gripped him with such force that it would mean a complete transformation in his ministry. A Sunday School Superintendent arose and told an experience resulting from Mr. Alexander's visit to his church the preceding Sunday, which deeply touched all who were present. He said:

"It took a great deal of courage in me to admit that I hadn't been living right. I have been superintendent and teacher in the Sunday School for 20 years; but there was one thing in my life that I felt ought to be eliminated. My wife and I get along happily, and we have five children. They annoy us sometimes, you know, and we would fly into a rage. I told my wife that we ought to get right with God, and thus be able to overcome that. Last Sunday I saw her get up and start down the church aisle; I couldn't stand that. I started after her, and we went down together. And our house has been a different place since, thank God."

At another luncheon tendered Mr. Alexander by Dr. J. R. Miller, the emphasis was placed upon personal work and family prayers. A prominent leader of the Presbyterian Church was so aroused that he began the custom of having a little prayer-meeting with the employes in his office every morning before beginning the day's work. The six or eight people in the office would meet together for 10 to 15 minutes while a brief passage of Scripture was read; then every one present would recite a verse of Scripture, and the little service closed with two or three brief prayers.

INQUIRY ROOMS OPENED

Yet another result of the Oak Park Church revival and of the Revival Luncheons was the opening of Inquiry Rooms in an office building in the heart of the business district of Philadelphia. Mr. Alexander had long had in mind something of the kind; and when he broached the plan to the young business men they approved the idea at once, and in a few days the rooms were opened. They were handsomely furnished through the generosity of a merchant of Philadelphia. It was planned that the most noticeable thing as one entered the rooms should be a framed placard reading: "How Long Since you Wrote to Mother?"

The aim of the room was to afford a quiet place to lead men to Christ, amid the rush of modern business life, and also to offer a place of easy access where men with spiritual difficulties could go and get expert spiritual counsel. From the beginning the rooms were successful. Scores of men found Christ in them during the first few weeks. Until the Philadelphia campaign ended they were in charge of Rev. W. S. Jacoby, one of the Mission party, and formerly Assistant Pastor of Dr. Torrey's Church in Chicago. His spirit-filled life to-day, and his past life, as a policeman, sailor and drunkard, made him an ideal man for the position, for he was enabled to cope with the problems of men in all walks of life.

During the first three days after they were opened, four men were converted outright, five backsliders were restored, and twelve were given spiritual help. Among the visitors were all sorts of people, business men, traveling men, drunkards and criminals.

When I asked Mr. Jacoby about some of the men who had come to him for help he said:

"One of the cases dealt with in the Inquiry Rooms was a gentleman who came in and said that there was something wrong with his Christian experience, and he wanted to know what it was. He had seen in others an experience which he had not, and he said, 'I want it.' For example, he told me of a young man who worked under him who was a habitual drunkard; the minute his wages were put into his hands he would go off to the rumship, and in a little while he would be penniless. He was becoming a hopeless case. One day recently this gentleman was in the Academy of Music, when he noticed, in front of him, the young man who had been a drunkard, singing 'Grace enough for me,' with such a look on his face as he had never seen there before. He met him shortly afterwards, and asked what had caused the change; and the former drunkard replied that he had gone one day to the Academy of Music, with his bottle in his pocket, and they had sung 'Grace Enough for me.' The power of God came upon him through those words, and he was converted, and had since become enthusiastic in his work for Christ."

Through the help of Mr. Jacoby the visitor quickly accepted Christ, and he, too, found peace. Mr. Jacoby also told of an attorney who came into the room, burdened with sin, but went out radiantly happy. He said:

"Another case dealt with was an attorney who came from the West to Philadelphia to transact some business, but getting acquainted with a woman and becoming enamored he was drawn away into sin, and for several years had been away from home and wife and going deeper and deeper into sin. He had almost come to the conclusion that he had committed the unpardonable sin, for he had once known God and Jesus Christ as his Saviour. In showing him the passages of Scripture necessary for one in his condition he finally, through God's Spirit, saw the truth that there was forgiveness and mercy for him, accepted it, and in leaving the room, said, 'My heart has not been so light since the day I was born.' "

At the close of the Philadelphia campaign the Inquiry Rooms were found to be so successful and helpful that they were continued for some time. For several weeks they were under the charge of Mr. F. A. Mills, who acted as a soloist in addition to Mr. Butler, during the last weeks of the work in Philadelphia. Each day a noon prayer-meeting was held by the men who were filled with a passion for souls, and a longing to keep absolutely right with God.

CONVERTS TELL THEIR STORY

Largely as an outcome of the "Revival Luncheons," there was held in the Academy of Music, near the close of the Mission, a remarkable converts' testimony meeting. It was for men only, although a choir of nearly one thousand voices, mostly women, occupied the platform. The meeting was led by Mr. Alexander, who delivered no set sermon, but conducted it largely on the lines of the Welsh Revival meetings. He called upon one after another of the converts to tell the story how their lives had been transformed by the power of God. The Holy Spirit was present in prayer; and the big audience of about three thousand men was deeply moved by the thrilling experiences of men in politics, business and the various professions. Among those who spoke were James Briggs, the converted police magistrate; John H. McBride, the converted real estate dealer; M. B. Lockyer, converted insurance man; Ben T. Jenkins, another converted real estate man and a former schoolmate of Mr. Alexander, and a number of personal workers including John Wanamaker, Dr. Cochrane, H. Wellington Wood, Allan Sutherland and Ben T. Welsh. After nearly two hours of song and stirring testimony, Mr. Alexander called upon those who would accept Christ to arise; and one after another quickly stood up in all parts of the building. After 68 had arisen, Mr. Alexander asked them to come down to the front of the building, and repeat in concert, "I accept Jesus as my Saviour, my Lord and my King." A Philadelphia newspaper termed the gathering "the most remarkable prayer and testimony meeting ever held in Philadelphia."

At the conclusion of the three months' campaign a great farewell meeting was held to praise God for the victories won. The great Armory was early packed with six thousand people, to say good-bye to the evangelists and unite in thanksgiving for the awakening.   Among the speakers of the evening were two Bishops and leading Philadelphia pastors of various denominations.   Dr. C. E. Bronson, a prominent Presbyterian minister, said:

"I feel sure that, when the religious history of Philadelphia is written, it will be said that the Torrey-Alexander Mission was one of the great religious movements in the two hundred years of Philadelphia's history."

XX

THE STORY OF MEL. TROTTER

At the close of the Philadelphia campaign, a number of business men, who had been set on fire with a passion for souls during the three months' Mission, accompanied Mr. Alexander as far as Washington on his way to Atlanta.

At Wilmington, Delaware, however, two meetings had been arranged. The Gospel singer and his party stopped there; and Mr. Alexander conducted two meetings which proved to be among the most remarkable ever held in the city. At the first one, in the afternoon, the Opera House was well filled, while at night it was packed to the doors; and for the hundreds unable to obtain admission an overflow meeting was held at a nearby church. At each service Mr. Alexander called upon the business men to give brief testimonies of Christ's power to save and to keep; and these deeply impressed the audience. In the evening he asked Melvin E. Trotter, to tell the story how his life had been transformed by the power of the Gospel. Mr. Trotter, who had been assisting the evangelists in the Philadelphia campaign, had been saved nine years before in Chicago when on his way to the Lake to commit suicide; and to-day has the largest rescue Mission in the world at Grand Rapids, Michigan. As he told the story of his redemption with passionate eloquence hundreds were melted to tears.

As the result of the songs and appeals of Mr. Alexander, of the testimonies of the business men, of the stirring address

MR. EDWARD ROBERTS TAKING FRIENDS TO TOURNAMENT HALL

by Mr. Trotter, and of the presence of the Holy Spirit in mighty power, about seventy persons made a public confession of their faith in Christ at the afternoon and evening meetings. The Secretary of the Y. M. C. A., who had arranged the meetings, was jubilant over the result.

The next morning Mr. Alexander and his party of business men took the train for Washington, where an audience with President Roosevelt had been arranged for noon, and a Gospel meeting in the New York Avenue Presbyterian Church for the evening. That was the church in which Abraham Lincoln had worshipped.

In his meeting with the President, Mr. Alexander, with characteristic generosity, gave up the pleasure of a private interview, in order to introduce nearly a score of his friends to the Chief Executive.

Late that night, after the inspiring Gospel service was over, Mr. Alexander departed for Atlanta. At the railway station, as one after another of the stalwart business men bade him good-bye, there were moist eyes and touching farewells. The scene reminded me strongly of those pictures recorded in the life of Whitefield, the great revivalist, when he would be accompanied a part of the way from one city to another, by a group of friends on horseback; and how at the hour of parting they would fall upon one anothers' necks, and weep for joy at the victories won, and for grief at the sad parting.

It was also at this period that Mr. Alexander was reluctantly compelled to part from Mr. Rupert Lowe, his secretary, who had been his friend and companion for nearly four years. Mr. Lowe was called back to his home in Geelong, Australia, to enter upon important business relations.

A THRILLING LIFE HISTORY

I now want to give my readers the life story of Mr. Melvin E. Trotter in his own words as he told it with thrilling effect on several occasions at Philadelphia, and at Wilmington, Delaware. He said:

"Brother Alexander likes to have me with him; I believe he loves me—I know he does—but he sort of takes me around as a kind of 'horrible example,' a 'Before' and 'After' taking advertisement. Did you ever see one of them? you know—a lean man up one side, and a big, fat, prosperous-looking one up the other side: 'Before' and 'After.' I'm 'After'—after the Lord Jesus Christ found me. He found me in Chicago one night nine years ago and more, and he saved me.

"I started out in life with as good a chance as any one you can find. My father would have let me go to school, but, of course, I did not need it. I knew so much more than the old man, so I did not get any schooling. I went out into the world and learned the barber trade; and at the age of sixteen I was drawing a man's salary. That's a bad thing for a boy. I was able to indulge in many things that did me harm.

"I got to know a great deal about four-legged Trotters. I was always stuck on the finest horses; and I was a good fellow. And I kept on drinking, and the first thing I knew I couldn't stop. The friends I had found that when they needed me the most I was not there; and they cut me out, and bye and bye I got down to drinking sheenies, three for five.

"And I couldn't help it. I tried to break away and get into the country. A man named Cook gave me a splendid big black horse, one of the best horses I ever drove, and I got a buggy and a job in the country. I moved out into the country, and made a lot of money. My wife would go with me to keep me sober, and I would stay stober awhile, and how I wanted to stay sober, and I'd say, 'I'll never take another drink as long as I live.'

ELEVEN MILES FOR DRINK

"One night I went to put my horse in a barn after a long drive, and took my wife to the house. It was snowing, and one of the coldest days in Iowa. All of a sudden the devil seemed to get hold of me. I had driven my horse nearly as fast as he would go; but I started him out again, and drove eleven miles and came back home with eleven big drinks inside of me, and three big quarts of whiskey in my buggy, and my wife was heart-broken. She looked into my face, and she said, 'I didn't know where you had gone, but if I could have walked through this awful storm I would have come to look for you.' I did not want to do that! I would have given my life if I could have stayed sober, but it wasn't in me.

"Another night I went on a drunk after I had been sober eleven weeks and three days, with a suspended sentence hanging over me. I went out into the country, and I was having a good time, and I drove up to a saloon, put my horse in the shed, and said, 'There's the old horse out there in the buggy; I want to give everybody something to drink, and just keep right on paying until the horse is drunk up.' I was just simply imbecile; there was nothing else to it. And I tried my level best. I do not look like a man that goes down easy, but I just could not stop it. I went on worse and worse, and finally I got back to the city again; and the drunks got oftener and oftener, and they'd get a little bit longer.

"I tried for six years to quit. There is no fun in that. Every time I would fall after promising my wife and my boy and myself that I would never take it again. Then when I would fall I would be just that much lower in my own estimation; I would hate myself. Finally when I would get drunk I would not go home. I got to staying away on a week's drunk, three or four days at first, and then gradually longer and longer. I would commit burglary in order to satisfy the awful craving for drink.

GOLD CURE USELESS

"They were trying to turn me off the whiskey, but they did not give me any remedy. You cannot tie a big fellow like me with a bit of ribbon. It needs something more than that. They tried the gold cure; and they gave me a hypodermic syringe and three bottles of medicine; but I sold the whole outfit in fifteen minutes for three drinks of whiskey. And I want to tell you they couldn't hold me with that thing. I needed Jesus in my heart before the old things could pass away and all things become new. That is my favorite verse in the Bible—II. Cor. 5: 17—'Therefore if any man be in Christ, he is a new creature; old things are passed away; behold all things are become new.' Present tense; you do not have to wait till you get to heaven before all this happens. The old things'—the old appetites, the old desires are passed away. Where are they? You can search me; I do not know.

"God gave us only one baby, and when the little fellow was two years and a month old I went to our little home one day—it had almost ceased to be a home—I went home after a ten days' drunk, and found him dead in his mother's arms. I

MR. ROBERT HARKNESS AND MR. ALEXANDER IN NEW ZEALAND

will never forget that day. I was simply a slave, and I knew it. It pretty nearly broke my heart. I said, 'I am a murderer. I am anything but a man; and I cannot stand it, and I won't stand it, and I will just end my life.' But I did not have courage enough. At my mother's knee I had been taught to say, 'Now I lay me,' and I knew there was a God; I did not dare face him; I couldn't stand suicide.

"Mrs. Trotter was alone with the little body when she laid it down, dead; and she turned away to God, and said, 'Father, I have had my thoughts on my baby more than on you, and now I want to turn away to you. You are all I have left.' Mrs. Trotter had never been away from our baby one hour from the time he was born till the time he died in her arms. She had a drunken husband, and her only joy and hope was in her baby, and, oh, how she cared for him! And she turned around from the dead child and she said, 'Lord, I am going to serve you, to help others in trouble. I have my husband'; and she began to pray for me. That's a thing that counts; when a wife gets hold of God without letting go there's something going to happen.

ALMOST DRUNK AT THE FUNERAL

"She led me into the little room and closed the door upon the three of us; and over the body of our dead baby, lying in the little white casket, she made me promise that I would not take another drop. I made the promise, put my arms about her, and told her I'd never touch liquor again as long as I lived, and the funeral was not over two hours before I staggered home so drunk I could not see. You know I could not help that. The devil had got hold of me.

"I went away from home, left my wife to get along as best she could; and I went clean down into the gutter. I went on down in sin till I was a hopeless, homeless drunkard. I was so far down that I had to reach up to touch bottom; and one night I made up my mind I could not stand it any longer. It looked as if there was no other way for me but to take my own life in the lake, along what they called the 'Viaduct Route,' where the railroad was reclaiming some land, and where all the suicides went over. Going down East Van Buren Street I went past a place; and I heard them singing inside, 'Throw Out the Life-line Across the Dark Wave.' I stopped just a little, and a man outside boosted me in. He said, 'Come on in, Fatty; just the place for you,' and in I went.

"Well, bless your hearts, it proved to be the old Pacific Garden Mission. That's the place in Chicago where an old bum is always welcome, where they will give him just as good a seat as they will when you've got your Prince Albert coat on, and where they will take just as good care of you as any place in all the world. I got a good seat, and I heard them singing. I went to sleep during the preaching, but I woke up when the testimonies started; and I heard the most marvelous stories I ever heard in my life. Why, men and women, I tell you that those boys in there were like these men here; they had found a new joy; they had been saved by the saving grace of God, some of them a week, some two weeks, some six months, some ten years, and there they were just filled with the Spirit instead of filled with sin and wickedness. And Harry Monroe got up and told how Jesus had come into his life and saved him. He said, 'Listen, fellows, God loves you,' and he pointed his finger straight at me, and God was in the whole business.

"Mr. Monroe gave an invitation, and I was the first man to raise my hand for prayer. I gripped my old cap and started down the aisle; and knocked over all the chairs in my way. Mr. Monroe got off the platform and helped me down front; we knelt down there, and he told me to pray the publican's prayer. Well, I did not know anything about it, but just what he told me to do I did. I heard the story that Jesus loved me, and that if I confessed my sin he was faithful and just to forgive my sin, and to cleanse me from all unrighteousness. The verse he stood me on that night was 'Him that cometh to me I will in no wise cast out'; and all of a sudden I remembered, so many times I had heard the story of the Cross, how Jesus went all the way to Calvary, and

> " 'None of the ransomed ever knew
> How deep were the waters crossed,'

and I saw Jesus, bearing his cross, men spitting at him and crowning him with thorns, all for my sin. I saw him starting up that awful steep hill with his cross, and falling under it. I got a glimpse of my Lord that I have never lost for an instant from that moment until this.

WAS A TOBACCO FIEND, TOO

"I did not have any money, and not much more clothes. I had a lovely overcoat, though. It was a bargain. I didn't stop to get measured for it. I bought it in a hurry. You know I wanted to catch a train; and I just picked out the biggest coat I could see; a friend of mine went back and paid for it. If you had taken the overcoat away from me I would not have had clothes enough to pad a crutch. I do not believe

I could have stopped a bread wagon on a bet. I was just as much a fiend for tobacco as I was for whiskey; and I didn't have the money to buy the one, so I had my right hand pocket filled with 'wet ones,' and my left hand pocket filled with 'dry ones.'

"A godly fellow took me to his home that night; my own brother Will. I want to tell you there were three of us boys, and all three of us tended bar, for my own father. My father was a drunkard, and my brothers and I were drunkards. But to-night brother George has a lovely Mission in Saginaw, Michigan; brother Will has a large Mission in Los Angeles, California; and I have one in Grand Rapids, Michigan. My old mother is not known outside of the little town she lives in in Illinois. She is a very quiet woman; if you would ask her to stand up here she couldn't do it; she has never seen a crowd like this. She's just a dear old home body, but she has seven children, and every one of them loves Jesus.

"Well I cleaned up that night. I just cleaned those dirty old things out of my pockets and started out right. Will stood and watched me, with the tears streaming down his face; he knew if I was ever going to get anywhere I would have to get away from that. I want to tell you right now there is just one thing I have never seen—and Mrs. Clark and Harry Monroe told me they had never seen—I never saw one man who had been saved from drinking and kept his tobacco that did not go back again. If I had stuck to that thing, I do not believe I could have been here to-night, standing before you; but God gave me the Holy Spirit in place of it; and I do not want it, and I have been able to go out and tell the story of my salvation.

"The next day I went to work. My brother bought me a coat, and put me to work at a barber shop; and I have never cost a man a dollar from that day to this. We had a compact little room; it was front parlor, back parlor, kitchen, pantry, bedroom and automobile shed all rolled into one room, and that was the best place I had ever been in, for Jesus was there. I set up the family altar, with a little bit of a Testament that cost two and a half cents. And I started to read. I did not know much where to read, but I said, 'I will start at the beginning; most books start there anyhow.' So I started off in the first chapter of Matthew; and the names got me up a tree before I got through the second verse. I got over into the second chapter, and began to read things. Then I would get down on my knees, and in the best way I knew how I would commit my way to the Lord; did not have any better sense than just expect him to lead me, and I would just place my hands in his, and ask him to keep us.

MEMORIZED SCRIPTURE

"Presently I got to reading the little Testament on the car. I was not long on newspapers. Well, you could not ride on a car seven miles from town, and let a lot of women stand up while you sat down and read a Testament. Well, I tried reading standing up, so I started to get a verse and to commit it to memory every day. The first year after I was saved I had 365 verses in my head, and, what is better, in my heart.

"I made $4.20 the first week after Jesus saved me; and my wife and myself lived on it and paid 60 cents car fares and a dollar a week rent, and never went back. I tell you right now we have been mighty badly bent, but we never went in debt and God took care of us. My wife never complained, although she came out of a splendid home. She said, 'I would rather live in one room and have my old man sober than live in a palace with a drunkard.' But I have paid $1,800 worth of debts since Jesus saved me, and it has been a pretty hard grind, too. I have just gone on, trusting him day by day, and made to-day count for God. I commit my way unto him every day before I talk to men; we just start the day together. I do not know very much about it, but I know this, that I was a poor old hopeless drunkard and Jesus saved me, and he keeps me all the way.

"My heart goes out to the drunkards; and I pity the poor girl on the streets. I pity her so that we have a home to take her to—not a Rescue Home that some one has paid for, but our own little home in Grand Rapids, and the door is always open to poor girls that want to live the Christian life. Sometimes we have no spare room, or we do not have the money, but Mrs. Trotter always says, 'Do not turn one of them away.' What is the reason for their being down in that life? Because some miserable scoundrel put them there. For every poor woman that has gone down into sin there is some man as black as Satan back of it. In the United States to-day there are 30,000 women who are really outcasts. Their average life is five years, so that 6,000 die every year, and 72 daughters go out of the homes of the United States every day of the year to fill up their awful ranks. Men, can you look me in the face and tell me that a woman that goes down into sin is any worse than you are. Some of these days you men that have a lovely home, and a good reputation in your neighborhood, and yet sin will meet judgment.

JUST "LET GOD MOVE IN"

"I went to work to find the old drunkards; and God has been giving me drunkards ever since. I have gone out in the power of the Spirit of God, depending upon him to do it. We find some cases that will just almost break our hearts. Nearly every scene that we see in our rescue work is a dark one; we get them when everybody else has done with them. But I am glad I am in it. It is the nicest work in the world; there is absolutely no worry; we just move out and let God move in. And I say to you my work is a pleasure all the way through; and if I had a thousand lives I would like to live them all for Him. By the help and grace of God I am determined to use the one I have for him. It is not much I can do, but I tell you it is a good deal He can do.

"I have only got one text, and that is, the blood of Jesus Christ, God's Son, can cleanse from all sin, and that takes in everything. I have just one remedy. I do not have to do like physicians do; go in and diagnose a case. I know that sin will cover it every time, and I know that the blood of Jesus Christ cleanseth us from all sin. When they begin to tell me their story I say, 'You just wait for my story before you begin to tell me; hold on just a minute; the blood of Jesus Christ, God's Son, will cleanse you from all your sin, and everything else will take care of itself.' 'And I, if I be lifted up, will draw all men unto me.' "

XXI

VICTORY IN ATLANTA

DURING the month of May, 1906, Atlanta was stirred as rarely before in its history by the revival campaign of Dr. Torrey and Mr. Alexander. Many of the marks of the old-time revival appeared in the meetings. Not a few were so deeply convicted of sin that they were in agony of mind and body. One drunkard, after having passed the hall, declared that he felt an invisible but irresistible force gripping him and compelling him to return; and he was so smitten with conviction that he threw his full whiskey bottle into the sewer and went back to the hall, where he accepted Christ. He then returned to his former employment.

Another characteristic of the work was the return of stolen money and the wide-spread payment of old debts throughout the city. In a single congregation one pastor declared that he knew of seven young men who were so convicted that they began to pay up old obligations.

Hundreds of Christian people in Atlanta were fired with a Pentecostal passion for soul-winning. They were so aroused that they led people to Christ in the street cars, in office buildings, on the street—everywhere.

PRAISE MEETING ON SIDEWALK

One evening while the campaign was in progress a man told me how a drunkard who had been on the point of commiting

MR. ALEXANDER AND MR. CHARLES COOKE, THE IROQUOIS INDIAN

suicide accepted Christ at noon on a down-town street and instantly became so happy that they had a praise and hallelujah meeting right there on the sidewalk. The same man told how he went into two offices, and the business men who occupied them knelt down and accepted Christ.

One day Mr. Alexander went into a dentist's parlor; and as the result of his personal work the dentist knelt and took Christ. The singing evangelist said:

"I went to have my teeth fixed a little this afternoon, and as I got through I put my arms around the dentist, and I said, 'You are a good dentist; won't you come to Christ?' He said, 'I have been wanting somebody to come here and speak to me ever since the meetings began.' They are hungry all over town. A friend and I talked with him a little while, got him down on his knees, and he sobbed like a child. I had to leave and go to the afternoon meeting, but I left the other two together. As I went out of the door the dentist called out after me, though he was on his knees, 'Ask the people to pray for me.' I have just had a letter from my friend, saying that the dentist was converted there on his knees this afternoon."

The meetings in Atlanta were held in a large Skating Rink, which was remodeled to accommodate 4,400 people. The campaign was supported by the most prominent business men of the city, including two millionaires, and a man who is at the head of about 73 country banks. The head of the Business Men's Committee was ex-Governor W. J. Northen.

SAM SMALL CAME BACK

Perhaps the most striking event of the entire movement was the return of Rev. Sam. Small to God after five years of backsliding. As my readers doubtless know, Mr. Small was one of the foremost evangelists of the country; but some years ago he drifted away from God, and had been living in Atlanta as a blackslider, writing for a local newspaper. One night he was sitting on the platform at the Skating Ring while Dr. Torrey preached on The Judgment Day. As he concluded his sermon and appealed for converts very few responded. Just as he was about to end the appeal a thrill ran over the audience as Sam. Small stood up at a reporters' table, and in a broken voice said:

"Dr. Torrey, I once accepted Christ and knew the full joy of salvation, but I have drifted away and God knows I need to repent, and God helping me I do now and here repent and surrender my life to him." As he finished his confession Mr. Small sat down, buried his head upon the table in front of him.

Not only the audience, but the evangelists themselves were deeply moved by the occurrence; and Dr. Torrey called on Mr. Alexander to pray. The singing evangelist offered a fervent prayer, saying: "Our Father, when we were boys we heard of Sam Small; and it encouraged our hearts when we saw what Jesus could do through him for men who were away down in sin. We do thank thee for the privilege of praying for him to-night; and we ask that thou wilt do such a work in his heart as shall last through all eternity."

Mr. Small's return to the fold created a deep impression throughout Atlanta and aroused widespread interest throughout the country. Within a few days after his confession Mr. Small received more than 100 letters of congratulation and encouragement, and among them invitations to begin revival meetings in two Northern cities.

The next day at a meeting for business men conducted by the evangelist, Mr. Small melted down the meeting by declaring that for years he had walked the streets of Atlanta, and not a soul had spoken to him about his salvation. He said:

"I have gone up and down the streets of Atlanta for the five years I have been away from God, with a hungry heart, and wished for some Christian to speak to me; but never has a Christian man spoken to me in all these years, and I felt a bitterness in my heart toward all Christian people. But as I listened to Dr. Torrey, I saw that my responsibility could not be shifted on to God, and I repented and came back to God a new man."

He had scarcely finished speaking when a man in the audience said: "I prayed for brother Small, and wanted to speak to him, but I felt that I was below him intellectually, and would not make any impression on him. I ask God to forgive me for not speaking to him."

Another got up and said: "I prayed for Brother Sam for years. I have his picture on the wall of my home, and I prayed for him every time I looked at it. I was on the eve of speaking to him several times, and hope God will forgive me for not doing so."

RESUMED PREACHING

Sunday Mr. Small preached his first sermon since his return to the fold in his old church here in Atlanta; and as a result two persons stood up to accept Christ. In the course of his sermon Mr. Small told how he had been drawn by the spirit of God and had been led to make a full surrender.

"Dear friends," he said, "if I could tell you the emotion that surges through my heart as I stand in this pulpit this morning you would rejoice with me; but it is sufficient for you to know that I have come back again into the fold. I feel like a deserter who has been pardoned by his chief. I have been a member of this church for a long time, and I want to begin all over again at home, for this is my church home.

"I cannot tell you how it came about, but I remember I was going to a lodge meeting to take part in an initiation, with never a thought of going to the Torrey-Alexander meeting in my mind. I was riding down town on the car, and as it passed the hall something seemed to say to me, 'Go to the Torrey-Alexander meeting.' So I left the car, went in through one of the side entrances to the rink, and took a seat up front. As I sat there and heard Dr. Torrey calling on those who had gone away from God to come back, something seemed to say to me, 'Why don't you stand? Why don't you stand? Why don't you stand?' I kept putting it off, but at last an overwhelming impulse came over me to stand; and I did stand, and by the grace of God I intend to stand the balance of my life.

"Oh, the joy that came into my heart, friends, when I rose and confessed that I had not been leading the life that I ought to and had gotten away from God. I can never fully explain the joy and peace that came into my life."

A "Revival Luncheon" was held in Atlanta which was attended by many leading business men. They told how deeply the city had been stirred by the movement and how they had been led to do personal work as never before. One well known business man, who had formerly run for mayor and had been backed by the whiskey element, arose at the table and told with tears and sobs how he had accepted Christ the night before. He said:

"I am 39 years of age, and have been a great sinner all my life. I had often thought about the matter of religion, and it prayed upon my mind, but I would dodge everything that pertained to Christianity. My wife would ask me to go to Sunday School or church with her, but I would always have an excuse. I went home the other evening, and went into the room where she sat. She had been to hear Dr. Torrey. She said, 'I want you to be a better man.' I said, 'Well, I want to be.' She said, 'I am going to pray for you right now'; and right then and there she knelt and prayed for me. It melted me; I couldn't stand it.

"First thing this morning I wrote off to my mother—she is 79 years of age—to tell her what I have done; and I would like to see her face when she gets that letter. I want you all to pray for me; and I want to work for God and make good for the time I have lost."

"OUT OF THE MOUTHS OF BABES"

One of the most beautiful features of the revival was the way in which the boys and the girls were fired with enthusiasm to get their companions converted. In one neighborhood sixteen boys have been converted, all as the result of a lady who accepted Christ on the first night of the meeting. The boys were so eager to have their companions saved that they held a prayer-meeting almost every night before they went up to the meetings at the auditorium. Ex-Governor Northen, in speaking of the leader of the boys, said:

"One of the boys here has been coming up to me for several nights with another boy, and saying 'Governor, let me introduce you to this boy; he has accepted Christ to-night.' Last night he came up to me, leading another boy as usual, and said, 'Governor, this is only half my boy; another boy helped me lead him to Christ.' And when I went out last night when almost everybody else had left the building and the lights were turned down, I saw seven little fellows down on their knees praying to God to give them more boys."

When the revival began Atlanta was honey-combed with card-playing and dancing Christians. Large numbers of these were led to give up these worldly practices and surrender themselves to God for soul-winning. One lady who had bought a new set of whist-boards took them back, and exchanged them for handsome little Bibles.

During the campaign, the revival fire broke out in curious and unexpected places. For two weeks two young men held noon-day revival meetings in the engineer's room in the basement of a big office building. Their little audience was composed of the engineer of the building, the elevator boy, and some painters and machinists; but the young men preached the Gospel with all the fervor of trained evangelists. As the outcome of their endeavor, three painters, a machinist and the elevator boy accepted Christ as their Saviour.

Before the revival closed Mr. Small's power as an evangelist seemed to come back to him once more. On the last Sunday of the campaign he addressed a large gathering of men, telling them how he had served the devil for five years, but was determined to serve God for the rest of his life and fight the devil till his last breath. As he spoke with thrilling eloquence, tears rolled down the faces of hundreds of strong men. At the end of his sermon some fifteen or twenty men, young and old, went forward and grasped the evangelist's hand, and declared that they would surrender their lives to God. Mr. Small said he had received invitations from many Northern cities to come there and conduct revival meetings, but that since he had served the devil in Atlanta he wanted to stay there for a time and endeavor to lead back to God some of the men he led astray.

At the conclusion of the last service in Atlanta, a beautiful scene occurred, when a considerable part of the audience, under the leadership of ex-Gov. Northern, marched to the Majestic Hotel, where the evangelists were staying, and held an impromptu meeting, during which the choir and others serenaded them with the "Glory Song" and other revival hymns.

A VISIT TO SAM JONES

It was during the stay of the evangelists at Atlanta, that Mr. Alexander paid a memorable visit to Sam. P. Jones, the great evangelist and lecturer, at his home in Cartersville, Georgia. Mr. Jones had been an interested visitor at the Atlanta meetings, and had cordially urged the singing evangelist to spend a day with him. Mr. Alexander gladly accepted the invitation, for he had long been an ardent admirer of the wise sayings and unique methods of the man.

Early one Saturday morning Mr. Alexander left Atlanta, accompanied by his brother, Robert Harkness, Charles Butler, Evangelist Ira Evans Hicks and the writer. We were most cordially entertained by Mr. Jones and his family; and Mr. Alexander declared that it was one of the pleasantest days he had ever spent. Following the death of Mr. Jones, Mr. Alexander wrote an appreciative article for the "Record of Christian Work," in which he said:

"We went up to Cartersville, and what a day it was! About such a day as I remember having with Mr. Moody when he was in Atlanta during the Cotton Exposition. I believe great men would spend more time with small men, if they knew what a help a few hours' conversation would be to their lives.

"When we reached his home we were made to feel at home, immediately. After getting acquainted with the members of his family, we went for a drive about the town; and then new beauties of his character began to shine out as he talked about his love for the people and how interested he was in their welfare. He showed us a big tabernacle he had built on a hill, which had been bought and given for the purpose by the town. He made it a point for years to hold at least ten days meetings in his home town annually.

"I plied him with questions constantly, for there were many that I had longed to ask him for years. He said when he first came to that town, with his family, there were twelve saloons there. He stated before an audience soon after coming, that even one saloon in that town was too many for his boy, and that they had to go. He kept preaching, praying, getting other people to pray, and working until they ran them out. They threatened to kill him, and did dynamite his barn. I asked him if a saloon could be legally brought into the town. He said 'Yes,' he supposed it might, but with a very earnest glance up into my eye he said, 'We have given them warning that if they won't go head first, they will have to go feet first.' I asked him how it was, and he said, 'We just keep the spiritual atmosphere of the town at such a temperature that the liquor seller cannot live here.'

"After the mid-day meal we sat on his broad veranda. He

was in a rocking-chair, with his little grand-child on his knee, we, all as close to him as we could get, asking him questions. And what answers he gave to us! I wish I could recall all of them. Among other things he said this, 'You cannot say it with your tongue if you haven't got it in your head.' Another striking sentence was: 'The men who leave their mark, on this world, are the men who have convictions. The men who have mere opinions slip through without leaving a trace.'

"The love and respect shown to him by each member of his famliy, and those who were his servants, was a proof of his home Christianity, which he had preached so constantly. I asked one kindly-faced colored woman how long she had been with them. 'Twenty years, sir.' 'And how do you like to live with them?' 'I could not live without them,' was her reply.

"I watched Mr. Jones as he walked about on the lawn, talking to us. I thought then he seemed very feeble, although his eye was clear and steady and his voice resonant and full. We all went back to Atlanta, repeating his sayings to one another, and each with a stronger determination to be better and truer men."

XXII

CONVERSION OF A FAMOUS PUGILIST

THE final Mission of the year before the summer rest period was held in Ottawa, Canada, in June, 1906. The movement resulted in a spiritual awakening scarcely less widespread in its influence than that of Toronto a few months previous. Not only the city, but the province was stirred by the revival. Ottawa being the capital of Canada, the effect of the Mission was felt throughout the nation. The names of about 1,500 converts were recorded, while hundreds of others were saved whose names were not recorded. The converts were from all classes and ranks, and included a lady of title, street railway men, and a well known pugilist and ex-saloon-keeper whose conversion thrilled the entire city.

The meetings in Ottawa were held in Dey's Rink, a big structure generally used for hockey matches or as a skating rink. In appearance it closely resembled the Drill Hall used by the evangelists in Plymouth, England. It was remodeled and fitted with seats to accommodate 6,000 persons, but on more than one occasion it was packed to the doors with hundreds unable to obtain admission. This was the more remarkable since the population of the city was only 60,000, with about one-half Roman Catholics. Among those present at the opening meeting were several from the Government House, including Lady Sybil Grey, daughter of Earl Grey, Governor-General of Canada.

A "SUNBEAM CHOIR"

One of the most beautiful events of the Mission was the presence one evening of a "Sunbeam Choir" of 500 boys and girls. Mr. Alexander said it was the largest "Sunbeam Chorus" he had ever had. The boys and girls were arranged on the rising seats at the side of the building, near the front, and presented a beautiful appearance. At one end of the throng of children were 100 boys with bright faces and shining eyes. Next to them were 400 little girls with equally radiant faces and sparkling eyes. In their costumes were all the colors of the rainbow. When, in response to Mr. Alexander's signal, their clear childish voices floated out through the arena many hundreds of hearts were touched and melted. Their favorite song was the "Sunbeam Song"; and it was thrilling to hear their clear, happy voices singing in unison:

> "I'll be a sunbeam for him."

At the conclusion of the sermon by Dr. Torrey, when the invitation was given, about 100 of the boys and girls in the choir stood up publicly to accept Christ, and went down to the front seats where the Way of Life was clearly explained to them, as well as to the older converts.

Like Toronto, Ottawa is one of the most God-fearing cities in the Dominion. The Sabbath is observed here with a strictness far surpassing anything seen in the States. By law no Sunday newspapers are allowed in the Dominion. A striking illustration of the prevalence of family religion was seen one afternoon, when Mr. Alexander asked all in the audience who had family prayers to raise their hands. Almost every hand in the audience was uplifted; and the Gospel singer declared it was the largest proportion he had seen in their tour of the World.

SPECIAL TRAINS WERE RUN

A unique feature of the work in Ottawa was the running of special trains throughout the campaign. The first was a special train from Pembroke, Ontario, 100 miles away. Another carried a party of 100 Christian Endeavorers and choir members who came from Toronto, 300 miles distant. A pleasant incident of that excursion was the spending of several days in Ottawa by some who were entertained by the Christian Endeavorers of the city.

The third Sunday of the Ottawa campaign was the red-letter day of the revival. At the afternoon and evening services not less than 14,000 people were in attendance, and over 300 converts were recorded. The afternoon meeting was for boys and girls; and was the largest gathering the evangelists had in America. Nearly 8,000 people, young and old, were present, the great structure being closely packed, with hundreds standing and sitting upon the steps leading to the choir platform. The musical part of the service was especially inspiring, Mr. Alexander having under his direction three choirs— the regular Ottowa choir, the "Sunbeam Choir" and nearly 100 members of his former Toronto choir.

The man who trained the two choirs in Ottawa—the regular choir, and the "Sunbeam Chorus"—was one of the interesting figures of the work there. His name was Charles H. Cooke, but he was a full-blooded Iroquois Indian. He was from a red man's settlement in the north of Canada, where his father was an Indian missionary. For several years he had lived in Ottawa, where he became director of a choir in a Presbyterian

Church.   Mr. Cooke is not only an expert musician, but a man of executive ability, having handled the choir arrangements in an admirable manner.   When I asked him to tell me something of his early life, he said:

AN INDIAN'S CHRISTIAN STORY

"I was born in 1870 down the Ottawa River, at Oka, which is an Algonquin Indian word meaning 'Pickerel.'   My people were all Roman Catholics, but just about the time I was born a general conversion of nearly all the Indians in the reservation occurred.   They turned Protestants and became Methodists.   It came about through one of the priests who had been educated for the priesthood finding a Bible.   He kept studying it in secret; and found it taught something very different from what he had learned.   He left the church, and persuaded his friends to renounce Roman Catholicism and follow the teachings of the Book.

Then a persecution came, and the Indians had to leave and go to Muskoka, Northern Ontario.   At about 16 years of age, I was converted through the preaching of my father, a native missionary to the Indians.   I remember that he would urge me, being his only son, to become a Christian that he might better urge other young men to become Christians.   The result was that I was never happy until I gave my heart to Christ.   Later I went to college, and became interested in music.   While there I was leader of the Glee Club.   I came to Ottawa in 1893, entered a church choir, and now I am director of the choir at the Stewarton Presbyterian Church."

A number of visitors came from long distances to attend the meetings.   One of these was Mr. H. Wellington Wood, of

Philadelphia, who gave up a pleasure trip to the seashore or mountains during his vacation, in order to get more fire and win more souls in the revival meetings. Another visitor was Benjamin M. Brown, of Cleveland, Ohio. Mr. Brown was a special insurance agent, making $5,000 a year, but he gave up three weeks' time to take part in the meetings and help win the business men of Ottawa to Christ. He is an enthusiastic personal worker. He believes it should be done with the persistency and business sagacity of an insurance agent. Mr. Brown is now one of the secretaries of the Presbyterian Board of Foreign Missions in Chicago; and he still makes personal soul-winning the chief business of his life; but, strangely enough, the man he helped most was a man far remote from the business world.

PUGILIST ALLEN SUCCUMBS

This brings me to the story of the most interesting and remarkable convert of the Ottawa campaign, Mr. Alf. Allen, the champion middleweight pugilist of Canada. One night he was wandering in a drunken condition through the streets of Ottawa. He had been on a spree for two months. Seeing people entering Dey's Rink, he accompanied them, led by God's Spirit. That night, drunk as he was, he found Christ; and he has been a saved and sober man ever since. The story of his conversion and transformation reads like a chapter from the Acts of the Apostles.

As Alf. Allen sat in the meeting that night, the sermon and the songs stirred his soul so that he had a longing completely to change his mode of living. At the conclusion of the service a worker led him down to the front, where, in God's mysterious Providence, he was successively dealt with by three of the best personal workers in the Mission. First, Mr. Jacoby talked and prayed with him like a brother. Then he fell into the hands of H. Wellington Wood, who, with his usual energy, drove the truths of the Gospel into the heart of the pugilist. As there were no meetings on the following day Mr. Allen did not leave his bed, lest if he should go outside he would be too strongly tempted to drink. On the following day, which was Sunday, he strolled out into the park before going to the Rink, and there met Benjamin M. Brown, a Cleveland soul-winner. With him he went to the meeting; and, after a stirring sermon by Dr. Torrey on "Heroes and Cowards," he went forward and publicly confessed Christ. As was the case with Sam Small in Atlanta, a thrill ran through the audience, as it was whispered about that Alf. Allen, the champion pugilist, was at the front. At the end of the meeting a large number of the choir gathered around the pugilist; and, as one after another grasped his hand, they sang again and again the chorus of the popular revival melody "Grace Enough for Me."

The next day when I talked with Mr. Allen, he declared he was through with prize fighting, and that he had never been so happy before in his life. When asked about his past career, he said:

HIS WRETCHED PAST

"I had never been in church but twice in my life; once when I was a boy, and once when I was married. I left home when a boy of 14, and went out to the Flathead Reservation in Montana, living with the wild people there for quite a few years. I came back, and have been here something like 15 years. I was in the saloon business four years. I have been drinking all my life, and living the hardest, wickedest life I knew how. I was drunk almost all the time.

"I made $20,000 fighting and running the saloon, and lost it in four years. About three years ago I lost my saloon. I was drunk for two years. I went home, and they tried to keep me straight; but I began to see green ribbons and snakes and hear dogs barking, and they couldn't do anything with me. Finally they sent me to the Central Prison, where I served six months, and came out last January.

"In April I fought Jack Monroe—the Butte miner—at Hull for eight rounds. Then I went down to Maine where I made over $200, and blew it in in a week's spree at Montreal. I came back to Ottawa, and in some way wandered into Dey's Rink last Friday night, after having been drunk for two months.

"I don't remember anything about the sermon. I remember that some one took me up front, and I promised to come again on Sunday night. To keep from drinking on Saturday I stayed in bed all day at my hotel.

"Now my old life seems away off; I don't want to think of it. I don't want to go near a saloon again, and I'll never put another glove on. I have no inclination for them. I never in all my life put in such a day as to-day. Yesterday was the happiest day of my life; but to-day is even happier than yesterday."

Following Mr. Allen's stand for Christ Mr. Brown went about with him day and night, building him up in the faith, and encouraging him to begin witnessing for Christ. Before the campaign closed the evangelists suggested to Mr. Allen that he go to the Moody Bible Institute. He eagerly welcomed the plan, saying that now his one object in life was to win others to the Saviour he had found. Through the assistance of several Christian friends and others, Mr. Allen went to Cleveland with Mr. Brown, where he gave a stirring testimony in the open air, and then Mr. Brown accompanied him to Chicago, where he never rested until he saw Allen installed in the Institute. And it all occurred within three weeks after the pugilist's conversion at the conclusion of a two months' spree. Many times I have heard Mr. Allen refer to that rapid metamorphosis from one life to another, and declare that the goodness of the Lord in being so gracious to him after he had treated Him so shamefully was past understanding. It melted down his heart to think of it.

At the Bible Institute Mr. Allen made excellent progress. At that time Mr. Alexander's brother, Homer Alexander, and another gentleman were conducting services at various Chicago churches, and frequently took Mr. Allen with them to give his testimony. It never failed to move the hearts of the audience.

When I visited the Institute I found Mr. Allen's face radiant with the love of Christ. The Devil strongly tempted him in Chicago, but he conquered through Christ. On one occasion he was sadly in need of funds when some sporting men offered him hundreds of dollars if he would only fight one battle and that under an assumed name. But the tempter was vanquished; and day by day Mr. Allen grew in grace and the knowledge of Christ as he spent hours studying God's Word and daily doing soul-winning. Once Mr. Allen grasped my hand warmly, and declared that for several days in succession he had had the unspeakable joy of leading one soul daily into a knowledge of the truth.

It is now over a year since Mr. Allen entered the Institute; and recently his grades in Synthetic Bible Study were among the highest in the class. He is one of the brightest trophies of God's grace during the American campaign of the evangelists. After a year or two of study Mr. Allen hopes to return to Canada, to carry on Mission work among his former companions and others.

CAMPAIGN STATISTICS

The Ottawa campaign closed six months of work in America during which nearly 15,000 publicly confessed Christ. This made a total of over 115,000 during the four and a half years' tour of the world, or an average of 25,000 per year. It constituted a world-wide work which, in many respects, had not been equalled in the history of the Christian Church. It was a triumph, not of men, but of prayer and of faith in God; and had it occurred in the days of old it would surely have found a place among the triumphs recorded in the eleventh chapter of Hebrews, where, through this faith, the heroes of old "wrought righteousness," "subdued kingdoms," and "turned to flight the armies of the aliens."

At the close of the movement in Ottawa Dr. Torrey returned to the United States; while Mr. Alexander hurried homeward to Birmingham, England, where his wife lay ill.

How Mr. Alexander was prevented from working with Dr. Torrey the next year, but, instead, made a second tour of the world, will be related in part two of this volume.

XXIII

EXPERIENCES ON SHIPBOARD

It was through the illness of his wife that Mr. Alexander was prevented from returning to the United States to continue his work with Dr. Torrey; but took, instead, the journey around the world with his wife that the sea air might completely restore her health. This course was decided upon, not only as the result of his own judgment and the urgent advice of the physicians, but with the hearty and cordial concurrence of Dr. Torrey.

So it came about that Mr. Alexander made a second-world tour; and, though it was undertaken primarily for the benefit of his wife's health, it also was a notable soul-winning journey, as the following pages will abundantly witness. It was not the writer's privilege to accompany Mr. Alexander on this second tour, but I met him in England immediately upon his return home, and a few days later worked with him almost constantly, securing from his own lips the graphic description, which follows, of the experiences of his wife and himself as they girdled the globe.

It was at his home, called "Tennessee," at Moor Green, Birmingham, England, that I met Mr. Alexander on his return from his second tour. He was in the best of health; and seemed to be thoroughly rested after the strain of over twelve years of almost continuous revival work. As I looked at his face, after a year's separation, I realized as never before the depth of the man's sympathy and the power of his big-hearted love. It is little wonder that everywhere he went, on the second journey, as well as the first, he won the good will and affection—of tens of thousands. He loves the Lord Jesus Christ; and it is the love of Christ shining out through his words and actions which draws people to him. It is simply a modern version of the eternal truth, "And I, if I be lifted up, will draw all men unto me."

As we sat in Mr. Alexander's study one morning in July, 1907, he began the narrative of his second journey by giving a brief itinerary of the trip, and relating some of their experiences on ship-board. He said:

MRS. ALEXANDER'S ILLNESS

"After four and a half years' work with Dr. Torrey, I bade good-bye to him in Ottawa, Canada, at the end of June, 1906. We had accepted invitations and arranged Missions in the States for the coming year, fully expecting to work together. I returned to my home in Birmingham, England, to spend my vacation with my wife, who had been too ill to accompany me to America. After four happy days together she had a sudden turn for the worse; and the doctors were hastily called in and performed a dangerous operation. At this critical juncture I cabled to America to praying friends; and indeed thousands of people on both sides of the Atlantic were praying for her recovery.

"Before leaving America I had written to a special Prayer Circle in the State of Iowa. When I am in trouble or need guidance, I always ask them to pray. I had told them that probably an operation would be necessary soon after I reached

INDIAN GIRLS IN A MISSION SCHOOL IN BOMBAY, INDIA

home; but it had to take place six days earlier than the date I had given. I cabled immediately beforehand to the praying group. One of the most godly members was away in another part of the State when the cablegram arrived. They were praying, but had not been able to send the message on to this member. The next day they received a letter from her saying that at a certain hour in the day she had such a strong impression that Mrs. Alexander needed help, that she was led out in an agony of prayer for a long season, and had wrestled with God for her.

"We were also praying earnestly here at home. The doctors made several visits each day. While they were with my wife, we would be downstairs praying that God would give them wisdom. She gradually grew better, and we all believe her recovery was in direct answer to prayer.

"The doctors said she must be kept upon the sea for many months to come to ensure a complete recovery. Our minds immediately turned to China where my wife's sister and her husband, Dr. Neville Bradley, had gone a year before to take charge of a C. M. S. Mission Station and hospital at Pakhoi, which is on the coast, about 400 miles south of Hong-Kong. My wife's mother and youngest sister had gone on before for a long visit with them. So we decided to go round the world, visiting China on the way. Leaving London on November 23, we made all the long journey chiefly by water. We visited Port Said and Colombo and the Straits Settlements, and reached Hong-Kong on December 29. We spent about two months in China, and went on to Australia, visiting the Philippine Islands on the way. After a month spent in visiting friends and holding meetings in some of the leading cities of Australia, we returned to England via America. The entire journey occupied about seven months.

THE OCEAN VOYAGE

"When we left England a large number of friends came to Tilbury Docks to see us off on the P. & O. steamship *India*. A young doctor, Hubert Gordon-Thompson, of Liverpool, was going out to assist my brother-in-law, Dr. Bradley, in his medical mission work; and so we had arranged to go on the same ship. His mother tenderly asked us to cheer her boy and be kind to him on the voyage, which of course we gladly did. As the tender left the side of our steamship, bearing our loved ones back to shore, a photograph was secured, showing Dr. Thompson's hand as he was waving good-bye to his mother in the distance.

"Before leaving, we had asked our friends everywhere to pray especially that, wherever we were on land or sea, we might be good witnesses for the Lord Jesus Christ, and the many opportunities that opened, and the results from some of them proved to us that prayer had gone up and was answered. By the time we had reached Port Said we had become acquainted with a large number of people. A clergyman came to see us while the ship was lying in dock; and told us about some American missionaries whom he had visited that morning, who had a school in the heart of the Arab town, and that they would be glad to see us. We three soon started to visit them; and we found a most interesting school, with about 100 pupils. The whole cost of running the school was only $150 a month—one of the cheapest missionary enterprises I have ever seen which was accomplishing anything.

We tried to encourage them in every way we could; and were interested in finding out the effect different Gospel hymns had had upon the lives of the pupils. They narrated story after story how the children went back to their heathen homes; and, even after they had married heathen husbands and were not yet Christians themselves, they would continue to sing the hymns, which God might use to their salvation. When they saw how interested I was in that part of their work, they took me into their little dining-room and showed me a small harmonium which Mr. Sankey had used for some time in his work in America. They treasure it with great care. After hearing some experiences of our own work in saving the lost, and listening to some of theirs, we closed our short visit with a time of prayer, which they said gave them a great uplift.

"Returning to our ship we went on our way, and were interested as we passed up the other end of the Suez Canal to hear from the lips of the Bishop of New Zealand, who was standing near us on the deck, that just a few miles thence was what was thought to be the place where the children of Israel passed across, and where Pharaoh's host was drowned. Each day that followed was packed with interest.

BETTING ON THE SHIP'S SPEED

"After we had been at sea a few days some of the men began to go among the passengers to collect money for sweepstakes on the day's run of the ship. When they approached me I did not understand at first what this money was to go for; and asked the collector if there was any form of gambling in it. He said, 'yes,' there was a phase of lottery in it. I told him that I would be glad to contribute to anything else that would be for the enjoyment of others; but I could not possibly join them in that. I noticed that almost everybody—men, women and children—joined in this kind of gambling. It seemed to grow more exciting each day, until they began to have what they called "Calcutta Sweepstakes." After the money is collected the choices are put up at auction; and one day a woman won 300 dollars by choosing the lucky number. I noticed a large number of passengers congratulating her, and crowding round her, and she seemed highly delighted. I watched this in its different aspects during the trip. I learned to know several young men who were on their way to the East, whither they were going to take positions in business. Some of them gambled so heavily that they had to borrow money before they could land at their destination. I talked with one Scotch boy, the son of a minister. My wife and I engaged him in conversation at different times when he appeared lonely; and we found that he was beginning to indulge in things on board which he had never done before, supposing that in order to be thought a man he must take up these practices. We were glad to see that he seemed to drop them again.

"In my conversation I found that many who were church members indulged as freely in the daily lottery as did others. One day I was sitting on the deck with an Australian gentleman. I was speaking in glowing terms of Australia and her people. He said that he was proud of Australia; but there was one thing that was becoming a great blight upon the country. He said he had been a member of the Government and had often made speeches against the gambling which was

spreading like wild-fire over part of the country. I compli-
mented him upon this stand. We were going into some
details about it, when I noticed two men making the regular
daily round to collect the sweepstakes on the run. I supposed
when they reached him that he would indignantly refuse after
such a warm arraignment of gambling. On they came. They
knew where I stood; and, passing me by said, calling him by
name, 'We want your money now.' He said, 'How much?'
They named the sum, and he sat up, put his hand in his pocket
and meekly handed it over with a smile.

"I said, 'I thought you were opposed to gambling in all of its
forms, and had made speeches against it?'

" 'Yes,' he said, 'I have.'

"I said, 'Why don't you quit it yourself? No man is ever
able to win a case by compromise. Here are young men on
this ship who look up to you as an example; and you go with
the crowd and gamble with them, and then go home and make
great speeches against it.'

"He said he had the same criticism passed upon his conduct before. Very soon they began to sell the sweepstakes at
the other end. He stood up and looked along the deck, and
said, 'Well, I am ashamed of myself. Here I have put my
money into that sweepstake, and the very form of gambling I
abhor has been encouraged with my money.'

GOSPEL SONGS IN THE SALOON

"When they began to prepare for the concert in the saloon
they asked me if I would sing. I told them I never sang
anything in public but Gospel songs. If they would like me
to sing one of these I would gladly do it. I sang the song,

'Was That Somebody You?' one of the most appropriate for an occasion like this.

"Another time I sang Mr. Harkness's new song, 'No Burdens Yonder.' I had some leaflets with it in, and gave them away to those who wanted them. Most of them were eager for them. Two or three asked for them that they might send them home to their wives. When I sang these two Gospel songs they knew where I stood; and it opened up several conversations. I have noticed that, on all of the boats where I have sung, some person with a heavy heart comes to me sooner or later; and I have the privilege of pointing him to Jesus. I heard various people playing the songs over on the piano and humming them quietly at different times afterwards.

"Dr. Thompson, my wife and I used to have our little time together in the evening to report the day's work, read a chapter and have a prayer. This was always a refreshing time. It did our souls good to kneel before our Father and get new strength to work among the scores of those who cared for nothing but drinking and card-playing.

"We reached Colombo, Ceylon, on a Sunday morning. I never expected any one would be there to meet us, for we were not acquainted with any one, but we were pleasantly surprised to be met by the Y. M. C. A. Secretary, who had read a book concerning our work, and knew that we were on board the boat. He took us ashore; and went with us to an English Church where we enjoyed a hearty service. The congregation was made up of both white people and natives. Outside the church there were cocoanut palms full of fruit—smooth, round, green balls. The clergyman took us all up to the

Church Missionary Society house for tiffin. It was a typical Ceylon bungalow with wide verandas, and a large open guest-room in front, separated from the dining and living rooms only by screens, so that it might be as cool and airy as possible. We found there two missionaries from Australia, who had been in our Missions five years before.

"At two o'clock we sailed away in another P. & O. boat, the *Delta,* for Hong-Kong. We went ashore at Penang, and at Singapore, where three young business men left their work and came down to the ship to welcome us. We could be there only a few hours; and they kindly volunteered to show us the place. What interested us most of all was to hear about the different lines of work these friends were carrying on. They hold various meetings, and Bible classes; and every Sunday morning some of them go down to the steamer docks about two miles away from the town, and go in and out among the sailors and stewards, doing personal work, distributing Christian literature, and inviting them to the meetings if they go ashore. In this far-away city wickedness of every kind is rampant; but it was beautiful to see these men standing true to our Lord and witnessing for him. We managed to introduce them to our young friend from Scotland, the minister's son. He had told us about his home on the moors, and the free simple life full of sea adventures up in the islands; and we wanted to get him in touch with the right kind of things in Singapore. We had a season of prayer on board the ship before we said good-bye to our new friends. Finding that they needed some Gospel hymn-books, I sent them some for their work, besides arranging for them to have a number of Mr. Moody's works."

XXIV

A NEW YEAR TEXT SELECTED

It will be remembered that during his first tour of the world, Mr. Alexander adopted a year text which led to several conversions, and the story of which was told and retold all over Christendom. During the second journey, a new one, was adopted, the narrative of which has already been a help and comfort to many. Mr. Alexander said:

"We spent our Christmas on the sea, and it was touching to see how the passengers vied with one another in making it a happy day. Very early in the morning we were awakened by the sound of singing just outside our cabin; and found that the stewards had gathered to sing the 'Glory Song,' followed by several Christmas Carols, in honor of the day.

"On reaching Hong-Kong we bade good-bye to our friends on board the *Delta;* but we had managed to do some personal work with several before leaving. I have never seen a description of Hong-Kong that did it justice. As we sailed into the harbor it seemed that anything we had heard of it came far short of what it really is. When our tender drew up to the dock, two friends were there to meet us, the Secretary of the Y. M. C. A., and Archdeacon Banister, who made us feel at home immediately. That afternoon at the Peak Hotel several Christian people promptly called upon us and gave us a warm welcome. Dr. Bradley came to Hong-Kong a few days later to take us back with him to Pakhoi.

"We spent New Year's Eve in that far-away place. There were only four of us in our sitting-room at the Peak Hotel—Dr. Bradley, Dr. Thompson, my wife and myself. I proposed that we should have a prayer-meeting that would last out the old year and into the new. We had a blessed time in prayer for about an hour; and when we rose from our knees I suggested that we should choose a Year Verse the first thing in the new year, to be our motto all through it. We easily settled upon that old verse which is so familiar to lovers of the New Testament, John 14: 1—'Let not your heart be troubled: ye believe in God, believe also in me.' We wondered why we were led to choose this, little dreaming how precious it would become to us before our journey was finished.

SHOUTED SCRIPTURE FAREWELLS

"In the short time that we had remaining in Hong-Kong, we enlisted several others to adopt this verse as their Year-Text also. The day we left the landing-stage for the small coasting steamer which was to take us to Pakhoi, a young doctor, whose acquaintance we had made, and the Y. M. C. A. Secretary were there to see us off. As our boat steamed out across the water, we waved farewell; and, instead of calling out 'good-bye,' shouted 'John-Fourteen-One' to them, and they answered with the same. As long as we could hear each other we shouted it back and forth. It reminded me of the time when I shouted 'Second-Timothy-Two-Fifteen' to the man on the back of the train in America, but I hardly hoped to hear from this as I had done from the other.

"Five weeks later I held a meeting in the theatre in Hong-Kong. The Y. M. C. A. Secretary who had called 'John-

Fourteen-One' to us from the landing-stage, told me that the manager of the press-room, where the printing of our song-sheets was done, had told him that he was a Scotchman from a Christian home, and that he happened to be down on the landing-stage one morning, and heard some people shouting 'John-Fourteen-One' back and forth. He said he was far from being a Christian; but it impressed him so much that he went home and took down his unused Bible and looked it up, and from that day on he was unable to get it out of his mind, and that he would like to see me. The last morning I was there, I had only a few minutes; but I went around and talked to him. I found him a fine Scotchman, but he needed the Lord Jesus Christ. I asked him if the influence of his father and mother had not followed him all the way out there, and he said 'yes.' He knew the way and was deeply impressed. He held my hand, while the tears started from his eyes. I could not remain longer, for my ship was sailing shortly. He did not decide immediately; but said that he would write me when he had decided. I have not received the letter, but I often pray for him.

"Everything was of interest as we sailed into Pakhoi. It was so entirely Chinese. The customs boat took us off the ship. In the distance, as we neared the shore, we saw some people in European dress; and it was most touching to see my wife's eagerness, as she looked through the field-glasses, to see whether they were her mother and sisters. It was a happy reunion. After our greetings, and when we had settled in our rooms, we met together; and our mother, Mrs. Cadbury, and our two sisters, Mrs. Bradley and Miss Beatrice Cadbury, all joined us in taking John 14: 1 as their Year-Text.

Another who took it with us was Mrs. Beauchamp, whose late husband was for many years a missionary in Pakhoi, and who now lives with Dr. and Mrs. Bradley. A few days later we went up to Liem-chau, 17 miles from Pakhoi, where the Year-Text was adopted by Mr. and Mrs. Wicks, and Mr. Norman Mackenzie, the only three English (C.M.S.) missionaries in that place.

"Let me show you how much each one of us needed just that verse, and how precious it has proved to us during the various experiences that have befallen us in the six months since we adopted it.

ACCIDENT TO MR. ALEXANDER

"One afternoon during our stay in Pakhoi we went out for a ride across the country. They have no roads out there; and one has to follow the rough paths as best he can. My horse was a fiery animal, and dashed across the plain where the country was very rough. In the middle of a gallop he trod into a deep rut and stumbled headlong, fortunately hurling me beyond the reach of his hoofs as he rolled over. I never knew anything about it until the next afternoon, for I did not recover full consciousness till then. My brother-in-law was with me, and managed to get me into a native carrying-chair, and had me carried back the two miles home. My wife was farther on in front; and a message was sent to tell her that I was seriously injured. She said her heart almost failed her as she followed on as fast as she could, for she did not know whether she should find me alive or not. She told me afterwards that her one comfort, every step she took, was our verse, 'Let not your heart be troubled.' She said she knew then why she had been led to take that as her Year-Text. It was an anxious time for all of them, and the verse was much comfort to the company.

"To our youngest sister, a few months later, there came one of the most trying times that can come to any one in this world. As she returned from China with Mrs. Cadbury, across the Pacific to America, in a moment of time she was deprived of her mother. During a heavy storm Mrs. Cadbury had started up the companionway, and had almost reached the top, when a sudden lurch of the ship threw her backwards. She fell to the bottom of the stairs, and received such injuries that she passed away, without having regained consciousness. Then it was that John 14: 1 became a living word to our bereaved sister.

"We were in New York City when we learned of the accident; and again this verse was our stay and comfort in the midst of our sorrow.

MISSIONARIES HAVE TO FLEE

"Many of my readers have seen the reports of the troublous times in Pakhoi and Liem-chau which have recently been experienced by the missionaries in those districts. I have just read of their striking experiences. Mr. and Mrs. Wicks were seated at their noon-day meal when they heard that the rebels were surrounding their house. They hurriedly escaped, leaving everything in their home, which was looted from top to bottom. They spent a few days in the house of a military official, guarded by soldiers; and later were escorted during the night-time by fifty soldiers down to Pakhoi. One night, during the disturbances, such rumors reached Pakhoi, that the Consul ordered the missionaries to take their wives and children and the other ladies on to a British ship which lay in the harbor. For that night Dr. Gordon-Thompson was left alone in the Mission compound, and was thus led to lean upon that verse—'Let not your heart be troubled: ye believe in God, believe also in me.' They returned to shore next day; and all the missionaries lived together in Dr. Bradley's house, as being the most central point of the Mission.

"It was during these fearful times, that Mrs. Bradley also received the sad news of her mother's death. I suppose no better verse in the Bible than our Year-Text could have been chosen for her at this time. The ladies and children had finally to leave Pakhoi altogether, and were sent to Hong-Kong, leaving behind the men of the Mission; thus bringing added anxiety to Dr. and Mrs. Bradley in their time of sorrow, in which the strength of John 14: 1 was revealed yet more clearly. I have just had a letter from Mr. Mackenzie, who is now in England on a vacation from his Mission field, in which he tells me that his mother is lying seriously ill in the hospital in this country, and that his books, furniture and home have all been destroyed by the rebels in Liem-chau. He was one of the number who most eargerly chose John 14: 1. He, too, is passing through a testing time, in which he finds his Year-Text is all sufficient for the need."

XXV

AMONG THE LEPERS AT PAKHOI

At Pakhoi Mr. Alexander had his first experience among lepers. He gave a graphic description of their condition and occupations; and told of the difficulties which occurred in connection with their printing the Bible, saying:

"Dr. and Mrs. Bradley fitted up two large rooms for us several hundreds yards away from their house. The man who was to wait upon us could not speak a word of English; so we had to do the best we could with signs, and a few stray words of Chinese which we could muster. Just over a low brick wall from us were the two leper compounds. Our rooms were at one end of the long hospital building; and in the leper compounds there were about ninety men and forty-seven women. I had read at different times of work among the lepers; and wondered if any one could go in and out among them without risk of infection. But soon it became a custom to go over and visit them, speaking to them through an interpreter. They were always keenly interested to talk on any subject we could introduce. They had Bible examinations while we were there; and we asked them to state some of their questions. I do not believe Bible students in this country would give better answers than they gave. Most of them could not read when they entered the compound, but have been taught to do so; and, now that some of them are well educated, they themselves help in instructing others. They have nice rooms furnished for them and so much allowance for rice. They do their own cooking. I recall especially the long low building bricked up at one side and open at the other, where there were probably fifty or sixty little Chinese fire places with quaint bellows at the side, which would quickly blow up their fire when they chose to cook a meal.

THE LEPERS' DAILY LIFE

"These lepers are very industrious. They spend a certain part of the day in a school room, where you would see little boys in their teens up to old men between 60 and 80 in the same class, eagerly studying the lessons planned by the teachers. At other times they are engaged in various occupations; some making baskets, others making twine. They are allowed to go out into the towns to sell their products and retain the proceeds of the sale. I think it is a wise arrangement. It encourages them in industry, and develops the individual. The work is supported mostly by funds received from friends in England. The women and the girls are taught to make lace. This, like the other goods made by the lepers, is disinfected; and some of it is exported for sale, the money being used to carry on the work.

"When we first stepped into their quarters, I expected to see some of the most morbid people that I had ever met; but, to my surprise, they were as cheerful as any other people we saw while we were away. One day one of the men was making some peculiar motions while he was twisting the twine. I stepped up beside him, and began to imitate him with his funny movements; and all of the men who had been watching me burst out laughing as heartily as a crowd of Englishmen would do. Their appearance is pitiful in the extreme, but one soon forgets as he sees their cheerfulness. Many of them were bright Christians. The leper who was the head Bible teacher for the compound had only one leg and had other deformities; but he was always kind and hopeful. In spite of their infirmities the lepers conduct a well-equipped printing office. Mrs. Beauchamp, who for years has been interested in that department of the work, told me how on one of her vacations she went to a printing office and learned how to set type and also to use a printing press. Then she purchased an outfit, and brought it back and fitted up these offices, which have given several of the lepers employment for years.

"The first morning I was shown through the office. One of the missionaries introduced me to the men; and I was especially struck with the face of the office foreman. He had such an open countenance, which beamed with love and gentleness. I asked Mrs. Beauchamp to interpret to him that I was sure he must love his Saviour, judged by his looks. She translated my remark. His face was radiant as he replied, 'My Saviour, Jesus Christ, is very precious to me; more precious than anything on earth.' I began to ask questions about the work; and found that Mrs. Beauchamp and her sister, Mrs. Horder, who had gone with her husband to England because of ill health, have been working for years on a Romanized version of the Bible for the Chinese.

PRINTING BIBLES FOR CHINESE

"It takes several years for the Chinese to learn to read the characters of their own language; but, by spelling with Roman letters in their local dialect, they learn it in a few months.

MRS. HUME AND SOME OF HER PUPILS IN INDIA

Many educated people object to the Romanized editions; but I thought one of the missionaries gave a very strong argument for it when she said that some of the lepers died in a few months after they entered the compound, and many of them died before they learned the Chinese characters. She preferred to put aside the whims of a few fastidious critics, and let the poor heathen know about Jesus Christ, no matter if the message was not conveyed to them in the highest literary form; thus following out Paul's injunction, 'by all means save some.'

"The printing press was not a very large one. They could print only a sixteen-page sheet on one side. They had no method of making the electrotypes; so, as soon as they printed a thousand copies on the sixteen-page sheet, the type had to be distributed and set up again for the next sixteen pages of the Bible. This is a long process, and not the way printing is done in this country. They had been about eight years printing the Bible. While I was there they printed the last sixteen pages of the old Testament, which completed the book, as the thousand copies of the New Testament had been printed first. They had stored away the sheets as they had printed them; and, as soon as the last pages were finished, they opened up the other cases, so that they might bind them into book form; when to their astonishment and dismay they found that the white ants had cut through almost every page of half the New Testament copies and had ruined the work of years. When asked what they were going to do, they said: 'We are going to start again and do it over,' and when I le´ : they

"Each day at Pakhoi was filled with interest; and our family were beginning the long task with undaunted courage.

Prayers morning and evening were rich with blessing.   I was glad to observe that through all the distractions, perplexities and cares of that large Mission station, my brother and his wife never lost sight of the main issue of their work, to lead people to a definite decision for Jesus Christ."

XXVI

A JOURNEY TO LIEM-CHAU

DURING his stay in Pakhoi, Mr. Alexander made a journey to Liem-Chau, a typical Chinese city, where a few missionaries had been doing heroic work for years. It was only a short time after his visit that the homes of the missionaries were looted, and they had to fly for their lives. Mr. Alexander said:

"I had heard much about the work at Liem-chau, 17 miles away, and was glad of an opportunity of visiting it. As we got into our Chinese carrying-chairs one day and started across the plain on our journey there, we made a long procession, and what an interesting trip it was! The rest-houses along the road, where the chair-carriers stopped for their rice, made interesting breaks in our journey. The moment we stood face to face with our Liem-chau friends we knew we were in the presence of Spirit-filled people. After our lunch we went out to look about the place; and on the hillside above us I saw a man of striking appearance, near to a Hindoo temple. He waved to the missionary who was with us, and I asked who he was. Mr. Wicks said that he was a Buddhist monk, and asked me if I would like to meet him. I said 'Yes; and we went up and I was introduced to him. Of course, he could not speak English, and I could not speak Chinese; but we had a pleasant conversation with Mr. Wicks as interpreter. I asked him many things about his religion and his work; and

he talked freely about them and invited me to see the temple.
I went in and looked about. He asked us to his private room
in the temple. While in there I began to talk to him about
Jesus Christ and his claims upon us. He seemed to agree
easily with all that I said; but said that he must make a living,
which he did by attending to his duties as a Buddhist priest.   I
had a copy of a Gospel Song pamphlet in my pocket; and
asked him if he would like to hear one of our songs. He said
he would be glad to hear it; and I sang one which we have
sung so much in our Missions everywhere.

> " 'I surrender all, I surrender all!
> All to thee, my blessed Saviour, I surrender all.'

and then asked Mr. Wicks to tell him what it meant and what
it brought with it.   As we were walking down the temple steps
I noticed a beautiful jade bracelet on his wrist; and spoke
about it.   He immediately pulled it off and gave it to me; and
I gave him a song book and a little pocketbook that I had; and
told him that I wanted him to remember that a man would be
praying that he might accept Christ as his Saviour.

CHINESE EAGER TO LEARN

"That night in the Wicks house we were eating our dinner
in one end of a large room on the ground floor, which was
partitioned off from the rest by a few wooden screens, when
we heard noises over the screens. Soon yellow faces began
to peer around the screens from the other side; and the missionary said it was a common occurrence. The people would
often creep in, to look at strangers, when they came. They
sent a message in to us to ask us if we would have some sing-

THE LEPER PRINTING OFFICE AT PAKHOI, CHINA

ing and talking after we had finished our dinner. This we did; and I found that they had already been using some of the hymns which we used in our Missions in this country. I told them of incidents in connection with different hymns we sang, which were interpreted by Mr. Wicks to them. Then my wife spoke for a little while. The women seated at one side of the hall, and men at the other, would ask questions back and forth, and seemed interested; and the crowd kept growing until it was so late that we had to ask them to go away. But the dusky faces were as inspiring as if they had belonged to white people, who could understand the English language.

"My wife and her mother, Mrs. Cadbury, stayed with Mr. and Mrs. Wicks in their house that night. Dr. Bradley and I went to another part of the city; and stayed with Mr. Norman Mackenzie, a young Australian, who had lived in the house of a Chinaman for five years. He explained to us how he would take his Chinese assistants and go through the country for weeks at a time, sleeping in the Chinese inns, talking about Jesus wherever he could get any one to listen to him. He had trained his colporters; and a unique part of his work I want to tell you about was this. He told me he sold almanacs. I said, 'What do you mean? Why do you sell almanacs?' He explained that the Chinese did not care nearly so much for a book that was given to them, as one which they had paid for, and that they all wanted reliable almanacs, if they could afford only to have one book. The Mission Board had prepared a splendid and reliable almanac, based on the Chinese calendar; and had printed on it extracts from the Gospel and Christian literature. They sold thousands of these almanacs at such a price that the Chinese wondered how it could be done; but they bought them, and in this way people were reached who could not be reached in any other way. There were only a few Christians in Liem-chau, but they stood firm and rejoiced in persecution. I should like to say here that missionaries are the most truly happy people I have ever met, although we often here at home pity them. It was beautiful to see what little note they took of all kinds of privations, which would cause plenty of grumbling in some Christian homes.

MINGLE HEALING AND EXHORTING

"The next morning the people began to come into Mr. Wick's big room from every direction. They had heard that the great English doctor would be there on that day. The room was filled with men and women; men on the one side and women on the other, with all kinds of diseases and pains. Mrs. Wicks had screened off a little room in one corner, for a consulting room and dispensary combined. While they were waiting to go in, one at a time, to be treated, and receive their medicine, the missionaries and native helpers were there with their Bibles, doing personal work all the morning long. There was a hum of conversation all about the room as they gathered in little groups. This was as fine a piece of personal work as I have seen in any after-meeting. Mrs. Wicks acted as interpreter for Dr. Bradley, while the women were going in; and I would ask every now and then what she was saying to the women, and found that she let no opportunity pass for getting in a word about their soul as well as their body. And she did it with such a warmth of love in her face, that, although I could not understand her words, I saw that her message was going home. Then Mr. Wicks interpreted when the men began to come in. I suppose a hundred and fifty people passed through the consulting room that morning; and they all received a message about Jesus Christ and his power to save.

"A fine-looking young Chinaman came up to Mr. Wicks; and asked if I would take a picture of him and his wife and baby, for they had never had a photograph taken. I told him I would gladly do it. He and his wife were both earnest Christians, and he was the school teacher. His name was Mr. So. After I had taken the photographs he brought his new Chinese Testament around for me to put my name in. I wrote my name and 'II. Timothy 2: 15' underneath it. He asked what I had written; and, as I told him, I saw a quick flash in his face, and he began to talk rapidly to Mr. Wicks. Mr. Wicks told me that he said 'Oh yes, those are the words that he called out to the man on the back of the train in the far-away country. I read the story in a Chinese paper that came from Shanghai.' I questioned him, through Mr. Wicks, and found that he remembered the whole story distinctly.

"The medical side to Mission work opens up places where nothing else would gain an entrance. The wife of a mandarin brought her little son over for an operation on his jaw; and then asked my wife and mother to call on her that afternoon. They went over with Mrs. Wicks, and made the acquaintance of the family. In this way the missionaries gain an entrance.

MISSIONARIES' HOMES LOOTED

"We were sorry when the time came to bid good-bye to our friends; and little did we think that the new home just built would so soon be looted and destroyed; for Liem-chau was one of the scenes where the recent serious disturbances and riots in China have taken place. Day after day the newspapers have told of the destruction wrought by the mob in this city, and the dangers which surrounded the foreign inhabitants. The house of our hosts, Mr. and Mrs. Wicks, was looted and everything in it destroyed; also that of Mr. Mackenzie.

"We have received recently a number of letters, telling of the thrilling experiences of our missionary friends and relatives in the midst of these disturbances in Liem-chau and Pakhoi. In one of them Dr. Bradley writes of the 'trying and anxious time' they have been passing through. On May 25th he says:

"Dr. Thompson arrived back early from Liem-chau on Thursday and reported all quiet, with the exception of a demand made by many hundreds of people for rice, which the officials were unable to meet, except by giving leave to the populace to help themselves at a large rice store, the Liem-chau Fu sitting in his chair at the time. On Thursday afternoon I went to Kotuk as usual, and when I got back just near home I was met by the English Consul's friend, telling me to go at once to the Consulate. I got there and found that a telegram had been sent from So, the teacher at Liem-chau, saying that the Wicks' house had been destroyed and that they had been wounded. The German Mission had been similarly treated. We were greatly upset; and the consuls and we missionaries met together to confer. We received another telegram, saying that the Wicks had escaped on horseback out of the city. It was decided for all the missionaries to be together in our house. Meawhile Thompson and I and our horseman set out on the horses to Liem-chau, hoping to meet the Wicks. We started in a heavy thunderstorm. So in about two minutes we were soaked to the skin. The roads were running with water in places over the horses' knees. Our one thought, however, was to get on, hoping to meet our friends. Where there were two ways, Thompson and I went one way, and A-Saam the other. On the other side of Kotuk we met, and here we stopped, as A-Saam had found the Wicks' coolie. We learned from him that the Wicks were safe in the Liem-chau Fu's yamen, and that they were unhurt.

"He told us that, as they were sitting down to tiffin, they were told that the new Chinese schools, which are of course entirely Chinese and run by the Chinese, no religion being taught of any kind, had been burned to the ground, and that the rebels were now coming to their house. They fortunately acted promptly and departed. Not being able, as we subsequently learned, to reach the Liem-chau Fu's, they went to the Chan-Toi's yamen, who is the head of the military, as it was not very far away. They had not been gone long before their place was entered and ransacked from top to bottom, all the windows were broken; the doors taken off and every article in the house carried off.

REFUGE TAKEN ON SHIPBOARD

"Thompson and I got back to Pakhoi just before seven. There was great excitement as the people were supposed to be marching on Pakhoi. The consuls had had a consultation and decided that all the ladies should go to an English ship, which had arrived that morning. We soon got things together, and the refugees started off. We were happy, but we must have looked a funny crowd, as it was just dark when

we started, and we all were carrying something, either a baby
or a handbag or a box of some description. We got to the
house, which it had been arranged should be occupied by the
men of the community. Here we got into sampans, and were
taken out to a junk, where we found all the other ladies and
children and a few of their belongings. The ship's people
did not expect us that night, and were taken unawares. They
were most kind, and the officers did all they could for us.
They turned out of their cabins, and made us as comfortable as
they could.

"Early next morning I-Shuk came on board with a note from
Thompson, saying that all was quiet, and there had been no
disturbance of any kind during the night. Mr. Blanchett and
I went off together, and came up to the compound. The
Liem-chau Fu and Hoppo had both sent telegrams, saying that
all the missionaries were safe and unhurt. We were glad
about this. It has been very difficult to find out from the
officials the exact state of affairs; and, as they have not been
able to bring the Wicks down yet, we fear that the city must
still be unquiet.

"Just before lunch yesterday all our party arrived off the
ship, and settled in this house for a night or two. We had a
happy time of fellowship together last night; and we all
retired, feeling that we were safe in our Heavenly Father's
keeping. There was no disturbance in the night, and we all
slept peacefully. We shall all keep together in case of emer-
gency. It looks as if things would settle down, although
those who know the Chinese best say that it is most uncertain; and, whilst there is no immediate danger or risk, it is
well to be prepared for whatever may turn up. The imme-

diate cause seems to be dissatisfaction at the taxing of the poor, which takes place to build the Chinese schools. This is borne out by the fact that the rioters first destroyed their own schools by fire and then attacked the Mission property.

VERY DISTURBED CONDITIONS

"In a later letter Dr. Bradley wrote: 'The reports about the insurgents are more reassuring. It looks as though they might be stopped from plundering any more by the government troops. Late on Wednesday night we were disturbed by a loud knocking. I went down and found two rifles and a hundred rounds of ammunition from the English Consul. Returned with thanks. We retained, however, some red flags in case of alarm, so as to signal to other people.'

"A few days later he wrote: 'Our Consul has had bad news about the Chinese troops' being hemmed in by the insurgents, about seven miles from Liem-chau, and that shortly Liem-chau would probably fall into their hands, and then it was a straight run to Pakhoi. The Consul requested that all ladies should leave the port. All our ladies decided to go. After seeing them off I went to the Consulate to find out what they wished us to do. He said that all the male members of the community should sleep at the Commissioner's house. Thompson and I then came to the Compound; and quieted, as best we could, the fears of the people. We had an early dinner and at seven o'clock, armed with walking sticks, made our way to the fortifications.

"'There were six of us all together—Mr. Bach, Mr. Jensen, Mr. Fletcher, Mr. Blanchett, Thompson and myself. We took turn on watch, one hour and a half each. It was a strange feeling as one passed up and down, listening for any sound of the rebels.

'Sunday, June 2nd. To-day all the services will be held as usual. I do hope that things will settle down quickly and that there will be no bloodshed on our account. We expect another British gunboat, and men are bound to be landed in order to protect life and property. The Germans expect another boat also, and eight hundred Chinese soldiers are on their way. I expect that all these provisions will make for peace, and will prevent any serious uprising.' "

MRS. ALEXANDER WATCHING A CHINESE FARMER AT WORK

THE GOSPEL SINGER IN CHINESE COSTUME

XXVII

AT HONG-KONG AND MANILA

Mr. Alexander's meeting in the Theatre at Hong-Kong drew a great throng; and was a striking tribute to the world-wide fame of his work. In describing the experiences of himself and his wife at Hong-Kong and Manila, the Gospel singer continued:

"The days before we left Pakhoi were busy ones, filled with small meetings of all kinds. Dr. and Mrs. Bradley wanted me to meet different groups of native workers and classes. A most interesting occasion was the assembling of the Mission servants and hospital helpers and evangelists; a splendid looking lot of people they were, too. Of course, we had these small gatherings composed entirely of men one time and women another. I could talk only through an interpreter, but grew to like it when I saw the deep interest the people took in all that we said to them.

"When we started down to the shore to board our boat, on the last day, the natives had secured four thousand firecrackers and wrapped them on a long pole, and two big, stout fellows took each an end and started in front of us. Just before we reached the water they set off the fireworks. This was their way of bidding us a ceremonious good-bye.

"We were accompanied to Hong-Kong by our mother, Mrs. Cadbury, her youngest daughter, and Archdeacon Banister who had been to Pakhoi to open the new church. We spent

a Sunday on board during the trip.   The only place where passengers could meet one another was the dining-room; and
we found the captain a kindly, cordial man.   On Sunday night
after dinner was over, we were sitting around the table, talking for some time.   Of course, there were not many passengers on that small boat, and nearly all were in the saloon
together, when my wife asked the captain if he would be
willing for the Archdeacon to read a chapter in the Bible
and have evening prayer, as most of them were accustomed to it when they were in their homes.   He said he
would be delighted to have him do it; so the Archdeacon read
and prayed.   Returning to Pakhoi a few days later on the
same boat, our mother made the same request of the captain,
and herself read the Scriptures.

A COSMOPOLITAN AUDIENCE

"While we had been in Pakhoi, the Y. M. C. A. secretary in
Hong-Kong had advertised a meeting for Europeans in the
Theatre Royal.   They had worked industriously and had
hymns printed; and much prayer was going up for a blessing.
I had been told that it was difficult in Hong-Kong to get a
crowd together for any kind of a meeting, religious or secular.
Those who were experienced in such things said that we
must not be disappointed if there were only a few people out.
The usual time for a gathering of that kind in Hong-Kong is
9 o'clock in the evening.   This was the time advertised.   I
went down thirty minutes before that time; and officials were
on the outside turning people away by the hundreds with the
statement that the theatre was packed.   A friend conducted
us up the back way to the platform.   Before we entered the

hall we heard the familiar strains of the 'Glory Song,' and
'Tell Mother I'll Be There.' They had grown tired of waiting; and some sailors who had been in our meetings in England had started these songs. I have never faced a more
eager audience than that. The Chinese Christians at Pakhoi
had promised to be praying during the service; and all
through the evening it would flash through my mind that those
native Christians were praying for us; and I realized that an
unseen Power was present.

It was as cosmopolitan an audience as I had ever faced.
Christian people who were familiar with the city said that
there were those present who had never been known to attend
any kind of religious service. Everybody sang, and sang
heartily. At the close of the meeting my wife and I went
down to shake hands with some of those in front. The first
man I shook hands with on the front row said, 'I was in your
meeting in Bradford, England.' The second said he was in
the meeting at Plymouth; and the next had been in the
Mission in Australia. A lady came to shake hands, saying
that she was from Bandigo, Australia, and knew Mr. Harkness, my pianist. A big, broad-shouldered fellow grasped me
by the hand, and said he confessed Christ five years ago in
Wellington, New Zealand, during our Mission there. I asked
him if he was still serving the Lord, and he said, 'Yes,' and
trying to win other men to Christ. I asked him if he would
come the next afternoon to the Y. M. C. A. and tell the meeting of Christian workers about his conversion and life since.
He said he would gladly do so; and his testimony made a
most striking impression on the meeting. Since then he has
spoken a great deal at gatherings of young men.

MEETING A CONVERT

"The day before the meeting in the Theatre I went to visit a new hospital that had just been built on the Peak, above Hong-Kong. As I stepped inside the front door I noticed a nice red-headed porter standing there, who saluted me politely, and said, 'Good afternoon, Mr. Alexander.' I said, 'Are you an Englishman?'

"He said, 'Yes.'

"I said, 'Where are you from?'

" 'Liverpool.'

"Were you ever in any of our Missions that we held there?"

" 'No, but I have heard about them.'

"How do you know me?"

"With a smile he said, 'I was in your Philadelphia meetings last February.'

"That was just one year from the time I was talking with him. I asked him if he was a Christian. 'Yes, sir, I was converted in your meeting on February'; and he gave me the exact date. 'I sang in your choir, and I was one of your personal workers after my conversion.'

"Then he put his hand in his pocket and pulled out a pocket Bible. On the fly-leaf were the references and directions which Mr. Jacoby, who was at the head of our personal workers at the time, had given to them. He also had his hymn-book, and had secured the autograph of Dr. Torrey, Mr. Harkness and myself. While we were speaking to the people down in the front of the theatre during the after-meeting on the Sunday night, he had been at work in the gallery and brought a wicked young fellow almost to a decision, and wanted me to have a few words with him. The man accepted

THE ANNOUNCEMENT OF MR. ALEXANDER'S MEETING AT HONG KONG

Christ, and the young fellow converted in Philadelphia made a beautiful prayer for him. I was glad to see a one year old missionary in Hong-Kong as the result of our Philadelphia Mission.

"It was a great joy to see the look of victory on the face of the faithful Secretary of the Y. M. C. A., who said they had never had such a meeting in Hong-Kong. God truly answered prayer at that time.

"My wife had a touching letter just before we left from a nurse in one of the hospitals on the Peak above Hong-Kong, in which she related how she had a friend in England who had wronged her, and whom she felt she could not forgive. She had received letters from her but would not even read them. She said that she had been to the theatre meeting on Sunday night, and at that time she had heard me speak about how impossible it was for the Lord to forgive us when we would not forgive our fellow-men. She had heard an announcement that I was to talk to missionaries the next afternoon, and came to that meeting. A still stronger reference was made to unforgiveness that afternoon; and, although she had before determined to cherish the unforgiveness in her heart, she felt that she must get right with God, and get the hatred put out of her heart. I was sorry my wife had not time to visit her; but she wrote, and we left the case in the hands of a godly woman to look after her, and could only pray that her heart would be made right.

"From Hong-Kong we took the Japanese steamer *Nikko Maru,* for Australia. As we sailed out of the harbor we both felt that God had been with us through all the happy visit, and would be glad if God should permit us to come again.

BRIEF STAY IN PHILIPPINES

"On our way down to Australia we touched at Manila, in the Philippine Islands. One bright Sunday morning we sailed into the bay and anchored. A tender came out from shore, and several people came on board the ship to meet their friends. I had no idea that I should see any one I knew, when a big hearty fellow came up and grasped me my the hand and said, 'Hello, Alexander!' And I turned and looked into the face of a man, who, with his wife, had been in my Bible Class in Waterloo, Iowa, a dozen years ago. He and his wife were now missionaries in Manila, and they insisted on my coming to their church that night to take a song service. He spread the news; and there was a full church that night. The pastor of another church heard that I was in the city; and, while I was at dinner, he sent a messenger to know if I could go over and sing once or twice at his church. I finished the song service at my friend's church; and went to the other church while the minister was preaching. They insisted, however, at the first church that I should go back before the service ended, which I did. I had only a few moments at each place, but at the close, at my friend's church, I sang 'Tell Mother I'll Be There,' and had the joy of leading an American soldier to the Lord Jesus Christ."

XXVIII

AMID FAMILIAR SCENES IN AUSTRALIA

IT was during his stay in Australia that the most thrilling scenes of Mr. Alexander's second tour occurred. The throngs which gathered at his meetings were fully as great as those which assembled during the Torrey-Alexander meetings a few years previous. The multitude at the Exhibition Building, Melbourne, was the greatest which ever came together for a religious service in the huge structure. In describing the events of the return visit to familiar scenes, Mr. Alexander said:

"The marvelous beauty of the trip from Manila through the Philippine Islands and down by the long north coast of Australia was beyond description; but the most interesting thing in all the world to me is a human soul. We had opportunities on that long trip of conversations with busy people about eternal things, which we probably could only have had in such circumstances. Our daily morning prayer was that God would open our eyes to see the opportunities, and give us wisdom and courage to take them when they came, which they did in many unexpected ways. Several people were on the boat who had been in our Mission in different places. One gentleman at the captain's table, where we sat, said he had often been in Royal Albert Hall, and had enjoyed the services so much that we must have a song service on board. This we did on the Sunday evening. We began it by my wife and myself's singing 'The Old Time Religion'; and soon the passengers joined in, for each one had a leaflet with the songs in it which we had used on the other boats. The simple melody seemed to warm the hearts of all in the room; and we felt like one big family. Then one song after another was called for; and I told incidents now and then about the songs. From that time until we reached Sydney, I heard the 'Old Time Religion,' and the 'Glory Song' hummed and sung every day from the stewards on up to the first-class passengers.

RENEWING ACQUAINTANCE

"What a different feeling I had as we went through the Heads at Sydney Harbor this time compared with my visit five years before. At that time I did not know a soul in Australia. This time I was going back to the people who had overwhelmed me with their affection during my first visit with Dr. Torrey. I felt sure in my heart that one person would be on the wharf to meet me—a man I had not written to nor received a letter from since I left Australia. And sure enough he was there. He was a godly man, who had taken an active part in our previous Missions, and who had in some way learned of our coming.

"We spent about four weeks, visiting Australia, and have brought away happy memories. From Sydney we took the train 500 miles to Melbourne. There we met the members of the old Mission Committee; and it seemed as if we could hardly believe we had been away five years. We began to plan the best way in which to meet as many of the friends as possible in the different towns. We arranged for two big choir practices to be held in the Melbourne Town Hall and a final Song Service in the Melbourne Exhibition Building; also for meetings in Ballarat, Geelong, Bendigo and Sydney.

"As we entered the Melbourne Town Hall for our first choir practice every available space was filled; and the officers were turning people away by the hundreds. With what a thrill of joy the memories of five years ago rushed over us as we stepped upon the familiar platform. After a few words of introduction by the Hon. James Balfour, I expressed my pleasure at meeting them again.

" 'It is five years,' I reminded them, 'since I first looked into your faces, and since then I have traveled far, and seen a great deal. But some of the best things I ever heard came from the lips of some people I met to-night. One young lady told me, just before this meeting, that while we were here before seven boys in her little country church—one of them her own brother—were converted, and have since given themselves to the ministry of the Lord Jesus. I cannot help referring to one song—a song that you all know—a song that everybody knows, who knows anything worth knowing. I mean the 'Glory Song.' That song was launched from this platform. Don't some of you remember it? Well, that old 'Glory Song' has gone on rolling round the world ever since. I was singing it down in Manila the other night; and a lady, who had been in our meetings in Philadelphia, said to me, 'Don't you ever get tired of the "Glory Song," Mr. Alexander?' 'Tired?' I said. Why, I felt like saying, 'Did you ever get tired of your mother?' Do you know, I've got that song in seventeen different languages. I know myself that there are seventeen million copies of it in books, papers and leaflets. One paper in London that has a circulation of a million copies printed the words and music three times. Get tired of it? I love that song so much, I couldn't let it go. I look at a Gospel song as a sermon—a sermon on wheels, and when you teach a good Gospel song to a man, it is like starting a wagon down a hill with the brakes off.'

AUDIENCE OF TEN THOUSAND

"At the second choir practice in the Melbourne Town Hall, a larger crowd came than had tried to get in before. At the close an appeal was made to those who would accept Christ and confess him that night; and many came forward and did so. But the greatest meeting of all was in the Melbourne Exhibition Building. The Song Service was advertised to begin at 8 o'clock. At 4:30 in the afternoon the first three people passed through the gates, and at 7:30 all the people that the building would safely hold had been admitted There were over ten thousand people inside; and many others tried to get in. The new songs were taken up in the splendid way Australians can sing. The Lord was with us from the first to the last. It was 400 feet from the spot where I stood to the back of the building. When I asked the people in the back gallery to sing a chorus, it sounded as if they were on a distant hill. We sang many of the old favorites. 'Tell Mother I'll Be There,' did not lose its power. Mr. Harkness's new song, 'Shadows,' was the one which seemed to take the greatest hold upon the people. To hear thousands of people in that great building singing Gospel songs so heartily was an inspiration; but best of all was the time when the invitation was given to them to accept Christ, and they began coming from all parts of the building, and their voices in unison, as they confessed Christ, was the sweetest music of all. As I slipped through the back door at the close of the meeting and got into a carriage, a few people at the back followed us. At the signal for the driver to go quickly, a big black-bearded man ran along behind our carriage and grasping my hand said, 'God bless you! If it had not been for your Mission here five years ago I would probably have been drunk to-night. Good-bye.' As we looked back we could see him still waving good-bye to us.

"Just before this meeting I went down and held a choir practice in Ballarat, preparatory to a big Song Service in the skating rink. During the practice I told an incident about the 'Glory Song'; how during our Mission in Bolton, England, a little girl, thirteen years of age, had attended the meetings, learning the songs, and among others the 'Glory Song.' The next summer after we had been there I received a letter from a lady, telling about her little daughter, and how one afternoon when they were at the seashore she was playing in the house and was singing the 'Glory Song.' She picked up her hat and called out 'Good-bye, mother,' and ran off, as they thought, to play. A little later her lifeless body was found at the bottom of the cliff. They thought she had been reaching for flowers, and losing her balance had fallen over. Her mother wrote me what a comfort it was to know that the last words on her little girl's lips were the beautiful words of the 'Glory Song.' A few days after relating this, I came back to Ballarat for the Song Service in the rink. As I stepped upon the platform, I had a letter handed me which I read to the great audience; and it is seldom that you see an audience touched more deeply than that one was. It was from a Ballarat mother about her boy, and she wrote:

A MOTHER'S TOUCHING LETTER

" 'Last Thursday I was in your meeting at the Church, and of course took home with me the hymn-sheet. On Friday my son played and sang the pieces for me just while he could snatch a few minutes after coming from his college in the afternoon and his return there in the evening. After breakfast on Saturday morning he went to the organ again and he played and sang them, and I joined in the singing while busy with my household duties. I went down to the dining-room to him for a few minutes, and he said, "Mother, I like 'Pray Through' best of all. I shall be able to play and sing them for father on Sunday." Then he kissed me and said, "I will go now," and that was the last time I saw his darling face until less than three hours after he was brought home, dead. I thought of the mother you told us of at Bolton, whose darling girl went out singing and was afterwards dashed to pieces.'

"The last afternoon we were in Ballarat the Mayor and his wife gave Mrs. Alexander a reception. She had never been to Australia before, and they wanted to make her feel at home; and the ladies of the city gathered in a large number, and it proved a most happy time. After the gathering the Mayor and his wife took us down to visit two invalids in their homes. I had called upon them five years before. One was a young woman who has had for years to gasp for each breath she took. It was a most pitiable sight, but she was one of the loveliest characters one ever meets. I shall never forget a little note she wrote me after my first visit, in which she said that she was so grateful that the Lord had sent her one other person to pray for, and instead of begging me to pray for her she was thinking of other people.

"We held a Song Service in the Mechanics' Hall, Geelong. This is the home of my former secretary, Rupert Lowe, who joined me when I was there and accompanied me for the next four years. He is now in business in this town. It was a delight to see him again, and hear of his activity in Christian work. The hall where we held our meeting was far too small for the crowds. We had a splendid Song Service. My wife and I were the guests of relatives of Mr. Lowe. We went with them down to their seaside home, "Colite," on the Barwon Heads, where we spent two days. At one time Mr. and Mrs. Howard Taylor were guests at the same place for three months, during which time Mrs. Taylor wrote that remarkable book *Pastor Hsi*.

HOME OF ROBERT HARKNESS

"From Geelong we went to Bendigo, the home of my pianist, Mr. Robert Harkness. He was with us; and we had looked forward with pleasant anticipation to visiting his native town once more. We stayed in his home; and it was an inspiration to meet his good old father and mother. The whole family came in one night—grown up sons and daughters and grand-children—and had a time of hymn-singing with Robert at the organ, as in days of old. I could easily see how the memories of times such as these would inspire him to write hymns.

"Mr. Harkness's father is one of the most honored and respected men in Bendigo. He was three times Mayor of the city; and, instead of giving an inaugural ball as had been the custom, he gave a picnic to 10,000 Sunday School children. Although seventy-eight years of age, he is still active in Christian work. He is a local preacher; and recently delivered a sermon commemorating his fiftieth year of residence in Bendigo.

"Mr. Harkness arranged for us to see one of the gold mines for which Bendigo is famous. The manager was super-intendent of the Sunday-school where he used to attend. We went down the mine shaft to the depth of 600 feet; and were piloted about with our candles in our hands to different sec-tions of the mine. We came upon two miners digging away in the rock; and I went over and shook hands with each of them. One man said he was a Christian; the other said he was not. While we were standing there looking about, Mr. Harkness suggested that I sing the 'Glory Song.' My wife and I sang the last verse, and when we reached the chorus I asked them all to join in, which they did. About the middle of the chorus, I noticed at my right an old miner coming out of an opening which I had not before noticed, with his candle high above his head, singing lustily a high part in the chorus of the 'Glory Song.' As we finished he was in front of us, and said, 'Will you not sing another verse? but I suppose you are too busy.' I stepped down and shook hands with him, and asked if he was a Christian man. He replied that he was not, but added, 'You almost got me last night. I was shaking from head to foot.' He was referring to the meeting we had in the church.

KNELT IN A GOLD MINE

"I asked him if he would give his heart to God right there and then; that it did not matter whether we were under the earth or above it, or whether we were in church or out of it; we could give our hearts to God at any time and anywhere. He said he would be at the meeting to-morrow night. I said,

'That is not the question. Will you accept the Lord Jesus Christ as your Saviour, and live for him from now on?' He hesitated a moment, and then the big Cornishman said, 'Yes, I will.' I turned to those around, and asked them all to kneel in prayer. They did so, pulling off their work-stained caps and reverently bowing their heads. Mr. Harkness and my wife prayed for him; and then I asked him if he would accept the Lord and confess him there, and come to the church the following night and publicly confess him. This he promised to do. We arose; and it was like heaven down there, 600 feet below the earth's surface.

"Mr. Harkness took us from one place to another, where he spent his boyhood days. I asked him to show us the place in the street where he was converted on his bicycle. He had not forgotten it; and showed us the exact spot where his decision for Christ was made. Then I asked him to show me the bicycle he was riding at the time. We went and hunted in the big foundry which his father owns, and finally discovered the remains of it up in a loft. The wheels had been taken away, but the body remained. Then he showed us the desk where he used to work in his father's office, and took us to the engine room where we saw the steam whistle upon which he used to play the 'Glory Song.' We also went to the hotel where I had stayed in Bendigo. In the story which Mr. Harkness often relates of his conversion, he always tells how the Spirit of God touched his heart as we came down the stairs together from my room in the hotel in Bendigo, where I had been urging him to accept Christ.

"Everywhere we went in Australia they gave Mr. Harkness a royal welcome; and were proud that one of their own number had become famous as a Gospel song-writer. Nowhere else was this shown more than in his home town. In our meeting in the theatre the first night at Bendigo I told that large audience that they should be proud of this Bendigo boy who had honored their town, and, more than that, thousands of people never knew there was such a place as Bendigo on the map until he got out of it.

CONVERSIONS DUE TO THE MISSIONS

"While staying here a gentleman told me that the religious denomination of which he was a member had accepted twenty-five candidates for the ministry in their church during the past year. It was their custom to have each candidate tell how he was converted, and if possible what led to his conversion; and nearly every one of the twenty-five candidates attributed their conversion to our Mission more than five years ago in that city. As we were coming out of the churchyard gate after the last meeting, the pastor introduced me to a gentleman who had a Bible class in the church. The teacher said that he was not in very much sympathy with our work while we were there before, but that he wished to say now that from his experience the work was solid. Out of a Bible Class of forty men, more than twenty of them were converted in our meetings, and they were all standing true, and several were doing splendid work as lay preachers.

"During our stay in Australia we made Melbourne our headquarters, returning to the same hotel after visiting the different provincial cities. Just before leaving on our way to Sydney, we heard a report of the work that had been in that hotel during our three weeks' stay. The maid who had been very kind to my wife came and said that during that time six people in the hotel had been converted. The last afternoon we spent in Melbourne was a touching one. The committee had arranged a tea just before our train left, to which they had invited the most prominent Christian people and their wives to meet my wife and myself. At this time they gave us a most pressing invitation to return to Australia and conduct a long series of Missions, which we hope sometime to do.

MEETINGS IN SYDNEY

"As we drew into the station at Sydney we were greeted by a great hearty fellow by the name of Virgo. All the Christian circles in Australia know and love him. He and I sang duets together and worked shoulder to shoulder in the former Melbourne Mission. He is now at the head of the Young Men's Christian Association in Sydney, one of the strongest organizations for reaching young men in that country. Under their auspices he had arranged two meetings for us in Sydney. One was to be in the Y. M. C. A. Hall on Sunday afternoon, and was exclusively for young men. It was impossible to get the Town Hall for the afternoon, but he had secured it for the evening service. The audience of men in the Y. M. C. A. was one of the most unique I have ever been in. They had picked their crowd, and had got together the very men they wanted to reach. From the first moment of the meeting to the close we felt the presence of the Spirit of God in mighty power. Although the hall would hold only 800 men, at the close of the meeting twenty-four big strong fellows marched down to the front and confessed the Lord Jesus Christ for the first time. At the beginning of the service we had the

'Glory Song,' of course; and they sang it so heartily that I asked them to name the place where they had first heard it. It seemed to me that nearly all parts of the world were called out—Newfoundland, all parts of the United Kingdom, India, Tasmania, New Zealand, China, the United States of America, including Alaska. I have just had a letter from Mr. Virgo in which he says the work has been continued ever since and many are being brought to Christ.

"For the evening service in the Town Hall, every inch of room that the officers would allow to be occupied was packed. The officers in charge of the building said that they had never allowed such a crowd to pass into the building before; and one came to me and said that there were five thousand people in the street unable to secure admittance. Some of the friends held open-air services and preached while we sang inside as we had done in Melbourne. We began at 7:30, and left off at 10:30, and when we came out people were still flocking about the entrance. I had not the opportunity of holding a choir practice before this Song Service, as in Melbourne; so at the afternoon men's meeting I had told the men my predicament, and asked all who would be in my choir that night to secure a ticket on leaving the building, for they knew the songs, and I wanted them to sit on the platform. That night I had a great platform of 400 seats filled with men who had only practiced in the afternoon. It was one of the most unique choirs I ever had, but they sang splendidly. I noticed three marines from a British warship in the harbor, sitting together in this impromptu choir. I saw their faces shining and noticed them singing so heartily, that I stopped everybody and asked them to sing all by themselves one of the new choruses we were learning. They did it effectively, thrilling the audience with their hearty voices.

AUSTRALIA'S WARM HEART

"What warm-hearted people the Australians are, and what wonderful singers! But best of all was when the invitation was given to those who would definitely accept the Lord Jesus Christ as their Saviour, to see them coming from all parts of the house. There were many who came down and publicly confessed the Lord.

"We sailed away the next morning out of the beautiful harbor of Sydney, looking into the faces of hundreds of those warm-hearted people who had gathered to bid us good-bye, and we were sorry to say farewell.

"One of the incidents we love to recall is that of a lady we met on the boat coming from Hong-Kong. She was a prominent lady in social circles; and she and my wife became great friends. On the morning we left Sydney, she came where my wife was packing in her room in the hotel, to bid her good-bye. My wife, being alone with her, had a solemn talk about her soul. She was melted to tears; and they knelt together and she said she would definitely accept the Lord Jesus and work for him—a happy ending to a ship-board acquaintance.

XXIX

JOURNEYING HOMEWARD ACROSS AMERICA

As Mr. Alexander went to China by way of the Suez Canal, and returned from Australia through America, he thus girdled the globe. And it is interesting to recall that the second trip was in the opposite direction from the first. He said:

"We sailed for Vancouver, Canada, on our way to the United States. Our first stop was at Suva, in the Fiji Islands. We were there several hours; and saw some fine specimens of natives. We also met a man who is at the head of a large part of the work which, in a very few years, has transformed the entire island from cannibalism to Christianity.

"When I came back to the ship that afternoon I found a letter awaiting me. I had noticed a war-ship in the harbor, and found that the letter was from one of the three marines who had been in my impromptu choir in Sydney and sung the chorus at my request on the night before we left. They had evidently sailed away the next morning. He spoke of the pleasure he had had in singing that night; and told me how among the hundreds who were on their ship only ten were out-and-out Christians, and that they had hard pulling sometimes, but God gave them strength to be true to him.

"We had many opporunities, on our long voyage, of personal conversation with our fellow passengers. After touching at Fanning Island and at Honolulu, we at last reached Vancouver, and started our long journey across the continent down

MR. ALEXANDER TAKING THE PHOTOGRAPH OF MR. NORMAN MACKENSIE

MR. ALEXANDER RIDING A WATER-BUFFALO AT MANILA

to New York. We stopped over Sunday at a little station in the Rocky Mountains, where we helped the pastor with the evening service, using the same song leaflet as before. Here in this place we saw the little room in a log building, now a telegraph office, where Ralph Connor used to preach to the men from the mines and the mountains. One of the ladies in the hotel used to play the organ for him in his little mountain church.

THE STOP AT CHICAGO

"We stopped at Chicago, and visited two places of world-wide repute, that stand out like mountain peaks in my life. One was the Moody Bible Institute, and the other was Pacific Garden Mission. My wife and I spoke twice in the Moody Institute, and once in the Moody Church; and attended two meetings at the Pacific Garden Mission. At the Moody Bible Institute we found many who had gone there from our Missions in England and from Australia and Canada, among them two young women whom my wife had led to Christ during our London Mission, and who were now just finishing their course preparatory to taking up their life-work. They spent their vacation last summer in Ottawa, Canada, during our Mission there. One afternoon I had them give their testimony during the song service in the church; and tell how they had been led to Christ and what they were doing then, and how much they were enjoying their training at the Bible Institute. A bright-faced young woman came and shook hands with my wife and me during our visit to the Institute at this time, and said she had come there from Ottawa, Canada. I asked her how she had been led there. She told us that she was in that Ottawa Church the day the two English girls told their story. She had been trying to decide what to do with her life; and their testimonies led her to decide to come to the Institute. I asked her if she was glad she came. 'Delighted,' she said.

"On the platform at the Pacific Garden Mission one night there were three men who are now well known in evangelistic work throughout the United States, but who had formerly been away down in sin. One of them, Harry Munroe, has been the leader of the Pacific Garden Mission for nearly fifteen years. Another, Melvin E. Trotter, came into that same Mission ten years ago, dirty, drunken, desperate. Mr. Munroe put his arm around him and led him to Christ; and he has never wanted a drink since, though the day before he would have taken the shoes from his feet to sell for a drink. He is now at the head of the largest Rescue Mission in America, at Grand Rapids, Michigan. The third was William Jacoby, who used to be Dr. Torrey's assistant in the Moody Church, Chicago, and is now engaged with him in his evangelistic work. Up till forty-three years of age he was a desperate character. Now he is one of the most Christian-like men I know.

THESE THREE GREAT COMPANY

"It was a great joy to take these three men down to the place where my wife and I were staying, to spend the night with us. I have never been in their company without receiving a great uplift. If my readers had come into our room that night, and had seen the joy upon the faces of these men, the kindliness in all of their actions, and their Christ-likeness, they would never have dreamed that these three had been rescued from the lowest depths.

It was while we were in New York, waiting for our boat to England, that we heard the sad news of the accident at sea to our mother. As soon as we heard the news we started back through Canada, where we met the train, bearing our sister and cousins and the remains of our dear mother. Returning to New York, we sailed for England on the *Oceanic,* reaching Birmingham on June 13th, about seven months after we had sailed eastward from London, suddenly plunged into sorrow that God alone could comfort.

XXX

AT NORTHFIELD AND ON THE BOWERY

AFTER a month in England Mr. Alexander had to hurry back to America to take part in the Christian Workers' Conference at Northfield, Mass., under the direction of Mr. W. R. Moody, leaving his wife to share in the sorrowful work of breaking up the desolated family home. After a two years' absence from the Convention he was warmly welcomed back by a host of friends. When he made his first appearance on the platform the people broke through the Convention rule and heartily applauded him, as well as his pianist, Mr. Harkness, who accompanied him. Mr. Alexander also had the assistance during the Conference of Melvin E. Trotter, W. S. Jacoby, Charles Butler and Mr. J. J. Virgo, of Australia, who came to the Conference at the Gospel singers' urgent request.

As was the case in former years, Mr. Alexander had charge of an hour daily during which he gave brief pointed talks, had stirring experiences from a group of personal workers, and led the people in singing new and old revival melodies. Throughout the Convention this hour was one of the most popular. A great crowd was always in attendance; and their singing was worth going far to hear. He also gathered and trained a large "Sunbeam Choir," which added greatly to the effectiveness of the Praise Service.

But from first to last Mr. Alexander kept this as the keynote of his daily hour, definitely winning people to Christ one

"TENNESSEE," THE HOME OF MR. CHARLES M. ALEXANDER AT BIRMINGHAM, ENGLAND

by one. Day by day by means of advice, by touching incidents and by testimonies from others, he drove the truth home
that every Christian must be a soul-winner if he is to follow
in the Master's footsteps. Near the close of the Conference
he said:

WEAK SPOT IN HIS MINISTRY

"I just found a man out there, a nice looking man, with a
strong face and a fine education, who said to me: 'I have been
pastor of a church for fourteen years, where I have eight
hundred members, but this personal work is what I have not
had. I am weak there.' The other night a young preacher
said to me: 'Last Sunday night after my wife and I watched
the souls being led to Christ here by personal workers, we cried
all the way home. We settled it on our knees that we were
going to do personal work. I have been preaching for two
years, but that has been my weak spot.' It is the weakest spot
you can have. You need not sympathize with yourself and
gloss it over.

"You will find a strength, a joy and a peace in your life
that you never knew before, if you will do personal work.
You say 'I am 65 years old!' That does not make any dif-
ference. One of the best workers I know is 84 years old.
She cannot walk very well neither, and has to be helped out of
the door; but she never loses an opportunity.

"Have you ever led a soul to Christ in your life? Do you
know of anybody you have led to Christ? What if you
should drop dead in your seat right where you are? What
could you say to God? Would you begin to make the excuses
you have been making to yourself? The Lord said: 'Follow
me, and I will make you fishers of men!' Are you fishing?

What would you think of a fisherman who had fished all his life and caught nothing? You would think he ought to be in the asylum.

"If it takes a long time to get the one you want, do not get discouraged. Keep after him. I got a letter from my wife yesterday. She told me about finding a woman that she and her mother had been after, I do not know for how many years. The woman would get drunk and everything like that, but they kept after her that much harder. Let us go after them and get them, no matter how long it takes. How long would you hunt for your son if you had lost him? If your little child were lost here on the grounds, how long would you look for it, mother? (Voice from crowd: 'Until she found it!') That is right; of course you would. How long must you keep after an unsaved soul? Until you land that soul. That is what I liked about Sam Hadley. It did not matter how often a man went off and got drunk, nor if he stole everything that he could get his hands on, when that man came back Sam would say: 'How do you do? Glad to see you back.'"

It was during Mr. Alexander's hour that many of the most melting times of the conference occurred. A number were led openly to confess Christ.

MEETING IN THE BOWERY

It was while in New York and waiting for a steamer to return to his home in England that Mr. Alexander received an urgent invitation from Dr. Louis Klopsch, proprietor of THE CHRISTIAN HERALD, to conduct a meeting at the well-known "Bowery Mission." He consented, and the result was a night of glorious victory.

As it had been announced that Mr. Alexander would be present at the meeting, a motley crowd of bums, drunkards, and men homeless and almost hopeless gathered at any early hour. The crowd in front grew so rapidly that the doors were opened before the usual time to prevent a disturbance. The meeting was for men only; and they poured into the hall, packing it to the doors; while some sat on the rear stairs and others stood throughout the service. It was a pitiable and touching sight that the throng presented. Scores were unkempt and woe-begone because of lack of work for weeks and months. Some were bloated and blear-eyed through dissipation. Some were stupid through drink, and fell asleep soon after the meeting began.

Mr. Alexander was piloted down into the Bowery district by Mr. John Callahan, Superintendent of Hadley Hall, and was accompanied by Mr. J. J. Virgo and Mr. Robert Harkness, of Australia, and his secretary, H. Bookmyer. After a few opening hymns, the Superintendent of the Mission placed the meeting in Mr. Alexander's hands. On rising to speak one of the first things the Gospel singer told the men was that he was glad to be with them, for it recalled memories of many happy nights spent in the Pacific Garden Mission in Chicago. Mr. Alexander told the men that there were two Australians on the platform, and he was going to ask one of them to sing a song that the other had written entitled, "He Will Hold Fast." He said that the singer, Mr. Virgo, came from Australia recently, and on the way over he sang this song among the third class passengers and many were helped by it. He said it was a song for those fellows who fear they can't hold out. Mr. Virgo sang it with power; and Mr. Alexander drilled the men on it again and again until they made the building reverberate with the melody. Following this the Gospel singer started up "The Old Time Religion," and after they had sung a verse or two he said:

SANG BECAUSE THEY HAD TO

"Down in a meeting in Melbourne there was a friend of mine sitting next to a great big fellow who looked sharply at him while he was singing this song. At length the big fellow said: 'What are you singing for?' My friend said, 'Can't help it.' Pretty soon the song began to warm things up, and the big man began to warm up, too. In a little while he was singing as lustily as the others. My friend turned round to him and said: 'What are you singing for?' He said: 'I cannot help it.' That is the kind of singing I like, when a man 'cannot help it.' I want you men to sing to-night, and I want you to mean every word you sing." By this time the meeting was enthusiastic; and Mr. Alexander had a firm grip on his hearers. He now called upon the men to sing softly and tenderly that cry of the soul for peace and pardon: "Pass Me Not, O Gentle Saviour." He then called upon Mr. John Callahan to tell how he was saved. Following a stirring testimony, he called upon the men to join heartily in singing another old favorite, "The Land that is Fairer Than Day." It brought back old memories to many in the audience. In answer to prayer God's Spirit was moving deeply on the hearts of the men. After the singing of several verses, Mr. Alexander briefly spoke to the men, in clear ringing tones which could be heard in the farthest part of the hall. He said:

"When I come to New York I do not go to the Cathedrals,

but to places like this where men are brought from death into life in Christ. I like to go before a great audience dressed in silks and satins, and get one of the men snatched from the devil's territory to speak to them. I love to be able to say to them, 'Look at him, and you dare not say anything against the power of God to save and to keep.'

"A great writer once said to me: 'What if Jesus Christ did not rise from the dead?' I said to him: 'The whole thing is a failure if Jesus Christ did not rise from the dead. You can talk from now until to-morrow morning, but when you are right up against the fact of a fellow who has been hounded out of every saloon in town, whom nobody will have anything to do with, what have you for him?' He said something with four syllable words, and went round and round the subject. I said, 'You are not getting anywhere, are you?' He said, 'Well, what would you do?' I said, 'Now you have come to a man who knows. If you want to go with me to-morrow morning I will show you dozens of men that have lived good, clean, Christian lives for a year, between our last Mission and this, whom no other power but the Lord Jesus Christ could have cleansed from sin. Have you anything like that?' The man wilted. He bowed his head and said: 'I hope you will get hold of my wife and boys when you come to London.' Do you see? Jesus Christ alone can save. Nobody has a monopoly of salvation. They may corner earthly goods, but they cannot corner Eternal life. The way to God is open.

INFLUENCE OF A TRACT

"One day a man in the Pacific Garden Mission in Chicago pulled out a little tract and said: 'Do you see that? It is called "Truth in a Nutshell." A man came up in the lodging house where I was staying the other night. He said: "Won't you come down to Pacific Garden Mission to-night?" I said, "No." "Well," he said, "Here is something to read." I looked and saw it was a tract. I was going to throw it at the fellow, but he passed out. I began to read it, as I had nothing else to do. I saw, in large black letters at the top of the page: "You are a Sinner," with a line under the you. I said: "I know that. Give me something new." I had been a drunkard for years. I had not been in a church in about fifteen years. I was just going to throw the tract down in disgust, when my eye caught another sentence on the next page, "God Loves You," with a big black line under "Loves." I said, "Hello, is that so?" For fifteen years I had been thinking that God hated me, but I read there "God Loves You." I turned around and read the tract through, and read it through again, and read it through again; and when I got up from there I was a saved man. I took Jesus as my Saviour that night. It was seven o'clock when I started to read, and it was 12 o'clock when I got through.' What God did for that man he will do for you, if you will give your hearts to him.

"In a few moments I want my friend Mr. Virgo to sing a song to you that has been used greatly all around the world in the salvation of souls. It is a song that has been criticized, but it gets men saved and that is more important. I carried it around many months in my scrap-book before I decided to use it. I will tell you how it was written:

"When President McKinley was in office in Washington his mother lay dying in Canton, Ohio, several hundred miles away. She sent word that she wanted to see her boy once more before she died. President McKinley chartered a special train and telegraphed 'Tell Mother I'll Be There.' A Gospel song-writer from the same state caught up the idea and wrote the song, 'Tell Mother I'll Be There,' which has been the means of bringing thousands to Christ.

"MY OLD MOTHER'S RELIGION"

"In connection with this song I want to tell you an incident that happened in Chicago. Two country boys went to Chicago to make their way in the world. One boy came from a good Christian home where they loved the Bible and had family prayers. He shared a room, however, with his infidel friend. One day the infidel boy said the other was a coward not to listen to the other side of the case. He said: 'We are going to have a lecture to-night, come along!' The boy from the good Christian home went, and during the lecture it seemed as if Christianity were torn to shreds. Men and women stood on the seats and waved their hats and handkerchiefs and made such a noise that you would have thought Christianity was being wiped off the face of the earth. As they were coming out after the lecture the infidel boy put his hat on one side of his head and said, 'Well, he knocked down everything in front of him to-night, didn't he?' 'Not everything,' replied the Christian boy, 'there was one thing he did not touch.' The infidel boy said, 'Well, I should like to know what that was?' The Christian boy said, 'My old mother's religion.' No matter how far down in sin you go, you cannot quite get that influence out of your hearts. Thank God! some of you don't want to do so. Men, make a full surrender to-night. Give Jesus Christ your heart. Come to your mother's God."

Mr. Alexander then called upon Mr. Virgo to sing "Tell Mother I'll Be There." As the famous hymn was sung prayerfully and tenderly, hearts all over the audience began to melt. While Mr. Virgo sang, Mr. Alexander pleaded with the men to decide the great question at once. During the first verse and chorus a number arose. Then as the song continued and was repeated, Mr. Alexander urged the men to have the courage to confess Christ publicly; and they continued to rise in all parts of the house. When over thirty had risen, the Gospel singer told the men that if they were in dead earnest about the matter, he wanted them to take a step further, to come out boldly and go into the room at the rear of the platform. The men responded at once; and a total of forty-three men arose from their seats and filed back into the room. It was a glorious sight to see that procession of sin-sick men going forward publicly to confess the Saviour who would bring them life more abundant.

At the close of the service, coffee and sandwiches were served to the men, and at length the night of victory was concluded. The Superintendent of the Mission declared it was the greatest night in the history of the work.

MR. ALEXANDER AT MONT-LAWN

While Mr. Alexander was in New York he had an opportunity to spend a Sunday at Mont-Lawn, The Christian Herald Children's Home at Nyack-on-Hudson, N. Y. The other distinguished guest was Admiral Sigsbee, who has long taken an interest in Mont-Lawn, and who is well known to many of the children who have been present when the admiral was among the speakers on patriotic occasions at the Home.

Dr. Klopsch always comes to the Home on Sunday, and the children always eagerly await his coming and the distinguished visitors that he often brings with him. This afternoon as usual they were clustered about the handsome entrance of the Home to watch for the Mont-Lawn's guests. At noon they began to arrive—Dr. Klopsch first, bringing Rev. Dr. Babbitt, the "grand old man of Nyack." He is the pastor who for nearly half a century has had charge of the parish and the church which he himself organized. Afterward came the members of Dr. Klopsch's household, bringing with them Admiral Sigsbee, who, having taken part in the Fourth of July celebration, enjoyed himself so much that he wanted to come again. Next came Mr. Charles Alexander, the singing evangelist. With him was his singing companion, Mr. Harkness. Then came the people, walking and riding, pouring in from Nyack and the neighboring towns and country. They came in such numbers that one wondered if even Mont-Lawn's capacious hospitality would be equal to the occasion. But of course it was.

IN MONT-LAWN CHAPEL

The beautiful chapel was fairly even before the children got in. With the organ playing, the long line of little folks filed into the house of worship in perfect order. It was wonderful to see how well they conducted themselves, especially as some of them were new arrivals of only two days before!

There was a hymn, a little talk by Dr. Klopsch, a prayer by Evangelist Alexander, and then the good pastor Babbitt rose to address the children. It is a beautiful thing to see a man who has lived through so many years of human experience with a face so sweet, and clear, and fresh; with a figure so straight and slender, a voice so gentle, a faith so undimmed. It made the hearers think of a time when childhood and old age would not be far apart, but only names for those who were pure and hopeful, reverent and at peace with God.

Dr. Babbitt spoke to the children about character building, about good boys and girls, and bad girls and boys, good acts and bad acts, good men and bad men, and how inevitably the goo came to their reward and the others to their punishment. He pointed out that the children before him were at the beginning of the road of life, and how important it was for the mto choose between good and evil and, cleaving to the one, destroy the power of the other, so that they might enjoy happy and useful lives. His words might have been summed up in these beautiful lines, "Sow an act and reap a habit; sow a habit, reap a character; sow a character, and reap a destiny."

After he had finished there was more Gospel singing. There is no mistaking the spirit in which that singing is done! If every good and healthy thing could be done with the same enthusiasm, how this old world would ring!

Then they gave the oath of allegiance to the flag.

THE STIGMA OF A LIE

Then, forming in line again, the children marched to the sloping lawn in front of the main cottage and sat down in platoons upon the grass. The visitors were seated nearer to the house on benches brought from the pavilion by many willing hands. Dr. Klopsch invited Admiral Sigsbee to speak. The Admiral, with his erect, soldierly bearing, and his clean-cut naval appearance, walked up to the cottage steps and spoke for a few minutes.

He told how the boys at Annapolis, when he was a "middy" there, always despised a liar. A boy might do a great many undesirable things, but they were not laid up against him; but once let him be caught in a lie, and his career was finished. Even when he went from the Academy into the Navy, the stigma of "liar" followed him. "The worst thing about a lie," the Admiral said, "is that, to be believed, it must counterfeit truth; in other words, it must impose upon the credulity, the trustfulness, the regard of some one. Therefore it alwoys does double damage; it injures the one who utters to it. There are times," the Admiral added, "when wisdom bids us hold back all of the truth, because people might not be able to understand it; but there never was a time when it was right or excusable to tell a lie."

AN OUTDOOR SERVICE

The Admiral's talk followed by hearty cheers. Then Mr. Alexander, making a platform of the piazza railing, led the singing, intermingling it with his little talks and evangelistic stories to the great delight of the whole audience. Then he broke into the famous "Glory Song":

> Oh, that will be glory for me: glory for me, glory for me!
> When by his grace I shall look on his face,
> That will be glory, be glory for me.

It didn't take the crowd long to learn that chorus. It is a favorite one with Mr. Alexander, and he has made it familiar around the world.

He next sang the beautiful Gospel song, "Tell Mother I'll Be There," and many an eye was wet with tears. He told how in rough mining camps, where the men's hearts seemed hardened to every good influence, that song, with its appeal to their love for their mothers, would bring them sobbing to confess their desire to be better men.

The little service ended with the whole audience singing "The Old Time Religion." This greatly pleased the visitors, for many of them had not heard it for years.

When the service was finished, Mr. Alexander asked everyone to shake hands with his neighbor, and so amid smiles and hanlshakings and little conversations and much good-will the visitors departed, leaving Mont-Lawn to the children and the sunset and the fast-falling twilight. A few days later Mr. Alexander was on the broad Atlantic bound for his home in England.

THE END.

12048